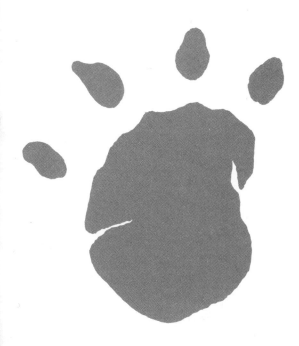

This book belongs to

_____

An Allen D. Bragdon Book

Sewing projects designed by Marsha Evans Moore
Recipes developed by Margaret Deeds Murphy

Distributed by Arco Publishing, Inc.
New York

THE TEDDY BEAR BOOK

I can't bear to

I LOVE YOU

sleep

Acknowledgments:

The author and editors would like to thank the following individuals and firms for their contributions to this book: The Crafty Teddy, Inc., a mail-order supplier, in Brooklyn, N.Y., for teddy bear hardwear and other teddy-making materials; Crompton Co., Inc., a fabric manufacturer in New York, for velveteen and corduroy fabrics; The Hired Hand, a shop in New York, for cotton print fabrics and sewing supplies for dressmaking and quilting; C.M. Offray and Sons, Inc., a ribbon manufacturer in New York, for ribbons and for permission to include *Bavarian Bear*; Wrights Home Sewing Company, a manufacturer of ribbon and trims in New York, for eyelet, lace, and ribbons; Bookbuilders, Ltd. for color separations; Type Positive and Werner Graphics for typesetting.

Staff for this book:

Editor in Chief Allen D. Bragdon
Consulting Editor Cecelia K. Toth
Project Design and Instructions Marsha Evans Moore; Janet Huffman Akhtarshenas (*Trinket Box, Jumpin' Rope Handles, Necklace, Lapel Pin, Cliff-Climber Magnets, Beanbag Bear*); Nadia Hermos (*Christine Crochet, Pierre Bear, Twin-Bears Sweaters*); Jean Wells (*Bavarian Bear*)
Recipes developed by Margaret Deeds Murphy; Lawrence Rosenberg (*Chocolate Honey-Bear Birthday Cake*)
Instruction Editors Amanda Claiborne, H.M. Graney, Hannah Selby, Mark Sherman, M.C. Waldrep
Captions A.D. Bragdon
Proofreaders David Gamon, Susan Rhodes
Art Direction Conrad Warre
Graphic Production Michael Eastman, Marta Ruliffson, Stephanie Schaffer
Line Drawings Marsha Evans Moore
Jacket Design and Color Illustrations Mejo Okon

Photography:

All photography by Photo Illustrators, New York, except the following: *Original Teddy Bear* (page 5), photograph courtesy of the National Museum of American History; *Buddy Bear* (page 49), Laszlo Studios, New York.

Published and Produced by
Allen D. Bragdon Publishers, Inc.
153 West 82nd Street
New York, NY 10024
Copyright © 1984 by Allen D. Bragdon Publishers, Inc.

Distributed to the retail book trade by Arco Publishing, Inc.
215 Park Avenue South, New York, N.Y 10003

Library of Congress Cataloging in Publication Data

Main entry under title:

The Teddy bear book.

"An Allen D. Bragdon Book."

Summary: Instructions for making traditional teddy bears with wardrobes and more than fifty other bear-related projects. Also includes a selection of recipes.
    1. Needlework. 2. Soft toy making. 3. Cookery. 4. Teddy bears. [1. Needlework. 2. Toy making. 3. Cookery. 4. Teddy bears] I. Moore, Marsha Evans. II. Murphy, Margaret Deeds. III. Toth, Cecelia K.

TT751.T43 1984 745.592'4 84-9311

ISBN 0-916410-09-9

Printed in the U.S.A
10 9 8 7 6 5 4 3 2 1

Bear Facts

This was the inspiration for making a stuffed bear-cub toy called Teddy. In November 1902 President Theodore Roosevelt went bear hunting in Smedes, Mississippi at a time when the state was wrangling with Louisiana over exactly where their common borderline was.

This cartoon drawn by Clifford Berryman, who was then on the staff of the Washington Post, ran in the paper during the hunt. The caption refers to a story, filed by a reporter at the hunt, to the effect that a small bear either blundered into the camp site or was captured and brought there for the president to shoot—which he refused to do.

This is the first Teddy Bear ever made. Mr. Morris Michtom, a Russian immigrant living with his family in Brooklyn, New York, was operating a small confectionary business there when he saw Clifford Berryman's cartoon. He admired President Roosevelt so he wrote a letter to the president asking his permission to manufacture stuffed toy bear cubs and market them as "Teddy's Bears." The president gave him permission in a handwritten note. Mr. Michtom's wife sewed up some samples which he successfully marketed through wholesalers, starting in early 1903. He named his new business the Ideal Novelty and Toy Company which, with a minor name-change, still operates in Brooklyn as the Ideal Toy Company.

This is T.R. Bear, who is also named for Teddy Roosevelt. You will meet him in this book. He stands 21" (53 cm) tall. His arms and legs move and his head turns. His body shape is similar both to Rose Michtom's original and to the now-classic teddy bears first designed in the early 1900's by Fraulein Margarete Steiff's nephew Richard, in Giengen, Germany. Though his body and expression may follow those classic patterns, his personality is uniquely his own, as you will see when you undertake to create him from the patterns and instructions on the following pages—in much the same way as an old woodcarver once created Pinnochio.

Contents

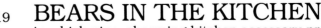

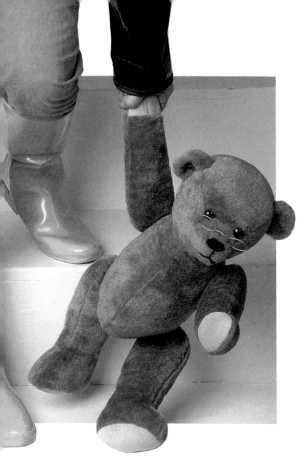

I AM T.R. BEAR, THE TRADITIONAL, heirloom Teddy Bear you are cordially invited to create, out of whole cloth, if you will forgive the expression. You will encounter other bears and other figures of speech in this book, you may also have to forgive. Bearnice is the greatest offender. You will first meet her formally about page 46. It's not that she doesn't appreciate when an old saying puts an idea well, it's just that she keeps trying to *adapt* it to the precise moment; but I have digressed.

I am called T.R. because those are President Roosevelt's (the first one's) initials. Theodore Roosevelt was president of the United States in the early 1900's at a time when some unusually appealing stuffed dolls, made with brown plush fabric, were named for him (they looked just like me). They captured the heart of the American public then and haven't stopped for breath since. If teddy bears had been invented when Theodore's cousin, Franklin, was president, these dolls might have been called Depression Bears. It doesn't have a ring to it, and I, the First Bear of this book, would have been stuck with the initials "D.B."—which would have been a shame.

In the first chapter, which is called "Heirloom Bears" you will learn to make me and three other, traditional, teddy bears of different sizes and personalities—all with fur and moveable limbs. We four are easily as attractive, and probably even more durable, than the ones Fraulein Steiff's factory has been making since 1907, I have made an

effort as well to keep an eye on things for you throughout the other chapters in this book in which instructions and patterns are given for making other kinds of bear dolls, decorations, useful objects, and original recipes—all of them inspired by teddy bears.

In an earlier incarnation, I constructed the costumes for Shakespeare's characters at the Globe Theatre—that was in the mid 1500's. For that reason I respect the precision and dedication that fine and imaginative tailoring requires. One must, for example, believe fully in the future to undertake to tailor a furry Pinnochio like me into being. As I have said before, "Soufflés rise and soufflés fall, but a well-made bear goes on forever."

My friend Buddy, another member of our group of four traditional teddy bears, has a different view. In contrast to me—a careful, vested bear who wears a *pince nez*, as Teddy Roosevelt did—Buddy is a bigger guy, softer-furred, more innocent-eyed. Buddy would help anybody in the group who needed his strength—whether they knew they needed it just then or not. His opinion about sewing projects goes something like this: "Sewing is a long-haul thing. You can make popovers in 40 minutes, get just as much credit for your effort in the next ten minutes, and still, maybe, have time left to locate a good honey tree before the sun sets."

Bearnice doesn't agree with him. She says, "If you counted up all the things in the world that were worth doing well, you would come up with your own five fingers." But then, she is a phrasemaker by instinct.

Bearnice's figure and temperament are both healthily maternal. She also comes equipped with an independent spirit. A while back, she made a mini-skirt for herself, when they were popular, but Buddy started calling her "Bear Knees," which ended *that.*

She keeps an eye out for the fourth, and much the smallest, member of the heirloom bear family. He was unable to understand our language when he first knocked on our door the day he jumped ship. He knew nobody in this part of the world and must have been hungry. Bearnice asked him what his name was, as he stood there silently on our doorstep. Since he couldn't understand what she asked, he didn't answer. "He's quite a small bear," I mumbled finally, thinking out loud.

"Sounds like a nice name to me," said Bearnice, "but how did you know it, T.R.?"

"It helps a little fella to have a big name," said Buddy, "He should hyphenate it too, to give it more class; look what that did for Napoleon Bone-apart."

So Quite A. Small-Bear he became, and neither he nor I will give you a straight answer if you ask how he came by that moniker. And nobody, but nobody, calls him by his first name alone; a little guy with a hyphen in his last name can get pretty feisty.

My skills as a tailor, and perhaps, admittedly, some self-

importance as First Bear of this book, have compelled me to stick in brief pieces of advice on the fine points of tailoring a first rank, traditional, fur-bearing, teddy bear. These are called "Bear's Pauses" by Bearnice because I wrote them myself. They are tucked into the margins here and there so you have to pause and read them before you go on with your work. You will recognize them by the mark of a bear's paw at the top of each one and my initials at the bottom.

Fortunately for us all, my mother is a talented seamstress and an understanding person. She agreed to contribute to this project by explaining some, perhaps unfamiliar, sewing techniques like how to enlarge patterns, make some embroidery stitches, and a few other points I may have left out. Those are collected at the end of the book and are referred to in the text as "Mama Bear's Sewing Basket" (which if you knew her, you would agree is a little too cute for her) or by this symbol ✄ .

I hope there is a baby in your family or someone you like has one, because the chapter called "Baby Bear" has a number of charming ideas in it. I like the Lickin' Good Bib and the Story Quilt best. "Bears in the Kitchen" is a chapter with quite easy projects that make appropriate gifts for others enlightened enough to appreciate bears. The recipes in Chapter Five are the most original and delicious from Mama Bear's recipe file. The best thing about them is that they are not all silly

and fattening. Even so, Quite A. Small-Bear likes every one of them, except for Forage Porridge.

When you get to the "School Days" chapter you will see Bearnice looking as cute as a bug's ear wearing her red sweater that matches a bigger child's sweater. That's also the chapter with the photograph of her looking stunning in her linen pinafore with the child-sized, matching, Goldilocks pinafore next to her. (It's the pink bow in her ear that does it, I think.)

The last chapter, called "Bears Bazaar," has ideas and patterns for relatively simple and very appealing items that can easily be mass-produced by cutting and sewing them in quantity as gifts or to sell at fairs and the like. Bearnice almost persuaded the editors to call that chapter "Bears in Batches." (Alliteration causes her judgement to career out of control.) I managed to reconnect her natural sensibilities by asking if we should also have a section called "Humans by the Hundreds." She said that I can be unstufferable sometimes. We were both right.

I look forward to meeting you in these pages and hope that you will have a good time making the projects you find there.

HEIRLOOM BEARS

"It may help you to notice in advance where all the pieces of my body will fit when you sew me together. By making T.R. Bear, you are bringing me to life, so as you cut the pieces, keep in mind that these patterns and materials may look like only pieces of paper, cloth, and yarn, but they are going to be parts of a body that is important to me."

Head Center

Ear

Head Side

Outer Arm

Inner Arm

Paw Pad

Foot Pad

Inner Leg

Outer Leg

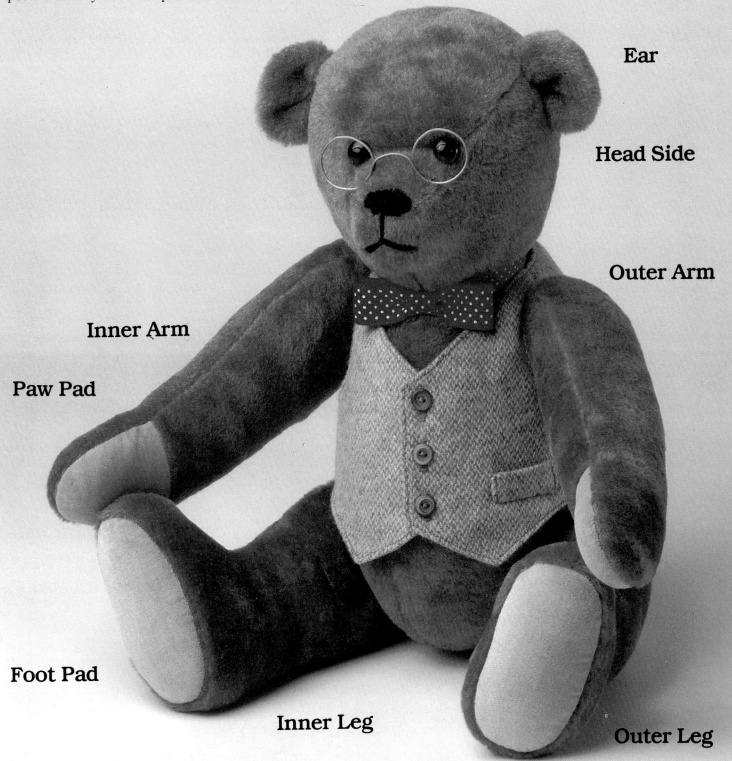

A Short Course in Bear Tailoring

This page tells you briefly what you need to do to create a sturdy, classic teddy bear—one that will be a lasting companion. The following pages will explain all the details, with illustrations showing how to perform each step. The sewing principles are the same as for dressmaking—and the section in this book called "Mama Bear's Sewing Basket" ✂ will help you out if some of the terms or techniques are new to you.

When you come across a "Bear's Pause," don't panic. T.R. has made his mark on our instructions by contributing advice on some unusual or especially important points about bear tailoring with fur fabric. His Pauses appear here and there on the sides of the pages. T.R. also asked for some space on the prior page to illustrate the names of the parts that make him a whole, three-dimensional bear.

Since T.R.'s parts are so important, they are in *italic type* in the instructions. They are also printed on the full-size patterns, so you can transfer them to the backs of the fur pieces as you cut out each piece. This will help you to keep track of which piece fits where as you assemble them. Then, when he is stuffed, T.R. will stand before you on your work table, a bear to behold. After that, if you like, he will go on to help you make bears with different shapes and to make other projects of interest both to bears and to their human friends.

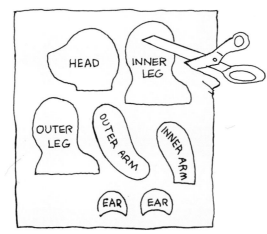

1. Trace full-size patterns from book, cut them out of fur fabric, then transfer the names of the parts and all markings to fabric pieces.

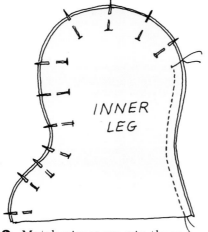

2. Match pieces up, pin them together, then sew them by hand or by machine. That's how you make the arms, legs, body, and head. Each section will have an opening for stuffing.

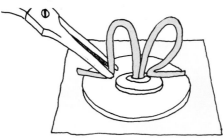

3. Join head, arms, and legs to body so they will swivel on disks and washers. Each joint is held firm by a cotter pin bent into the shape of a crown.

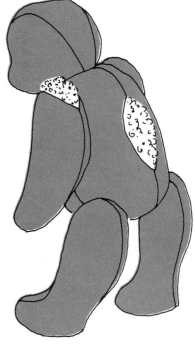

4. Stuff each piece with big wads of polyester, poking stuffing in firmly with a chopstick. Then stitch up stuffing openings carefully by hand.

5. Sew eyes tightly in place with doubled carpet thread. Sew ears on, cupped slightly forward. And finally, stitch nose and mouth, handsomely, with black Persian yarn.

Tools and Materials

On the next two pages we show you exactly what tools and materials you will need to construct "T.R." and the other classic heirloom bears. Although the information here applies directly to T.R., any variations for Buddy Bear, Bearnice, and Quite A. Small Bear will be specified at the beginning of those instructions. Taking those alterations into account, you will then be able to refer back to these pages as a checklist for all of your bear projects.

In addition to telling you what you need, we explain briefly what each item is for. We also offer some suggestions for potential substitutions (for instance, a razor blade instead of scissors, or real velvet instead of velveteen). Dimensions are given in both inches and metric measures since some items may be sold either way depending on where and when you purchase them.

A few materials may be hard to find in local shops—real glass eyes, or growlers, for example. In the last page you will find the names and addresses of firms that currently sell them by mail.

Pencil for marking fabric. Pastel pencils or chalk are more accurate and legible than lead pencils. Ink may bleed through to the fur on the other side.

Dressmakers Shears. 7-8" (18-21 cm) long with "bent-trimmer" design for cutting fabric. The handles are offset so the bottom blade can remain parallel to what is being cut: this makes cutting fabric around a paper pattern much easier. *Alternative:* single-edge razor blade.

Scissors. 5-7" (13-18 cm) long with sharp, pointed tips, for precision in snipping stitches and trimming fur fabric.

Utility knife for cutting out the disks used in crown joints. *Alternative:* a drill with 3" and 1½" (4 cm and 7¼ cm) hole cutters.

Drill with ⅛" bit (3 mm) for drilling center holes in crown joint disks. *Alternative:* an awl, but only if using cardboard disks.

Awl for making holes in fur fabric, felt, and cardboard. *Alternative:* a thin knitting needle.

Sewing Machine for assembling pieces.

Pins for holding fabric in place while, or instead of, basting.

Embroidery Needle for basting, slipstitching, etc. Size 7-9. *Alternative:* sharps.

Toy-making Needle at least 4" (10 cm) long for sewing on eyes. *Alternative:* any long, strong needle that can take carpet thread.

Yarn-darner Needle for embroidering nose and mouth. Size 16-18.

Long-nose pliers for bending cotter pins in crown joints.

Chopstick for poking stuffing into corners. *Alternative:* eraser end of pencil, blunt end of knitting needle, etc.

Optional: *Wire Cutters* for taking apart practice crown joints. (Straightening cotter pins can be frustrating.)

Optional: *T-pins* (about 6) are helpful when attaching ears and making mouth.

Tracing paper for making paper patterns. 2 sheets, 19" x 24" (48 x 60 cm) or equivalent. Available at art supply stores.

Fur fabric ½ yard (50 cm), at least 54" (140 cm) wide, or equivalent area. See pages 14-15 for fabric swatches, color samples, etc.

Velveteen for paw pads (palms) and foot pads (soles of the feet). 8" x 10" piece (20 x 25 cm). *Alternatives:* velvet, real or fake suede. Color range from beige to tan.

Interfacing for stiffening paw pads and foot pads. 8" x 10" piece (20 x 25 cm). Fusible (iron on) interfacing is easily available, but should be used only with velveteen, since ironing can damage other fabrics by melting or flattening the pile.

Sewing thread same color as fur fabric for all machine sewing. 1 spool.

Carpet thread or *Buttonhole twist*, same color as fabric, for all hand sewing. 1 spool.

Optional: *Beeswax block* for coating carpet thread or buttonhole twist, to add strength and smoothness. Essential for uncoated threads (though some may already be coated with silicon finish).

Felt for protective pads in crown joints. 9" x 12" or ⅛ yard (23 x 20 cm or ⅛ m). *Alternative:* leather.

Wood board for crown joint disks. ¼" (5-7 mm) thickness. 9" x 12" (23 x 30 cm). *Alternatives:* masonite, cardboard. Buy cardboard in ⅛" pieces for proper thickness.

Cotter pins for crown joints. 3/32" width, 2" length (3 mm x 5 cm). 5 for making the joints, but have extras on hand for practice and mistakes. Thicker pins are too hard to bend, longer pins won't be tight enough.

Steel washers for crown joints. 7/16" (1 cm) diameter with a 3/16" (1 mm) hole for making the crown joints. 10 total.

Polyester Stuffing. 1 lb. (450 gm) bag. *Alternatives:* older bears were stuffed with anything from sawdust to horsehair to kapok. Polyester is the most washable, durable, and firm. See page 37 for more details.

Glass eyes. 14 mm diameter. 1 pair. *Alternatives:* safety eyes, also called post-and-washer; black shank buttons. See page 36 for more details.

3-ply black Persian yarn for embroidering facial features. 1-2 yards (1-2 m). *Alternative:* any other black sport-weight or tapestry yarn.

Optional: *Growler Box* for making bear noises. *Alternative:* music box. See page 28 for details.

Growler Box

Music box

Drill with ⅛" bit

Scissors

Pins

3-ply black Persian yarn

Squeakers

Safety eyes

Sewing thread

Carpet thread
or Buttonhole twist

T-pins

Dressmakers' Shears

Awl   Embroidery Needles

Velveteen for paw pads

Beeswax block

Ruler

Sawdust

14

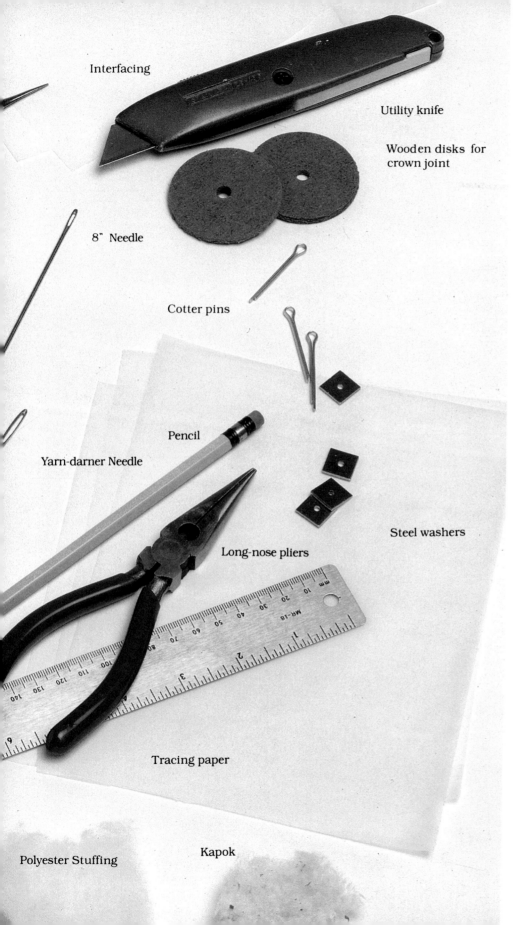

Interfacing

Utility knife

Wooden disks for
crown joint

8" Needle

Cotter pins

Pencil

Yarn-darner Needle

Long-nose pliers

Steel washers

Tracing paper

Polyester Stuffing

Kapok

Stuffing Materials

Polyester Fiber Stuffing is the best, most readily available material for stuffing bears. It is lightweight, durable, easy to work with and washable. It can be purchased at fabric and variety stores usually in 12 ounce 1 or 2 pound bags. It comes in a variety of qualities, so choose one that is soft and fluffy and of even consistency.

Kapok is a natural fiber which surrounds the seed pods of the ceiba tree. It was once commonly used to stuff bears, but it is not easy to obtain today and is more expensive than polyester. Although kapok doesn't tend to bunch up as much as polyester fiber, it is more difficult to work with. The individual fibers are lightweight and tend to float about in the air. When stuffed it is heavier than other stuffings and may make a large bear heavy.

Sawdust was a stuffing once used for teddy bears that is enjoying a comeback among traditionalists today. It can be purchased in 1 pound bags or found in woodworkers' shops. Make sure that it is clean, doesn't contain splinters, and that the bear's fabric is dense enough so the sawdust will not come through.

Foam rubber pieces can be used to give a pliable bouncy feel to a bear. They are inexpensive, readily available, and washable. However, foam pieces contain static electricity and stick to everything in the area. When working with foam pieces, do not try to stuff them in firmly. Simply fill the body parts up to the top and let the foam remain fluffy.

Cut-up fabric scraps or old stockings are not the best material for stuffing. They tend to be heavy, too firm, and sometimes lumpy. However, if you have nothing else available you can try using small pieces of the softest materials on hand.

15

Cinnamon-colored fur fabric: ⅜"
(1 cm) pile. sleek look. smooth feel.
For all sizes of bears.

Cinnamon-colored fur fabric: ½"
(1.25 cm) pile. fluffy, shaggy look.
For cuddly medium to large bears.

Brown fur fabric:
½" (1.25 cm) pile. smooth
and luxurious feel. For
medium and large bears.

Beige fur fabric: ¾" (2 cm) pile.
soft and fluffy feel. For large and
extra-large bears.

Grey fur fabric:
⅜" (1 cm) pile.
soft feel. fluffy
appearance. For
medium and large
bears.

Brown upholstery plush fabric: ⅛"
(3 mm) pile. woven backing. smooth
velvety feel. For bears of all sizes.
good for paw and foot pads.

Wrong side (the back) of fur fabric has a
knitted backing which stretches for well-
shaped bears.

Honey-colored fur fabric: ³⁄₁₆"
(5 mm) pile. velvety appearance.
smooth feel. For small and tiny bears.

Fur Fabrics

Light cinnamon-colored fur fabric: ¼" (7 mm) pile, soft, smooth feel. For small to medium bears.

Fur is a Teddy Bear's most important characteristic. So give some consideration to the kind of furry fabric that you purchase. Look at the swatches shown here to see some of the possibilities—some are shaggy, some are smooth, some are sleek, some are fluffy. These qualities are determined by the length, the composition (what fibers are used), and the density (how close together the fur is) of the pile. Of course, the way a fabric will look depends a lot on the size of the bear you are going to make. For example, a short-pile fur will seem full when worn by a small bear. A bear made with a medium-length fur will seem quite fluffy. A large bear made with short-pile fur will have a velvety appearance. Long fur will give a soft and cuddly feel.

The first Teddy Bears were made from plush fabrics of mohair or wool in the early 1900's. Originally mohair was a firm pile fabric made from the fur of angora goats. It is dull and has a distinct scent, especially when wet, as does wool. Modern day "mohair" plush is usually a blend of wool and cotton, so it has no special scent.

Most fur fabrics today are a blend of man-made fibers such as nylon, polyester, acrylic, and modacrylic. Although they tend to be a little shinier than real fur or mohair, they are inexpensive, durable, and available in a wide range of colors and textures. They usually have a knitted backing that is extra pliable, so it conforms well to a stuffed shape and gives a little when hugged.

Fur fabrics are sold by the yard or as remnants in fabric stores or in the sewing departments of discount and variety stores. For plush fabrics, check upholstery stores and interior decorating sections in department stores. As for prices, remnants are usually your cheapest bet. You can pay up to twice as much when buying by the yard. More luxurious fur coating fabrics can cost up to twice as much again. While cost is one concern, so is quality.

Check fabrics for durability by folding the fabric with the fur side out and examining the folded edge. If the hairs are sparse, the fabric will quickly show signs of wear. Some fur fabrics are washable and others only dry-cleanable. When you buy the fabric, try to find out what the fabric is made of and how to clean it safely. A tag is usually attached to remnant pieces and bolts. If this information is unavailable, you will have to test a scrap before washing the whole bear because the fabric may pucker or run.

Yes, some bears are made with real fur. Real fur skins from a used fur coat can make a luxurious "conversation-piece" bear, though the skins must be sewn by hand.

Modern-mohair fabric: ³⁄₁₆" (5 mm) pile (available in other lengths), firm feel, densely woven. For small to medium bears.

Real Fur.

Honey-colored fur fabric: ⅜" (1 cm) pile, densely woven, luxurious, fluffy, and full appearance. For medium and large bears.

Making the Patterns

The patterns here are for T.R. Bear, a classic heirloom teddy who stands about 18" (45 cm) tall. If you want to vary the size and make T.R. either larger or smaller, check "Mama Bear's Sewing Hints" for instructions on enlarging or reducing the pattern size. To use the patterns for T.R. as shown, copy each pattern piece directly onto tracing paper. Be sure to copy all of the markings—labels, dots, X's, etc. In short, be as precise as you possibly can. The most important lines are the seams, marked with broken lines. The outer solid lines are exactly ¼" (2 mm) outside the seams. That ¼" difference is called the "seam allowance."

You do not have to transfer the broken lines to the fabric if you can stitch exactly ¼" in from the edge of the fabric all around. Although marking the seam allowance on the fabric helps you to visualize the stitches you are going to make, almost all sewing machines have indicators to help you follow an exact seam allowance as you sew.

When you have finished transferring all of the markings to the tracing paper patterns, carefully cut out the patterns along the outer solid lines.

*An experienced tailor, to whom I was apprenticed early in my career, told me "Measure twice, cut once." What he forgot to tell me (probably because it was so obvious to him) was that when I am working from printed patterns and see "**CUT 2**" on a piece, it usually means to cut one, then turn the pattern over before I cut the other one. This is especially important when one piece will be on the right side and the other on the left side. Of course, if I double the fabric before laying out the pattern and cutting, I automatically get the reverse side.*

T.R.

Cutting and Marking the Pieces

Laying Out the Patterns
Place the furry fabric, wrong side up, on a flat surface—the floor, or a work table if you have one. Turn the fabric so the nap of the fur runs toward you from top to bottom. Arrange the pattern pieces on the wrong side of the fabric with the arrows running in the same direction as the nap of the fur.

You don't have to use our suggested layout to arrange the patterns on your fabric. If you have a different width of fabric, you may have to make your own layout—but watch the nap direction, and make sure you have enough room to reverse the patterns and cut the pieces for the opposite side of the bear.

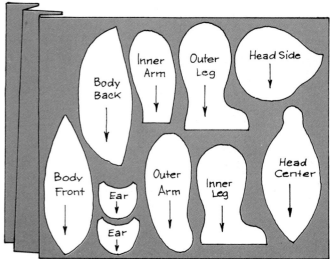

A Suggested Layout

Cutting the Fabric

When you have arranged all the pattern pieces on the fabric, pin them securely in place so they won't slide around while you cut. Insert the pins into the backing only. If you wish, you can trace around the patterns with chalk or pastel pencil after they are pinned down, and then cut along the lines. (Don't use felt-tip markers because they might bleed through to the fur side.) The tracing method has an advantage because you can reverse the patterns and mark the pieces for the opposite side before you start cutting.

Cutting Check-list for Furry Fabric
Head Center (cut 1)   Ear Pieces (cut 4)

Cut out one from each of the following pattern pieces, then reverse and cut out one each for the opposite side.

Back	Inner Arm	Inner Leg
Front	Outer Arm	Outer Leg
Head Side		

Use a pair of sharp scissors or a single-edge razor blade to cut out the pieces of fabric. Try to avoid cutting the fur; cut through the backing only. The fur pile will separate by itself as you cut. If you use a razor blade, be especially careful not to press so hard that you cut the fur. If you prefer to use scissors, it helps to cut in short strokes and slide the scissor tip on the furry side close to the backing as you cut.

Velveteen and Interfacing

You will need to cut the Paw Pads and the Foot Pads from both velveteen and interfacing material. Since velveteen is a lightweight fabric, it must be backed with interfacing to add strength and stiffness. Although the Paw Pads and the Foot Pads are small pieces, lay out the patterns and cut out the fabrics carefully, flop the patterns to make the reverses, and copy all of the markings.

*When you stroke my fur it lies down or it stands up, depending on which way you rub it. Tailors call that hairy grain the **NAP** of the fabric (fake fur, corduroy, and velveteen, for example, are all fabrics with a nap). Rain runs off a bear better if the nap of the fur lies flat when you stroke it downward from head to toe. The arrows printed on the patterns show the direction in which the nap of the fabric should be lying when you pin on a pattern. (One way to remember nap direction is to notice that when a cat "naps," it lies down.)* T.R.

*When you mark the fur or velveteen fabric on the wrong side, **INK** or felt-tip pens might bleed through and stain my fur. I'd surely be blamed for the mess, so please mark with something that doesn't use ink—like pastel, pencils, or chalk.* T.R.

Marking the Pieces

After you cut out the fabric pieces, copy the markings from the patterns onto the wrong side of each one. The placement marks, represented by X's, must be copied precisely. Position the pattern on the fabric piece and make a slight pinprick at each X. Then take the pattern off and mark the X on the fabric immediately. Also use a pin to mark the area for the nose on the head center. Make a series of pricks and then connect the dots as you mark the fabric.

The other markings are less crucial, but still important. The dots and notches are reference points for stitching instructions. The arrow reminds you which way the nap runs. The label helps you to tell arms from legs and backs from fronts. You may also want to indicate on the pieces that have reversed doubles which piece is for the right-hand and which is for the left-hand side of the bear. The patterns printed in this book are all for the left-hand side; the reverses are for the right-hand side.

Some of the markings—the X's and the area for the nose, to be precise—have to be indicated on the right side of the fabric as well as on the wrong side. On the right side, mark all of the X's with tailor's tacks, and mark the top border for the nose area with basting stitches.

The full-sized patterns you see on the opposite page, and those immediately following, are the ones you must trace to make me, T.R. We have printed them in tints of blue, and sometimes grey, so you can see them more easily when the pattern pieces overlap. The marks around the edges are ruled at 1-inch (2.5 cm) intervals. If you want to **enlarge or reduce** these patterns, you may connect the lines to make a grid of squares.

Bearnice is a slightly smaller bear than I am. To make patterns for her, draw a grid of 7/8"-inch (2.25 cm) squares and transfer the lines inside my patterns into those. Quite A. Small-Bear is the same noble shape as mine also, but on an even smaller scale. Draw a grid with 5/8-inch squares to reproduce his patterns from mine. If you have access to a photocopying machine that reduces, Bearnice's patterns are 87.5% of these patterns; QASB's are 62.5%.

Crown Joint Parts

You don't have to mark the pieces: just cut them out. Later on, remember that the larger pieces are for the head joint, and the rest are for the arms and legs.

From felt or leather:
2" (5 cm) diameter pads—cut 8
3½" (9 cm) diameter pads—cut 2
From wood or cardboard
(⅛" - ¼" (4-6 mm) thickness): 1½" (4 cm) diameter disks—cut 8
3" (7½ cm) diameter disks—cut 2

If you are cutting wood, use a utility knife, a small craft saw, or a hole saw. A pair of scissors will do for all other materials, although it might be easier to cut cardboard with a utility knife.

Finally, on each wood or cardboard disk, cut a hole in the center. On wood, use a ⅛" (3 mm) drill bit. The hole must be large enough for the legs of the cotter pin to fit through, but small enough to catch the head of the pin. On cardboard disks, use an awl.

Complete List of Pattern Pieces

Body Front	Outer Leg	Head Side	Paw Pad
Body Back	Inner Arm	Head Center	Foot Pad
Inner Leg	Outer Arm	Ear	

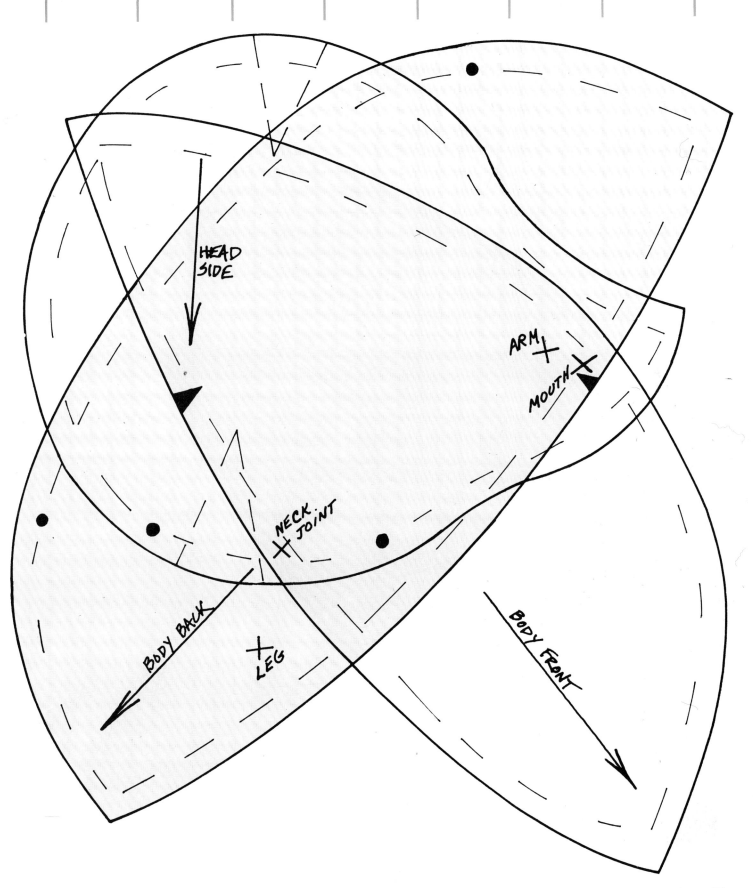

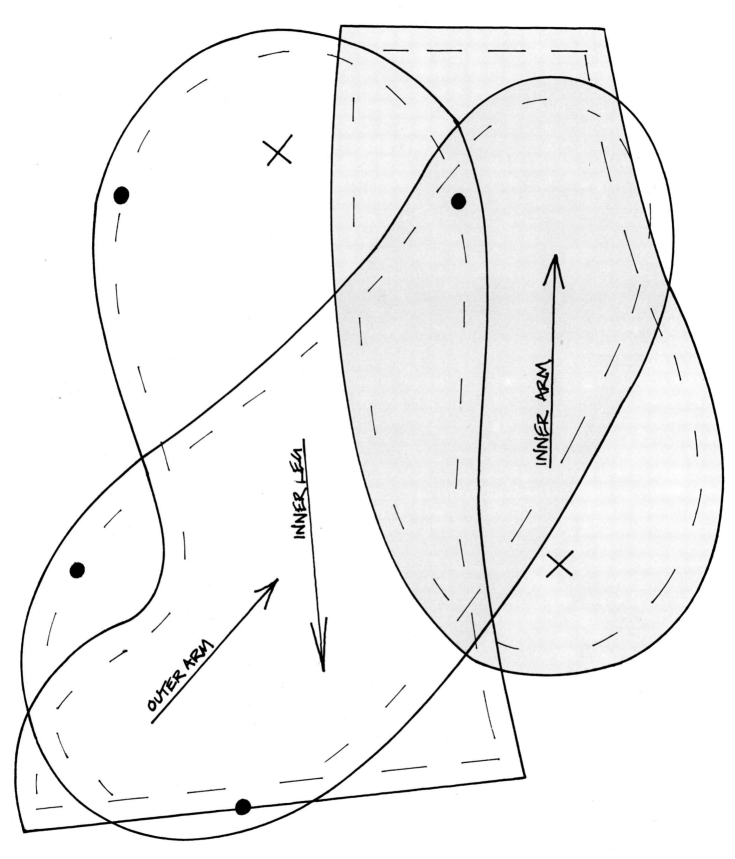

INNER LEG

INNER ARM

OUTER ARM

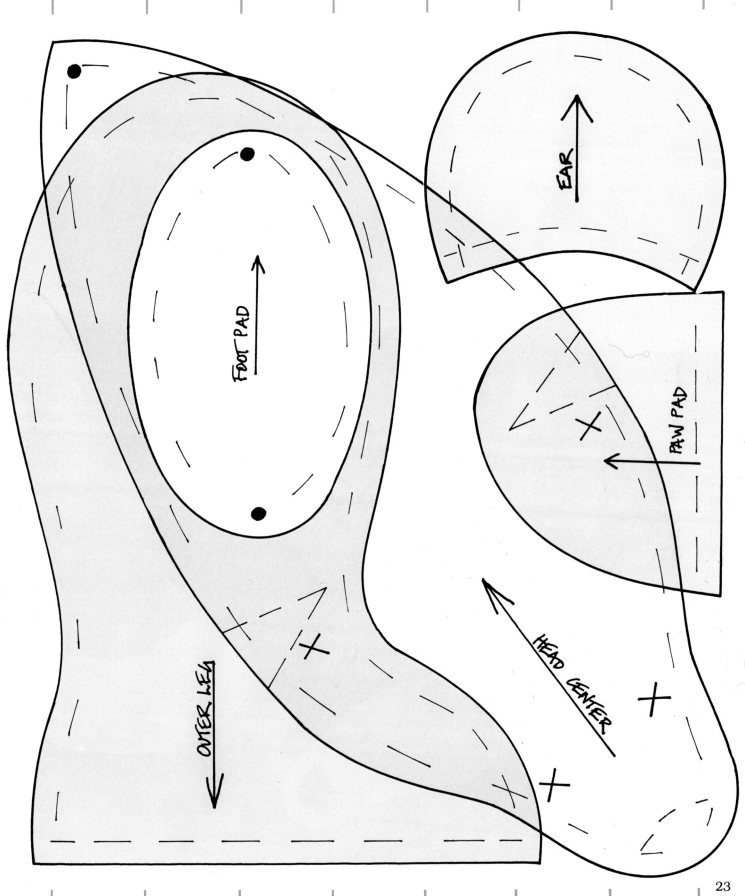

FOOT PAD

EAR

PAW PAD

OUTER LEG

HEAD CENTER

23

Sewing The Pieces Together

Arms. First attach the velveteen fabric to the interfacing to make the pads for the palms of both paws. The interfacing stiffens the fabric. Some types are sewn on, while others are fused to the fabric with a hot iron. If you use fusible interfacing, follow the instructions on the interfacing package instead of our instructions, but test a scrap piece of velveteen first to be sure that the ironing doesn't flatten the velveteen's pile.

When you have made both pads, sew one to the paw-end of each *Inner Arm* piece of fur fabric. Then, with the right sides together, sew the *Inner Arm* piece to the *Outer Arm* piece for each arm to make two open-ended sacks. Leave the shoulder end open to insert the stuffing later. Turn each arm right side out. Fold under and baste the ¼" seam allowance along the stuffing opening.

1. *For non-fusible interfacing only:* Pin, then baste interfacing to wrong side of velveteen. Trim interfacing close to stitches to reduce bulk.

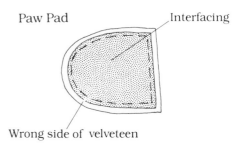

Paw Pad · Interfacing

Wrong side of velveteen

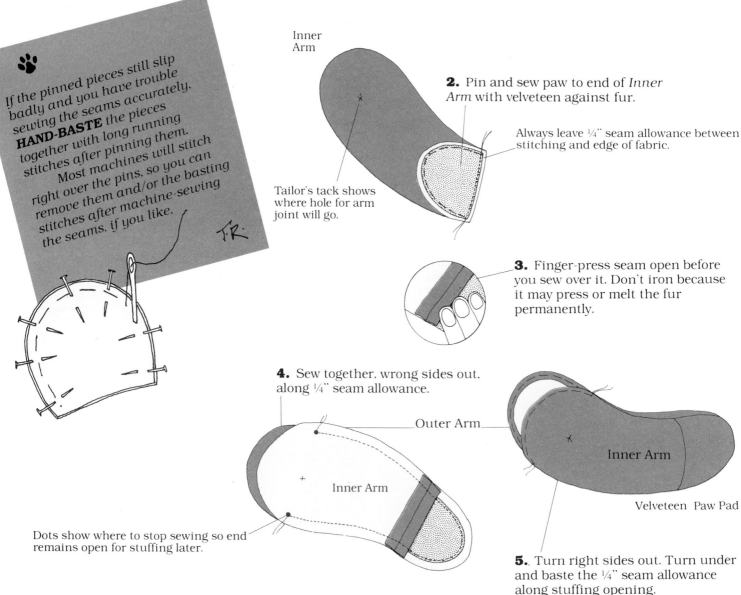

If the pinned pieces still slip badly and you have trouble sewing the seams accurately, **HAND-BASTE** the pieces together with long running stitches after pinning them.
Most machines will stitch right over the pins, so you can remove them and/or the basting stitches after machine-sewing the seams, if you like.

J.R.

Inner Arm

Tailor's tack shows where hole for arm joint will go.

2. Pin and sew paw to end of *Inner Arm* with velveteen against fur.

Always leave ¼" seam allowance between stitching and edge of fabric.

3. Finger-press seam open before you sew over it. Don't iron because it may press or melt the fur permanently.

4. Sew together, wrong sides out, along ¼" seam allowance.

Outer Arm

Inner Arm

Dots show where to stop sewing so end remains open for stuffing later.

Inner Arm

Velveteen Paw Pad

5. Turn right sides out. Turn under and baste the ¼" seam allowance along stuffing opening.

Legs.

The tricky part of the first step is matching the edges of the *Inner Leg* with the larger *Outer Leg*. Pin them so they line up exactly all around. The outer sides will be slack, but when the legs are stuffed they will look just fine.

After you have made the pads for the soles of the feet, but before you pin and baste them to the foot end of the leg, make sure the dots on the wrong side of the pad line up with the seams on the front and back of the leg. Don't worry about which side is the heel and which the toe. On T.R. they are exactly the same shape.

1. With right sides together, stretch smaller *Inner Leg* to meet edges of *Outer Leg*. Pin or baste securely before sewing.

Leave opening at top for stuffing.

Tailor's tack shows where hole for leg joint will go.

Inner Leg

Opening for *Foot Pad*

2. Sew *Outer* and *Inner Legs* together. Leave bottom open for *Foot Pad*.

3. *For non-fusible interfacing only:* Pin, then baste interfacing to wrong side of velveteen. Trim interfacing close to stitches to reduce bulk.

Interfacing

Wrong side of velveteen

4. With right sides together, fold out seam allowance around bottom of foot and pin it to edge of *Foot Pad*. Once pad is fixed in place, stitch it to leg.

Dots on *Foot Pad* match front and back seams of leg.

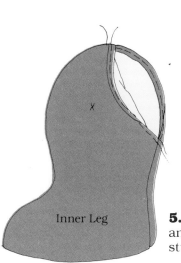

Inner Leg

5. Turn right sides out. Fold under and baste ¼" seam allowance along stuffing opening.

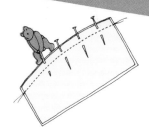

Because furry fabric is so slippery and smooth, it is especially important to **PIN** pieces together before you sew them. Also, as you pin you smooth the fur away from the seam line. This keeps the fur from getting caught in the stitches of the seams and giving me a thread-"bear" appearance, if you will pardon the expression. Insert the pins at 1-1½" intervals, perpendicular to the seam.

I recommend a pin cushion or magnet to keep loose pins safe and handy. Better still, make an embroidered Bear-maker's Ribbon like the one I am wearing. It helps you keep from misplacing your scissors all the time, too. See instructions for Needleworker's Ribbon in Bear's Bazaar.

T.R.

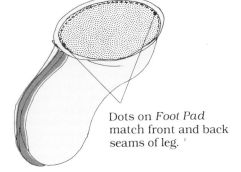

Body. First you sew each *Front* piece to a *Back* piece, matching them up along the notched edges. This makes the seams that run up the bear's sides under his arms. Then you sew the two halves of the body together along the seams that run down the bear's belly and up his back. When you are through, part of the back seam will be left open for working on the joints and for stuffing. You also leave a tiny hole at the neck area for the pin that attaches the head.

2. Pin the two halves together.

3. Do not sew over seam allowance for side seam. As you sew toward it, push the allowance out of the way, and stop sewing about one stitch length from side seam. Secure thread end as you would any other seam.

1. Match up notches and pin side seams together, then sew.

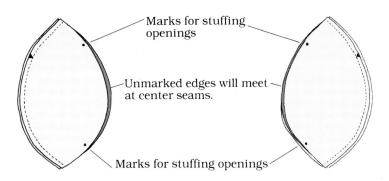

Marks for stuffing openings

Unmarked edges will meet at center seams.

Marks for stuffing openings

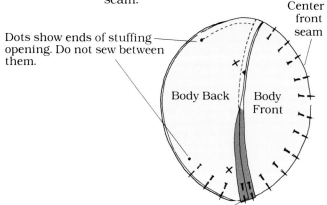

Dots show ends of stuffing opening. Do not sew between them.

Center front seam

Body Back

Body Front

4. Finger-press side seams open.

5. Start sewing one stitch length from side seam. Make sure the end is secure.

Leave a ⅛" (3 mm) hole at the seam.

Side seam

6. Sew over the finger-pressed side seams.

7. Sew all around to lower dot on back.

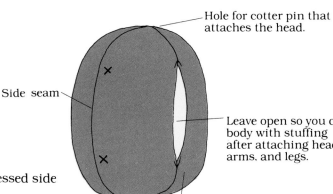

Hole for cotter pin that attaches the head.

Side seam

Leave open so you can fill body with stuffing after attaching head, arms, and legs.

Back seam

8. Turn right sides out. Fold under and baste the ¼" seam allowance along stuffing opening.

Head. See "Mama Bear's Sewing Basket" ✂ if you need to know more about sewing and clipping darts. The rest of the sewing is simple enough. Sew the *Head Sides* together between the nose and neck opening; then sew the *Head Center* on, starting from the back of the neck opening, stitching all the way around the nose and returning to the neck opening.

Note that the instructions for attaching safety eyes are optional. Glass eyes are attached only after the bear is stuffed.

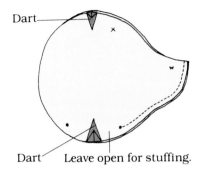

Dart

Dart   Leave open for stuffing.

1. Stitch darts in *Head Side* and *Head Center* pieces.

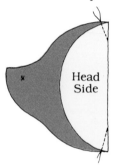

Head Side

Tailor's tacks show positions for facial features

2. Clip the center fold of the darts and press them open with your fingers.

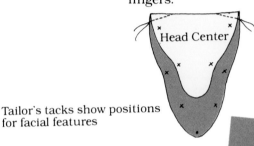

Head Center

3. With right sides facing, pin and sew *Head Sides* together along center front seam that runs from nose to neck.

4. With right sides still facing, pin *Head Center* piece to each of the two *Head Side* pieces, matching up darts.

5. Use pins to match dot on *Head Center* to dot on each of the *Head Sides*. (The three pieces meet at one spot.) Start sewing from dot on one of the *Head Sides*, and sew all the way around to the dot on the other.

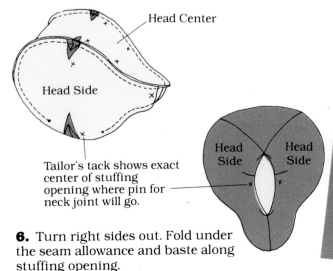

Head Center

Head Side

Tailor's tack shows exact center of stuffing opening where pin for neck joint will go.

6. Turn right sides out. Fold under the seam allowance and baste along stuffing opening.

Head Side   Head Side

I love kids, so I worry if there's any way they might hurt themselves by playing with me. The only thing I can think of is that if one of my eyes should ever come off, some little child might swallow it. **SAFETY EYES**—also called post-and-washer eyes, may not be as nice and bright as glass eyes, but they will never fall off. You decide which is best, but remember to attach safety eyes before you stuff the head.

Back Section

Eye   Shank

7. Make a small hole at each eye position with an awl or small knitting needle.

8. Insert shank of the eye through hole.

9. Turn head inside out, then press back section (washer) securely onto shank.

T·R·

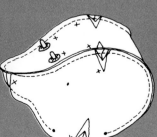

EYES

Just like human beings, a teddy bear's eyes reflect the individual's spirit. Your bear's expression, even character, is determined both by the placement of the eyes on the face and by your choice of materials (glass, button, embroidery, felt, or, for little children's bears, plastic safety eyes). You can make your teddy's mood chipper and cheery, or pensive and melancholy—or anything in between.

Spend some time experimenting with different locations. Avoid getting the eyes too high on the face or too close together. Your decisions will determine how your teddy will look out on the world (and the world in on your teddy) for ever and ever. You'll find some ideas about positioning eyes in the "Expressions" section in this chapter.

Glass puts a real glint in a bear's eyes, but it's not a wise choice if you are making a bear for a very young child, since glass eyes are easier than other types to pull off and swallow. And, of course, they occasionally break. Sizes range from tiny (3 mm) to huge (25 mm). And colors include amber, blue, pink, and white. You usually buy them in pairs, one at each end of a straight wire.

1. To make loops, cut wire about ¾" (2 cm) from each eye.

2. Form a loop out of wire, using needle-nose pliers.

3. Attach eyes following instructions in the section on "Making the Face."

Safety eyes are good for bright-eyed bears destined for small children. Their design makes it difficult for children to pull them off and possibly swallow them or choke. There are two types of plastic safety eyes: lock-and-washer and those fitted with a sewing loop. Some bear makers find the sewing-loop type easier to attach and more secure. Safety eyes are attached *before* the head is stuffed. Make sure you position the lock-and-washer type exactly before pushing the washer in, since it is extremely difficult to take it out.

Washer

Push washer onto stud.

Buttons make very good eyes. You may have perfect ones in your button box right now just waiting to become eyes for some bear. You can create any expression you want with buttons because they come in such a wide range of colors, shapes, and sizes. To attach shank buttons, see the instructions in the "Making the Face" section.

Shank buttons   Flat button

Embroidered eyes are ideal for bears going to live with small children and for bears you want to be able to wash. Eyes can be embroidered directly onto any bear's face that is covered in short fur or a low-pile fabric. The eyes can be squares, circles, or ovals, or even a circle within a circle to show both iris and pupil. You can make raised and shaped (dimensional) embroidered eyes. For each eye, use a button, a piece of fabric (cotton, linen, or wool are good choices), and embroidery yarn or floss.

Felt eyes also work well on bears for small children and, if the felt is colorfast, the bear will be washable. Felt eyes are easy to make, too.

Growlers, Squeakers, and Music Boxes

An older bear like T.R. might make a low growl if you tip him over. A smaller bear, who is softly stuffed, may squeak when you squeeze him tightly. Another more talented bear might play a lullaby when he or she is wound up. All of these special effects are options that you can choose to take when you are ready to stuff your bear.

If you cannot find growlers, squeakers, or music boxes in stores near your area, see our list of Mail-order Suppliers at the end of this book.

Insert sound devices like these in the bear after the body is mostly stuffed and you are ready to sew up the stuffing hole in the back. You may also retro-fit an existing bear by opening the back seam and removing some stuffing to make room for a sound device.

Growlers and squeakers are cylindrical containers with holes in one end. When tipped, a weight presses on a bellows forcing air past a reed, making a big bear growl or a small bear squeak.

1. Cut a piece of strong, lightweight fabric, such as voile or organdy, wide enough to go around the cylinder and long enough to cover the ends.

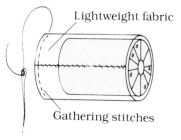

Lightweight fabric

Gathering stitches

2. Wrap fabric around cylinder, turn under one edge, and whip stitch edges together.

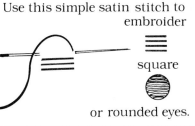
Embroidered eye with button

1. Trace outline of button on fabric. Draw lines for iris, pupil, and highlight, if desired, then embroider.

2. With embroidered image at center, cut circle twice as large as button. Run gathering stitches around the edge.

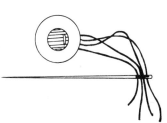

Gathering stitches

Very strong thread, 12" (30.5 cm)

Tie knot here

3. Thread each button with 2 lengths.

4. Turn fabric, eye side down, center button on fabric, and gather edges of fabric tightly over back of button. Stitch edges across button.

5. Thread into large needle and attach to bear, following directions for attaching glass eye.

Felt eyes

Slip stitch

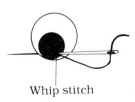

Whip stitch

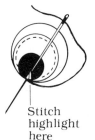

Stitch highlight here

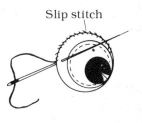

1. Cut black (small), brown (larger), and white (largest) circles from felt and stitch together. Or, you can use just 2 circles.

2. Whip-stitch edge to face. For rounded effect, push stuffing behind eye before stitching to face.

---

3. Gather and stitch both ends tightly. Insert cylinder so end with holes in it is against inside of fur.

Carpet thread or buttonhole twist

Stitch end with sound-holes to fur

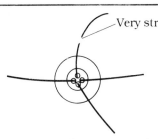

4. Stitch fabric cover to fur fabric inside body with carpet thread or buttonhole twist. Don't let stitches show. Tightly pack space around cylinder with stuffing.

Music boxes have winding keys that can be unscrewed from the shank that sticks out of the metal case.

1. Unscrew key and cover music box in sturdy fabric as shown for growlers and squeakers. Push shank through fabric cover.

2. Stitch covering to inside of fur as for growler, in exact center of top of bear's back.

3. Make a hole in fur for shank and screw on winding key so shank will not slip back through hole. Pack stuffing around music box to keep it in place.

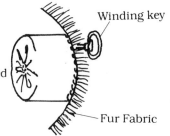

Winding key

Music box covered with fabric

Fur Fabric

Jointing and Stuffing

T.R.'s head, arms, and legs attach to his body by means of five crown joints. The actual assembly of the bear is easy; but putting together a firm, strong joint can be a little difficult, even for experienced joint makers who are simply out of practice. If you are not already skilled at making crown joints, follow through the crown joint training session below. If you have made them before, but feel a little rusty, you should at least make a practice joint or two ahead of time. Use extra cotter pins and scrap fabric until you get back the touch.

How to Make a Crown Joint

T.R.'s five crown joints are the most complicated part of his anatomy. However, since they enable him to move his head and limbs, and to hold them in any position, they are really what make him the outstanding teddy bear he is. The trickiest part of making a crown joint is getting it to hold tight. A successful joint must be so tight that you will probably think it is too tight to move. (After the bear is stuffed, the joint will loosen slightly so that the limbs will move easily.) The first try rarely turns out as well as the third or fourth, so it helps to practice making joints out of spare scraps of furry fabric and extra cotter pins.

For your practice joint, have on hand:

- 2 Metal Washers
- 2 Wooden or Cardboard Disks
  (Use two of the disks that you have already cut. They can be reused in T.R.'s actual joints.)
- 2 Felt or Leather Pads (These can also be reused.)
  Cotter Pins (Cannot be reused. You need one per joint, but have enough extras on hand to cover mistakes.)

For tools, you will need:

An awl or a thin knitting needle for puncturing the fabric.
A long-nose (needle-nose) pliers for bending the cotter pin.
Wire cutters. Actually, you don't really need these, but they come in handy when you want to take apart a joint.

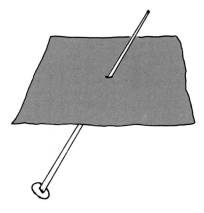

1. Using an awl or a thin knitting needle, pierce a hole through both pieces of fabric from the wrong side and through the centers of the two felt pads. The holes should fit the shank snugly.

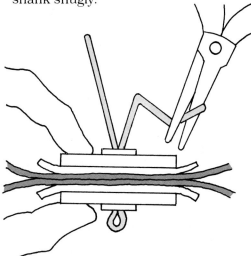

5. Grip the same leg half-way between the top and the first bend, and make a second bend upward.

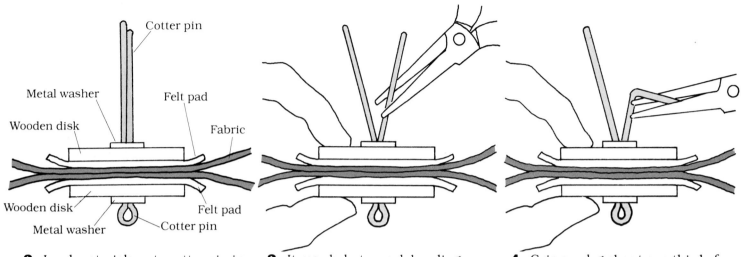

2. Load materials onto cotter pin in order shown. The furry sides of the fabric pieces face each other.

3. It may help to mark bending points at one-third intervals ahead of time. Pinch joint tightly with your free hand while you separate the legs of the cotter pin with a long-nose pliers.

4. Grip one leg about one-third of the way from the washer. Pull upward—hard—as you bend it back and away. Keep pinching joint in your hand as you work. It helps make the pressure tighter.

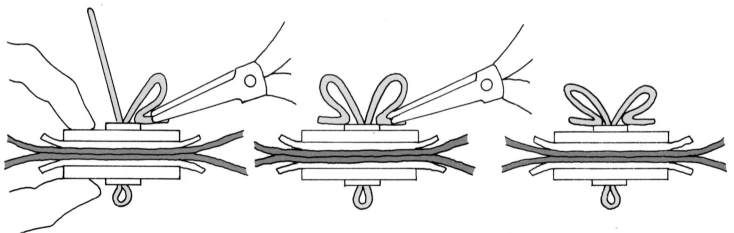

6. Push the second bend as far as you can toward the top washer to form a loop.

7. Squeeze the second bend securely against washer and base of cotter pin. (Now, at last, it's okay to relax your other hand.)

8. Bend other leg the same way, then pull both loops out away from each other and slightly down, for extra firmness.

Congratulations. You've just made a crown joint. If you can barely manage to turn it, it is made correctly. If the joint moves freely before you stuff the bear, then it is too loose. The reason for making the crown joint tight is so that the limbs will hold any position in which you put them. Loose crown joints result in a down-and-out teddy bear who will remain limp and unresponsive all his life. If your joint is loose, remove and discard the cotter pin. (Use a wire cutter if you have one.) Do not straighten out and reuse the old pin; too much bending weakens the metal.

Although almost everybody makes mistakes at first, it doesn't take long to get the knack of making crown joints. And when you've got the hang of it, the achievement is worth the hard work and frustration. Just think how good you'll feel as you effortlessly turn out firm and sturdy crown joints—almost as if you were born to make teddy bears.

Stuffing and Attaching the Head to the Body

If you have some questions on the details of how to stuff a bear, turn the page and refer to the list of stuffing hints. When stuffing the head, use your fingers to massage the head into its correct shape as you stuff. Also, stuff the nose first because it is hardest to reach.

Just before you seal the stuffing opening, put in a cotter pin with a washer, large disk, and large pad loaded on it. Seal the stuffing opening tightly around the pin's shank, with the pin positioned between the placement marks at the center of the opening. Insert the pin into the neck hole of the body, finish loading the cotter pin, and bend the pin's legs into a crown. Press the pieces of the joint as firmly as you can while you bend the legs so the joint comes out tight.

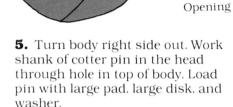

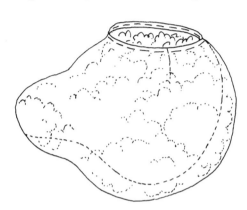

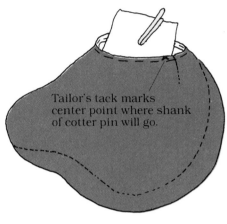

5. Turn body right side out. Work shank of cotter pin in the head through hole in top of body. Load pin with large pad, large disk, and washer.

1. Firmly stuff nose area first, then fill the rest of the head with large handfuls of stuffing. Massage face with your fingers as you stuff it to settle stuffing evenly into the correct shape.

3. Place loaded pin inside opening. Pack stuffing around its edge, but not on top.

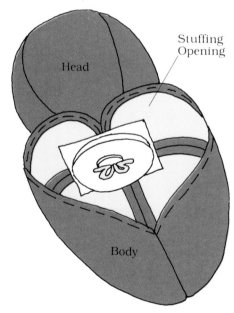

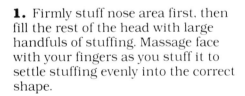

Is the head packed firmly and evenly? Is the pin straight in the center at the tailor's tack?

Close opening permanently by slip-stitching with carpet thread.

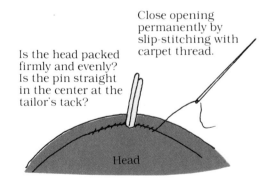

6. Press pieces firmly together as you bend cotter pin to make a crown joint. The joint for the head must not turn loosely. It will loosen with use.

If head is not centered on the body or tips to one side, the disks are not level or the cotter pin is not centered. You may have to cut the pin, open the seam, and redo the joint.

2. Load cotter pin with a washer, large disk, and large pad.

4. First pin seams together. Slip-stitch around opening by hand so pin is held firmly.

Attaching the Arms and Legs

All four limbs are attached in the same way. Start with an arm or a leg and match its placement mark to the corresponding placement mark on the body. Puncture the fabric, put the right sides together, and join the body and limb with a crown joint.

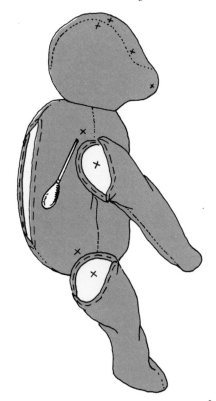

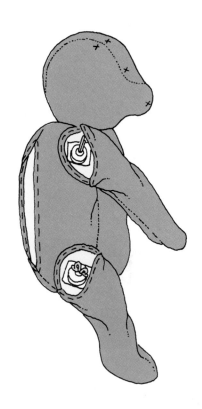

1. Use an awl or knitting needle to make holes at the two matching spots for the joint marked with tailor's tacks.

Work on one limb at a time so you can remember where holes are.

2. Load cotter pin. Put your hand through the stuffing opening in the back. Poke end of pin through the hole for the limb.

3. Attach arm or leg by pushing cotter pin out from inside of body and through the matching hole in the limb. Then load and bend legs of cotter pin into a crown.

Just one word of caution: do make sure to distinguish the right arm and leg from the left arm and leg. One little mix up and T.R. will end up having to walk backward all his life. The toes should point forward, and the arms should curve slightly upward with the paws facing inward toward the body.

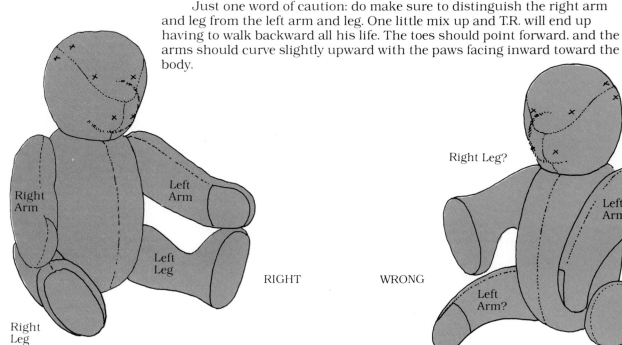

Right Arm

Left Arm

Left Leg

Right Leg

RIGHT

WRONG

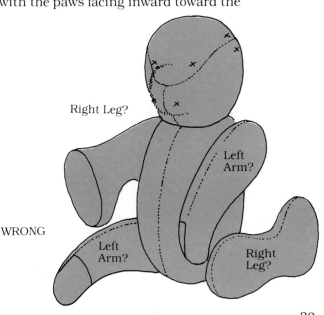

Right Leg?

Left Arm?

Left Arm?

Right Leg?

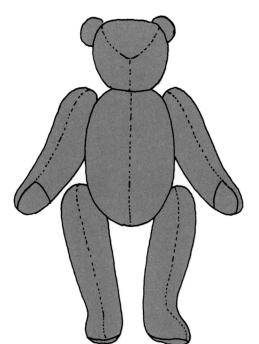

Stuffing the Body, Arms, and Legs
The perfect bear is stuffed firmly and evenly all around. He doesn't have a lump on one side of his head. He doesn't tip over to one side when you try to stand him up. He doesn't have a flimsy nose or a hollow toe. He should be huggable and squeezable, but not limp or lopsided. Here are several hints to make sure your T.R. inherits a fine physique:

1. Whenever possible, insert stuffing in healthy handfuls (roughly the size of a bread roll). Large bunches of stuffing rarely clot into lumps.

2. For all sections of the bear, stuff irregular or hard-to-reach parts first. When you worked on the head, you began by stuffing the nose firmly. On arms and legs, stuff paws and toes first and work your way up. Use a chopstick to pack stuffing firmly in areas difficult to reach with your fingers.

3. Pack stuffing especially firmly around the crown joints. You must not be able to feel the joints at all when you are done.

4. If lumps develop, you don't necessarily have to take out all of the stuffing. Try a vigorous massage to work loose clotted material.

5. Use your hands to mold the shape of each part, especially the face, as you stuff it until it is firm.

6. Test firmness of each part before you stitch up the opening. Pin opening shut, and give the part a squeeze. All T.R.'s parts should be equally firm and huggable.

7. Try not to let stuffing get caught in seams when you sew openings closed by hand.

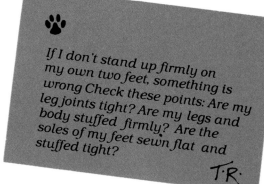

If I don't stand up firmly on my own two feet, something is wrong. Check these points: Are my leg joints tight? Are my legs and body stuffed firmly? Are the soles of my feet sewn flat and stuffed tight?

T·R·

Although the order in which you stuff each part is not really important, it seems natural to start with the body, and end with the arms and legs. After you finish stuffing each section, pin it shut and go on to the next. Stuff the entire bear before you slip-stitch the stuffing openings closed. That way you can re-open some sections to make last minute adjustments. Usually you will just need to add stuffing to one or two parts that didn't fill out properly. However, don't get frustrated if you realize that you need to take out all of the stuffing and adjust a seam at the last moment. It's only natural that mistakes become apparent after the whole bear is stuffed.

Making the Face

Eyes Except for safety eyes, all other types of eyes are tied to the head by their shanks. In some cases—often with glass eyes—you will have to make your own shanks. See the "Eyes" section earlier in this chapter.

1. Double a 48" (120 cm) length of carpet thread so it measures 24" (60 cm).

2. Insert needle just below tack marking top of ear.

3. Bring needle out on same side at tack for eye.

4. Leave 6" (15 cm) of doubled thread extending so you can knot it later.

5. Enlarge the hole where the needle came out with an awl or knitting needle so it is just big enough for the eye shank to slip through.

6. Thread eye shank onto needle, then insert needle into the hole.

7. Bring needle out at Head Side at a spot the ear will cover guiding the eye shank into the hole as you pull the thread tight.

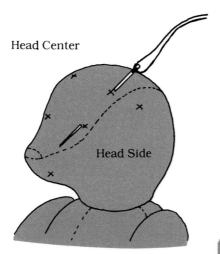

Head Center

Head Side

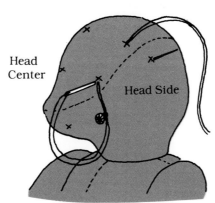

Head Center

Head Side

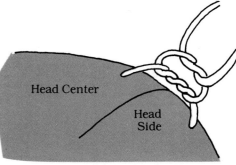

Head Center

Head Side

9. If you can squeeze the head while you finish tying the knot, the eye will fit extra tight.

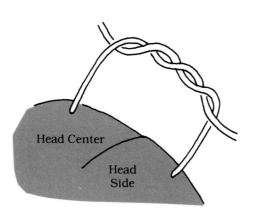

Head Center

Head Side

8. Tie the first half of the knot with an extra twist to help hold it tight while you tie second half of knot.

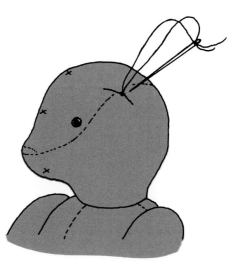

10. Trim ends of threads to about 3" (7 cm). Thread both ends back through eye of needle and pull them into head directly underneath knot.

You can change my expression if you want, by changing the places we show for my eyes and ears, or by sewing the nose and the lines of the mouth differently (see "Expressions" at the end of these instructions). Of course, I am partial to the straightforward, traditional T.R. look—alert eyes, erect ears, graceful nose, and stiff upper lip.

T.R.

Ears. One thing about ears: they are perfect handles for determined tugs by little fingers. Be sure to take three or four extra stitches to strengthen both corners of each ear as you slip-stitch it to the head. When you cup the ears forward, the corners will be closer together and the fabric will give. You can then pull the fabric back just a bit to cover the dart seams.

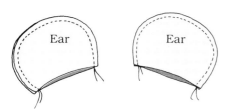

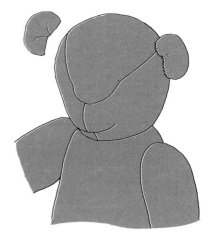

1. Sew ears, wrong side out, along outer edges. Leave bottom open.

2. Turn ears right side out. Fold under and baste the ¼" seam allowance along bottom edges.

3. Pin ears in place between tailor's tacks so they are cupped slightly forward and cover the knotted thread holding the eye.

4. Slip-stitch ears in place, taking several reinforcing stitches at both ends of each ear.

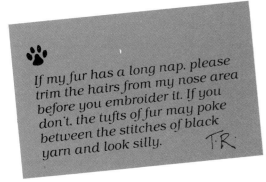

🐾 *If my fur has a long nap, please trim the hairs from my nose area before you embroider it. If you don't, the tufts of fur may poke between the stitches of black yarn and look silly.* T.R.

Nose You use the same thread for both the nose and the mouth, so don't be surprised at how much will be left over when you finish embroidering the nose. You also have plenty of thread for making as many stitches as you need to completely cover the nose area, so make those satin stitches very close together.

The top of the nose is marked with basting stitches put in when the pattern was cut. The bottom is the seam of the *Head Center* piece.

1. Thread a crewel needle with a 24" (60 cm) length of black yarn and knot one end.

2. Insert needle at center of nose and bring it out at the top corner. Pull it through so the knotted end sits against the fabric.

3. Stitch all the way across nose area with vertical satin stitches. Cover knot in middle and basting stitches on top of nose area.

4. Bring out the last stitch for the nose on bottom border of nose area at center seam.

Mouth.

The simple stitches that make the mouth determine the expression on your bear's face more than any other factor. You might want to check the "Expressions" section for possible variations. However, for the traditional T.R. look, just use the marks already positioned on the *Head Sides.*

1. No matter what expression you choose for your T.R., you will start making it by marking the three positioning points. Use T-pins to mark any points that are not already indicated by tailor's tacks:
Point 1: On T.R.'s right *Head Side*
Point 2: On center seam, ¾" (2 cm) below nose
Point 3: Exactly opposite Point 1, on T.R.'s left *Head Side*

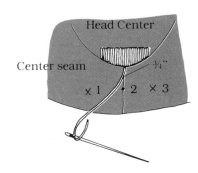

2. Run needle into point 1, toward point 2.

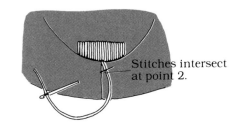

Stitches intersect at point 2.

3. Bring needle out at 2 so that it runs between the yarn and point 1, forcing the stitch to pass point 2 on its way toward 1.

4. Run needle into point 3, and out at top center border of nose. You're almost done.

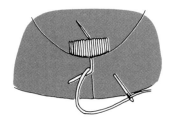

Remove tacks and pins as you pass each point.

5. Pull yarn so that all mouth stitches rest against the fabric, but not so tight that it looks strained. Fasten end of yarn with tiny stitches underneath nose embroidery. Then clip yarn close to fabric. That's all there is to it.

6. Give your T.R. a big hug and welcome him into the world.

Bear Bath T.R. will stay clean a long time, but eventually even the tidiest bear will start to look a little dirty. Most modern fabrics used to make teddy bears can be cleaned by giving your bear a quick sponge bath and blow dry. Have on hand: a washcloth, sponge, mild soap, 2 or more terrycloth towels, comb, and brush. Buy a comb and brush especially for your bear, so you won't get any human hair oil on the fur.

Test your dirty bear to make sure he is washable. Apply a small amount of suds to the upper part of his inner leg, where the fabric won't show if it gets damaged. Rinse the spot and press some white paper towels over the wet area. Wait a few minutes to see if the towels pick up any color from the fur. If not, you have a perfectly washable bear and may proceed.

Make warm, sudsy bath water by following the instructions on the soap package. Place your bare bear on a towel next to the water. Then gently apply the suds to the fabric with a sponge or washcloth, starting at the head and working down. Don't leave the suds on the fabric more than ten minutes or it might soak into the stuffing. During the whole bath, only the fur should get wet.

The parts of your bear's body that are made from yarn, leather, felt, or suede may not be washable. Either test them like you tested the fur, or try to keep the soap away from them.

After you have finished soaping your bear, rinse the washcloth in clean water. Wring the cloth out well and wipe the suds from the fur. Continue rinsing the washcloth and wiping the fur until all the soap is removed.

If you have a very dirty bear, repeat the washing process again. When you finally have him clean, dry the bear with a towel. Comb his fur in the direction of the nap, and then blow dry. Finally, brush the fur into the nice fluffy style that your bear likes best.

Three Finishing Touches for T.R. Bear

1. Keep his seams from showing any more than necessary. When you sew furry fabric on a machine, the long hairs tend to get caught under the stitches, even if you're careful. Take a pin or a needle and pick them out again, so he'll be nice and fluffy along the seams.

2. Brushing your bear will clean off any little scraps or left-over stuffing, and it will help pull out any spare hairs that are still caught in the seams. A dog-grooming brush for short-haired dogs is probably the best bear brush around. Its soft bristles are perfect for teddy bear and dog fur alike. Wash the brush well, though, if you have already used it on a dog. T.R. doesn't mind dogs, but he does hate to smell like them.

3. If fur partially obscures the stitching that forms the mouth, carefully trim it away with a pair of scissors.

Expressions

It is a known fact that teddy bears are capable of feeling every emotion known to humans, perhaps some others too. Each of the heirloom bears in this chapter has a special look that expresses his or her character, but you may decide that the bear you make should have a different sort of expression. When you have stuffed your new bear and are about to add the features to its face, look at the head shape or slope of the shoulders for hints on how it feels about life. You might think "Oh, she's so serious" or "He looks like he's just waiting to get into trouble." These pages tell you a little about how to form each part of the face so it contributes to the personality your bear will have.

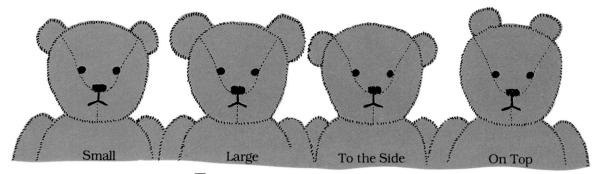

Small Large To the Side On Top

Ears.

The ears are a very distinctive part of a bear's anatomy. Their size and shape should be in keeping with the bear's character. For example, a staid, serious bear wouldn't look right with big floppy ears. Since the ear pattern is a simple shape, you should feel confident enough to do a bit of your own pattern-making. You can draw ears that are a bit larger or smaller, or ears that are curved differently. If you like, test several ear shapes by cutting up some of the scraps of fur. Then try pinning the ears on in different positions and at different angles.

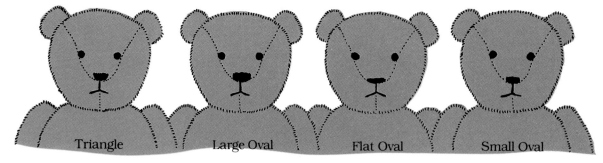

Triangle Large Oval Flat Oval Small Oval

Nose.

The nose may not be a bear's most expressive feature. But it is, after all, right in the middle of its face. Traditional bears have embroidered noses of many shapes and sizes. Triangles and ovals are the most popular shapes. You might try cutting out shapes from scraps of black paper or fabric and placing them on the nose area. When you have decided on the nose shape, take a few basting stitches to remind you where the borders are. Another option to consider, especially if you are making a light-colored bear, is using brown, beige, or pink yarn. Most bears, however, look great with the traditional black noses and mouths.

Happy Smile   Needs Friend   Stubborn   Serene

Mouth.

Like people, teddy bears have very expressive mouths. The traditional teddy bear mouth is an upside-down Y-shape. The expression of the mouth is determined by the length and the angle of the stitches that form the slanted branches of the Y. To experiment with different mouth expressions, cut two small pieces of yarn and pin them on the face along the lines of the mouth. On a traditional, no-nonsense bear like T.R., the mouth slants downward in two straight lines. To make a wide-open smile, like Buddy's, place the lines straight sideways. If they slant upward the bear may look silly. You may also leave slack in the stitches to form a curve, like Bearnice's, which makes her look warm-hearted but perhaps a bit formal, even shy. If the fur doesn't hold the curve of the yarn in position, take a few overcast stitches, using black thread to tuck it in place.

Serious Bear   Cross-eyed Bear   Innocent Bear   Silly Bear   Shy Bear
Close   Too Close   Wide   High   Low

Eyes.

The eyes, of course, are the windows of your teddy bear's soul. Take the eyes you've selected and try placing them on the face. Close-set eyes like T.R. Bear's give him the serious look of the original German Steiff bears. But if you get them too close together, your poor bear will be cross-eyed. Wide-set eyes like Buddy's look innocent and relaxed—some people think they are the most attractive for a bear. Put the eyes down low on the face of a very shy or a very young bear. Put them up higher for a woeful bear or a silly one.

(Left) T.R., the senior, ranking bear in this book, takes his responsibilities seriously when it comes to helping his three friends. Quite A. Small-Bear (being given a boost by T.R., bottom), Bearnice (standing on the bottom shelf), and Buddy, who got to the honey pot first and has just told everyone it is empty. All three of T.R.'s friends are made the same way he is, with a few minor variations. Patterns and instructions for making all three appear on the following pages, starting with Buddy, the largest.

(Below) Buddy Bear has spent all afternoon picking raspberries and blackberries at the edge of a mountain forest on a hot August afternoon. He has just sat down to enjoy all he wants of his second favorite food, when he hears Quite A. Small-Bear shouting with glee at having found a honey tree. What to do?!?

How to Make Buddy Bear

T.R.'s best buddy is a different sort of bear. All of his parts are a little unlike T.R.'s, so Buddy has a whole new set of patterns. He has a darker color, shaggier fur, and he has coal-black button eyes instead of T.R.'s brown glass ones. With all these differences, however, you will find that you can make Buddy almost entirely by following the instructions for T.R. There are new directions for sewing on Buddy's paw pads, and for attaching the head to the body without a crown joint. Some of Buddy's differences, such as the new facial expression, are worked out in the placement marks on the new patterns, so you do not need new instructions.

Since you will make Buddy Bear primarily from the directions for T.R., read the following checklist carefully so you know exactly at which steps to refer to these pages to make changes for Buddy:

Materials.
Same as for T.R., *except:* for his eyes, two black shank buttons, ¾" (2 cm) diameter; reduce the amount of wood and felt for crown joint parts so you have just enough for the four smaller joints only.

Cutting the Crown Joint Parts.
Don't make the disks or pads for the large crown joint.

The Patterns.
Cut and mark Buddy's pattern pieces in the same manner as T.R.'s.

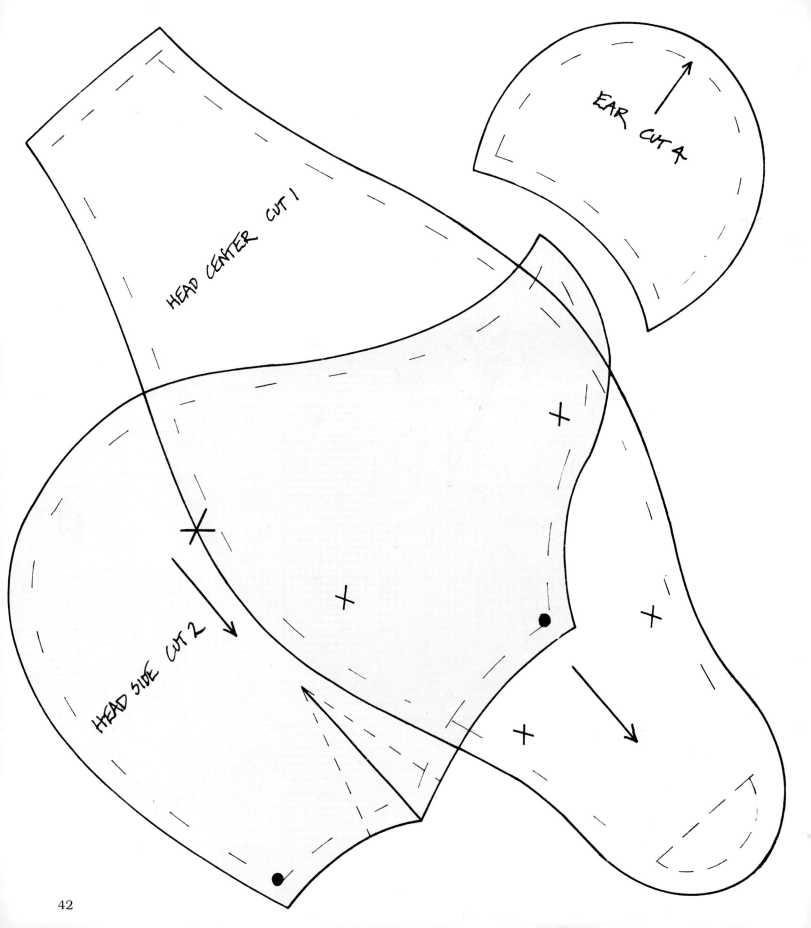

HEAD CENTER CUT 1

EAR CUT 4

HEAD SIDE CUT 2

42

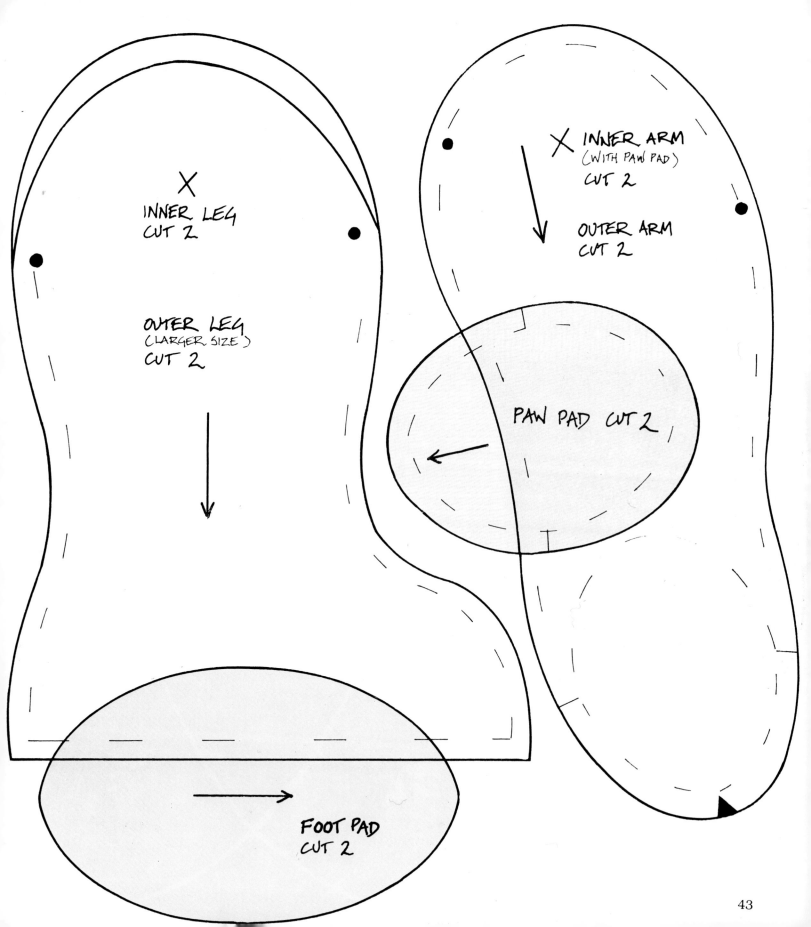

X
INNER LEG
CUT 2

OUTER LEG
(LARGER SIZE)
CUT 2

X INNER ARM
(WITH PAW PAD)
CUT 2

OUTER ARM
CUT 2

PAW PAD CUT 2

FOOT PAD
CUT 2

Making the Arms.

Buddy's paw pad is oval shaped. Since it doesn't have a flat edge like T.R.'s. Buddy's pad is attached to his arm differently.

1. Trim the interfacing along the dotted line that runs around the edge of the piece.

2. Fuse the interfacing to the wrong side of the velveteen.

3. Clip the edges of the velveteen.

4. Fold the velveteen over the interfacing, taking little tucks, then baste.

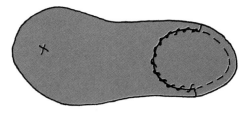

5. Baste the *Paw Pad* to the right side of the *Inner Arm* with the unhemmed edge flush against the edge of the arm piece.

6. Slipstitch the hemmed edge of the *Paw Pad* to the *Inner Arm* with carpet thread.

Finally, finish the arm according to T.R.'s instructions.

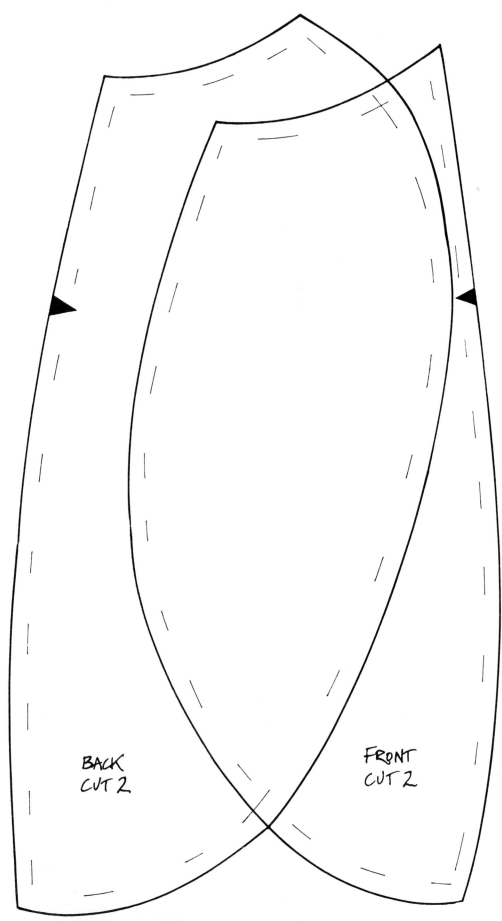

BACK
CUT 2

FRONT
CUT 2

Making the Body.

Buddy's body has a stuffing opening at the top, instead of at the back like T.R. Start sewing Buddy's pieces together at the side seams, following the instructions for T.R. For Buddy's center seams, however, make the following adjustments:

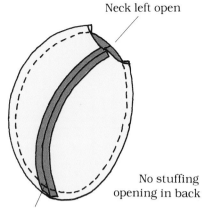

Neck left open

No stuffing opening in back

Finger-press the side seams before you sew over them.

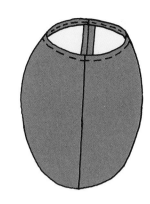

1. Stitch the center seams all around the body, except for the neck opening.

2. Turn the right sides out. Fold under and baste the ¼″ seam allowance along the stuffing opening at the neck.

Making the Head.

Buddy's head is almost the same construction as T.R.'s. However, there are only two darts (one on each *Head Side*), and the *Head Center* does not taper off at the neck. After you make the darts as shown on the patterns, sew the *Head Sides* together as in T.R.'s instructions. But, when you are ready to pin the *Head Center* to the *Head Sides*, follow these instructions:

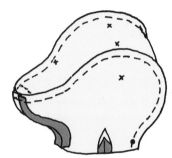

1. Match the dots at the base of the neck to the dots at the base of each *Head Side*. Then sew around the *Head Center* from dot to dot.

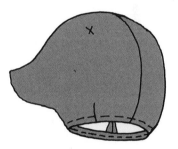

2. Finish the head by turning it right side out. Fold under the ¼″ seam allowance and baste along the stuffing opening.

Stuffing and Attaching the Head to the Body.

Attach the arms and legs first. Although T.R.'s head went on first, for Buddy bear the head goes on last. After the arms and legs are on, stuff both the body and the head. Instead of attaching them with a crown joint, you will simply slip-stitch the two neck openings together.

1. Pin the neck openings together first. Make sure both the body and head are firm before you start to sew.

2. Align the center seams. Or, you can make the head tilt slightly to one side by attaching the head just a little off center. Experiment until you find a pose you like.

3. When you're ready, slip-stitch the neck openings together with carpet thread.

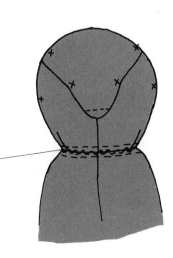

How to Make Bearnice

Bearnice resembles T.R. even more than Buddy does. She's just a bit petite in comparison, with a slightly more feminine head pattern. She also has a lighter complexion and daintier eyes. Fortunately, Bearnice and T.R. are constructed in the same way, so once you have the right materials and the right patterns, you can proceed, using the instructions for T.R.

Materials for Bearnice.

Use the materials listed for T.R., but use lighter colored fur with a longer nap and smaller (10mm) glass eyes.

Reducing the Patterns for the Body, Arms & Legs.

There are two methods for reducing the patterns for T.R. to fit Bearnice's size. If you have access to a photostat machine (some print shops, or perhaps a local newspaper, will have one) have the pattern pages for T.R. reduced to 87.5%.

The alternative is to re-draw the patterns yourself. Complete the grid lines on T.R.'s patterns pages at 1″ intervals, and, on a separate sheet of paper, draw the grid lines at 7/8″ (22 mm) intervals. (See Mama Bear's Sewing Basket for an easy way to draw the grid.) On the reduced grid, copy the pattern seamlines square by square to ensure accuracy. Then, add 1/4″ (6 mm) seam allowance to the edges of the patterns.

Copy the patterns for the body, arms, and legs, including the *Paw* and *Foot Pads*, but do not copy the patterns for the head. As for the crown joint pieces, they remain the same size.

One thing about Bearnice is that she always has an apt phrase for whatever situation she finds herself in. Sometimes it's an almost recognizable old saying, sometimes it is pure Bearnice. Here, having discovered that Buddy's honey pot is completely empty—in fact licked clean—she tells him, tartly, "A fool and his honey are soon parted; that's why you can't keep a girlfriend for long." Later in this chapter there are patterns and instructions for making Bearnice's cotton print dress and pinafore of fine linen.

The *Head Side*, *Head Center*, and *Ear* patterns are already reduced to match Bearnice's smaller body. Trace them, cut out, and mark, in the same manner as for T.R.'s patterns.

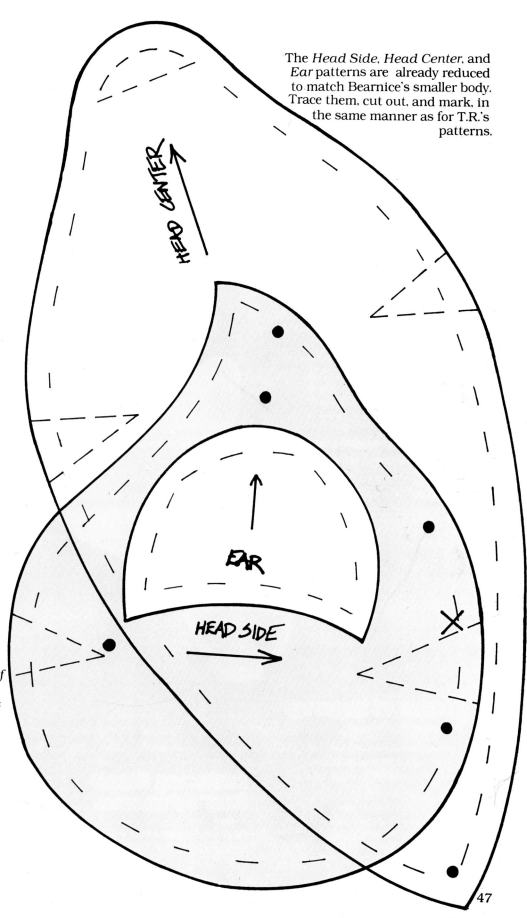

47

How to Make Quite A. Small-Bear

He's not a blood relative to T.R., but he looks just like him—the same patterns and all. The only difference between T.R. and Quite A. Small-Bear is that Quite A. Small-Bear is quite small.

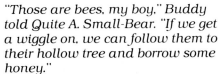

"Those are bees, my boy," Buddy told Quite A. Small-Bear. "If we get a wiggle on, we can follow them to their hollow tree and borrow some honey."

"But won't they get mad and sting us?" said Quite.

"That's why you're made of fur, son. And they'll make some more honey; bees were born to be busy."

Patterns for Buddy's denim overalls and Quite's sailor suit appear later in this chapter.

Amounts of Material for Small-Bear.

Use the materials listed for T.R., but in smaller amounts as follows:
Fabric: ¼ yard of 60"-wide fabric (¼ m of 150 cm-wide). You may want to use a shorter pile than T.R.'s, so Quite A. won't look too fuzzy.
Velveteen and interfacing: 7 x 7" each (18 x 18 cm).
Wood and felt for crown joint parts:

4 x 12" each (10 x 30 cm).
Stuffing: ¾ pound (375 g) polyester.
Eyes: 10 mm glass eyes.
Black Persian yarn: 1 yard (1 m).

Reducing Small-Bear's Patterns.

Follow the instructions for reducing Bearnice's patterns, except this time reduce to 62.5%, or make a ⅝" (16 mm) grid. Also, reduce all of

T.R.'s pieces, including the head. Remember to keep the seam allowances at ¼".

Unlike Bearnice, Quite A. Small-Bear has smaller crown joints too. Cut the small disks at 1¼" (3 cm) diameter, the large disks at 2¼" (5½ cm). Cut the small pads at 1½" (4 cm) diameter, the large pads at 2½" (6½ cm). The cotter pins remain the same size.

Outfitting T.R. and His Three Friends

Of course a bear's fur all by itself is more than suitable clothing for a bear. It is durable, wrinkle-free, and has no buttons to come loose or zippers to stick. However, T.R.'s knowledge of human nature led him to design some clothes for himself and his friends that would be appropriate to their personalities. He knew, wise old tailor that he is, that once people have made a doll, even a bear doll, they often develop an irresistible need to dress it up, somehow. So, leaving nothing to chance, he asked Buddy to help him run up the following designer wardrobes: for himself, a no-nonsense vest and a polka-dot bow tie; for Buddy, a pair of durable denim overalls and a red bandana; for Bearnice, a cool, calico-print dress with puffed sleeves, and a white pinafore with a ruffle; for Quite A. Small Bear, a classic sailor suit with middy blouse and white shorts, plus a red nightshirt. His patterns and instructions are found on the following pages. Color photographs of the bears modeling these classic items may be found on the jacket, and here and there throughout the book.

*T.R. is trying to teach Buddy some sewing skills and elementary tailoring, but it is an uphill job. In Buddy's opinion, cooking is much more in his line. "You get results faster," he says, "and nobody else can ever be certain whether you made a mistake or not—except toast, of course. As Bearnice says, 'all a blueberry pie has to do is fit just right **inside** where no one can see it.'" If you need a little help with your sewing skills and terms, too, see "Mama Bear's Sewing Basket" in the back of the book.*

49

T.R.'s Vest

After checking the better men's stores, T.R. has selected a conservative wool (100 percent of course), three-button tweed vest. Lest the vest give him too stolid an air, T.R. has brightened up his outfit with a red-and-white polka dot bow tie. The wire-rimmed *pince-nez* are appropriate because they are the type worn by President Teddy Roosevelt, for whom T.R., and all "teddy" bears, were named. Furthermore, this type of spectacles was worn by German professors at the turn of the century when the first teddy bears were made by Fräulein Steiff. T.R.'s body is patterned exactly like those early German bears.

Materials

For vest: 9″ x 28″ (22 x 67 cm) piece each of wool tweed and lining (cotton or synthetic)
Matching thread

Buttonhole twist or top-stitching thread
Three ⅜″ (1 cm) buttons
A 3″ by 5″ piece interfacing

For tie: 2 pieces red grosgrain ribbon with white dots: ½ yard (44 cm) ⅝″-wide (1.5 cm); 8″ (20 cm) ⅞″-wide (2.2 cm)
Red thread

For glasses: 10″ (25.5 cm) piece of #16 gauge galvanized wire

1. Cut interfacing for center front ending at broken line to reinforce fabric behind buttons and buttonholes. Fuse or baste it to wrong side of wool front pieces. Press under ¼″ (6 mm) side seams of lining pieces.

2. Right sides facing, stitch linings to front pieces, leaving side seams open. Clip seams at corners and curves and press open. Turn right side out and press.

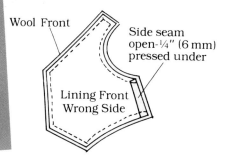

Wool Front
Side seam open-¼″ (6 mm) pressed under
Lining Front Wrong Side

3. Stitch darts in both wool and lining back pieces. Right sides facing, stitch back wool pieces together, then stitch back lining pieces together. Press seams open, then press side seams under ¼″.

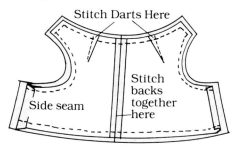

Stitch Darts Here
Side seam
Stitch backs together here

4. With right sides facing, stitch lining to back leaving side seams open. Clip seams at corners and curves. Press seams open and turn right side out.

Pocket Flap

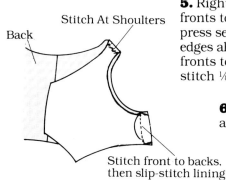

Back
Stitch At Shoulters
Stitch front to backs, then slip-stitch lining

5. Right sides facing, stitch wool fronts to back along side seams and press seams open. Slip-stitch lining edges along side seams. Slip-stitch fronts to backs at shoulders and top-stitch ⅛″ (3 mm) from edges.

6. Make 3 buttonholes on left front and sew buttons on right front.

7. For pocket flap, cut piece of wool tweed 2¼ x 1½″ (5.8 x 3.8 cm). Press under ¼″ all around. Fold in half lengthwise and slip-stitch edges together. Folded edge up, slip-stitch to lower left side of vest.

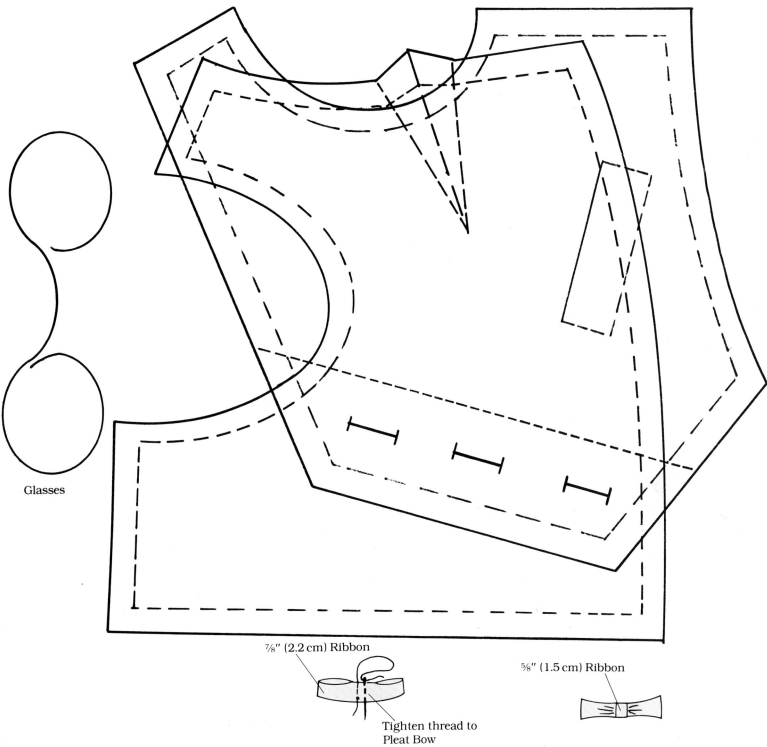

Glasses

⅞″ (2.2 cm) Ribbon

Tighten thread to
Pleat Bow

⅝″ (1.5 cm) Ribbon

Accessories

For glasses, use pliers to bend
wire into shape shown in pattern.

1. To make bow tie, fold ends
of ⅞″-wide (2.2 cm) ribbon
to center, overlapping ends ½″
(1.25 cm). Sew ends together. Stitch
along center, pull thread, and knot to
pleat bow.

2. Fold 2″ (5 cm) piece of ⅝″ (1.5 cm)
ribbon around center, overlapping
and sewing ends in back. Place ⅝″
ribbon around T.R.'s neck, trim end
to overlap ½″ (1.25 cm) in front, and
sew ends together. Sew bow to
overlap.

Buddy's Overalls

Buddy's down-home hard-working approach to life requires an unpretentious all-purpose wardrobe—what could be better than these smartly-cut but very serviceable blue denim overalls? The red bandana-print kerchief in the pocket reflects Buddy's cheery character (and keeps his nose dry when he gets the sniffles).

Materials

½ yard (46 cm) blue denim fabric.
4½" (11.5 cm) square of bandana fabric for kerchief.
Blue and red thread.
Two ½" (1.25 cm) red buttons.

Note: if denim contains sizing, wash and dry it before cutting.

Note: use blue thread unless otherwise indicated.

1. With right sides facing, stitch fronts together here and backs together here.

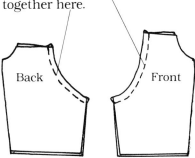

2. Fold under and press ½" (1.25 cm) on top of pocket and stitch in red thread ¼" (6 mm) from fold. Turn under ¼" along other edges. Stitch side and bottom edges of pockets to left front here.

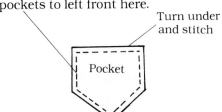

3. Then, right sides facing, join front to back, stitching along side and inner leg seams.

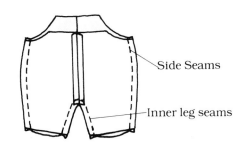

4. Zigzag or overcast longest edge of facing. Then, with right sides together, stitch facing to top edge of front. Clip seams and corners.

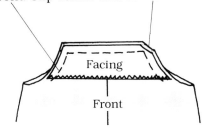

5. Turn under ¼" (6 mm) along underarm and back edges. Top-stitch ⅛" (3 mm) hem in red thread.

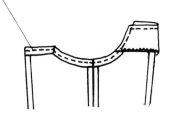

6. Fold each strap piece in half with right sides facing. Stitch seam along pointed end and long edge. Clip corners and turn right side out.

7. Stitch ⅛" (3 mm) all around strap using red thread. Make buttonholes.

8. Sew straps under back edge of overalls so they cross in back.

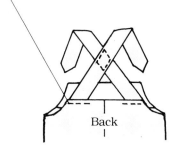

9. Sew buttons here.

10. Turn under ¼" (6 mm), then ½" (1.3 cm) along leg bottoms and top-stitch hem in red thread.

11. To make kerchief, turn under ¼" (6 mm) all around bandana square and stitch in red thread ⅛" (3 mm) from edge. Fold and insert kerchief in pocket.

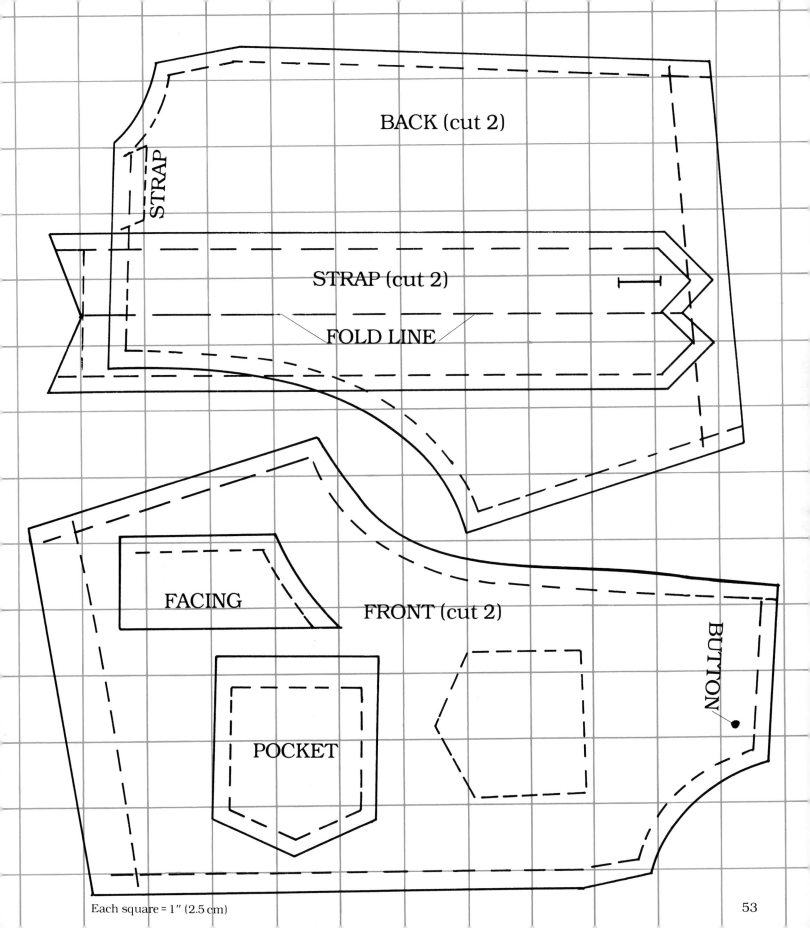

BACK (cut 2)

STRAP

STRAP (cut 2)

FOLD LINE

FACING

FRONT (cut 2)

POCKET

BUTTON

Each square = 1″ (2.5 cm)

Bearnice's Wardrobe

Bearnice will never deny she likes frills. Thrills she's not too certain about. She has selected a beruffled cotton-print dress with a bow at the neck, quite a traditional ensemble, but gently fussy too, just like Bearnice. And she tops off the dress with a crisp, old-fashioned, lace-trimmed apron of the sort her own Grandma Bear might have worn.

Making the Dress

Materials

- ½ yard (44 cm) 45" (114 cm) cotton-print fabric
  Matching thread
- ½ yard (44 cm) ¾"-wide (2 cm) eyelet ruffling
- 12" (30.5 cm) piece elastic
- 2 snaps
- ¼ yard (22 cm) ⅜"-wide (1 cm) yellow ribbon

1. Right sides together, stitch backs together along center seam line below dots.

2. Press right-hand side under ¼" (6 mm) along upper center back, then stitch.

3. Trim ¼" (6 mm) from upper center back of left-hand side, then turn under ½" (1.25 cm) twice and stitch hem.

4. Stitch front to backs along shoulder seams.

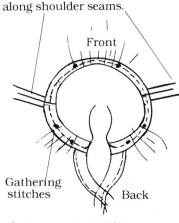

5. Press under ¼" (6 mm) along neck edge, then make rows of gathering stitches along this edge. Gather each back neck edge between dots to 1" (2.5 cm) and center front between dots to 1¼" (3.2 cm).

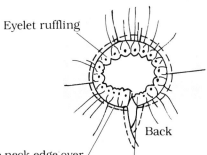

6. Place neck edge over bound edge of eyelet ruffling with ½" (1.25 cm) of ruffling extending on each end of neckline. Stitch close to ends.

7. Hem ends of ruffling even with center edges of dress back.

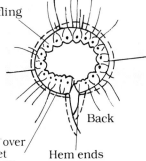

8. To make casing along lower edge of sleeves, press under ⅜" (1 cm) twice and stitch along inner edge of casing. Insert 5¾" (14.7 cm) piece of elastic in casing, then stitch across ends.

9. Make row of gathering stitches along top edges of sleeves. With right sides together, gather sleeves between dots to fit armholes of dress, then stitch armhole seams.

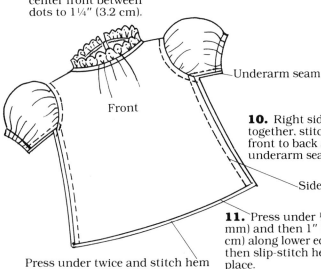

10. Right sides together, stitch dress front to back at side and underarm seams.

11. Press under ¼" (6 mm) and then 1" (2.5 cm) along lower edge, then slip-stitch hem in place.

Press under twice and stitch hem

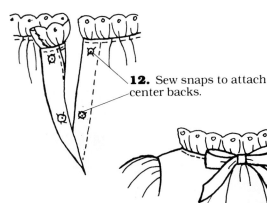

12. Sew snaps to attach center backs.

13. Tie yellow ribbon into small bow and sew it to center front of neck.

Making the Apron

Materials

- ⅜ yard (35 cm) white handkerchief linen or any lightweight cotton such as lawn, broadcloth, or muslin
  White thread
- ½ yard (44 cm) ¾" (2 cm) lace ruffling
- 1 yard (92 cm) ¼" (6 mm) lace edging
- ¾ x 18" (2 x 44 cm) strip lightweight interfacing

In addition, cut out the following fabric pieces:

- 1 apron skirt 28 x 6¼" (70 x 16 cm)
- 1 waistband 16 x 1¾" (41 x 4.5 cm)
- 2 shoulder straps 8¼ x 1½" (20.5 x 3.8 cm)
- 2 ties 9½ x 1¾" (24.2 x 4.5 cm)

1. Fold apron top in half, right sides together, and stitch along both sides. Clip corners and turn top right side out. Top-stitch ⅛" (3 mm) from folded edge.

Fold

Apron top

Stitch sides, then turn and stitch along fold

Fold straps and stitch here

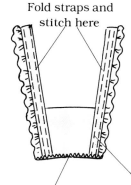

4. Zigzag or overcast lower edge of top.

2. Right sides together, fold shoulder straps in half lengthwise and stitch along long edge. Turn straps right side out. Press each strap flat with seam on one edge. Place folded edge over gathered edge of lace ruffling, then stitch along edge of straps.

3. Line up lower edges of top and straps and lay one strap along each side of apron top, overlapping ¼" (6 mm). Stitch along inner edge of strap.

5. To hem apron skirt, press back edges under ⅛" (3 mm) twice, then stitch hem in place.

6. Press long edge under ⅛" (3 mm), then 1" (2.5 cm), then stitch hem in place. Stitch row of lace edging on right side over hem, turning under ends of lace.

7. Fuse or baste interfacing to wrong side of waistband, with 1 edge along center.

8. Make rows of gathering stitches ½" (1.25 cm) and ¼" (6 mm) from top edge of apron skirt.

9. Right sides together, gather skirt to waistband, beginning and ending ¼" (6 mm) from end of waistband. Stitch ½" (1.25 cm) from edge. Press under ¼" (6 mm) on remaining edges of waistband and fold it in half lengthwise. Slip-stitch long edge in place, then slip-stitch ends together.

10. Place center of waistband over lower ½" (1.25 cm) of top and stitch along edge of waistband. Hem long edges of ties. Make pleat in one end of each tie and stitch it under end of waistband.

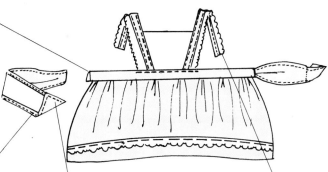

11. Press under ⅛" (3 mm) on other end of each tie, fold end diagonally, and stitch it in place.

12. With apron on Bearnice, adjust back ends of shoulder straps under waistband. Stitch them in place along top edge of waistband.

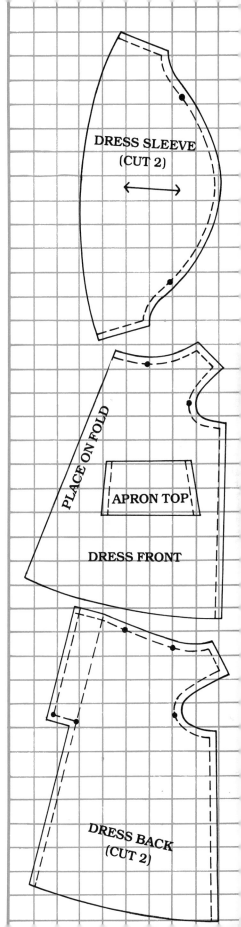

DRESS SLEEVE (CUT 2)

PLACE ON FOLD

APRON TOP

DRESS FRONT

DRESS BACK (CUT 2)

Shorts and Shirt

Materials

¼ yard (22 cm) each white and
  light blue cotton fabric
  White and light blue thread
10″ (25.5 cm) piece ¼″ (6 mm) elastic
  3 sets snaps
13″ (33 cm) piece ½″-wide (1.25 cm)
  red grosgrain ribbon

Note: Patterns are shown reduced;
one square equals 1 inch (6 mm)

Quite A. Small-Bear models his
sailor suit on page 48 while Buddy
takes him for a ride in the
wheelbarrow in search of honey.

Shorts

1. Right sides together, stitch 2 fronts, then 2 backs together, along center seam lines.

2. Right sides together, stitch fronts to backs along sides.

3. Along top, press under ⅜″ (1 cm) twice, then stitch along edge leaving a ½″ (1.25 cm) opening.

4. Insert 10″ (25.5 cm) length of elastic through casing. Stitch ends of elastic together and stitch casing closed.

5. Turn leg bottoms under ¼″ (6 mm) twice, then stitch hem.

6. Right sides together, stitch front to back along inner leg seam.

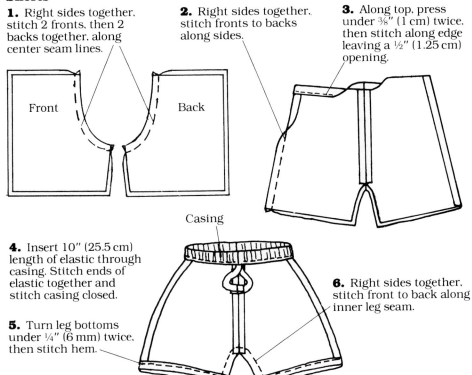

Front   Back

Casing

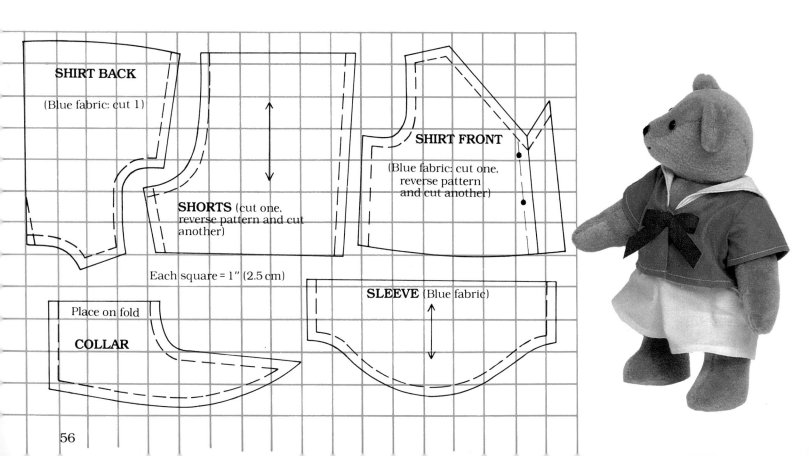

SHIRT BACK

(Blue fabric: cut 1)

SHORTS (cut one, reverse pattern and cut another)

Each square = 1″ (2.5 cm)

SHIRT FRONT

(Blue fabric: cut one, reverse pattern and cut another)

Place on fold

COLLAR

SLEEVE (Blue fabric)

Shirt

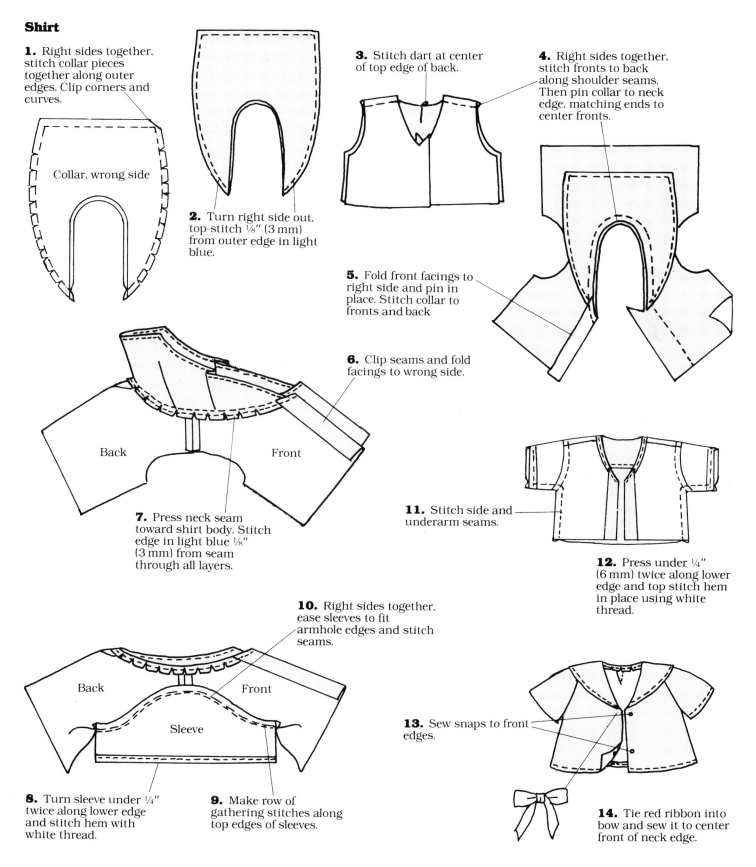

1. Right sides together, stitch collar pieces together along outer edges. Clip corners and curves.

Collar, wrong side

2. Turn right side out, top-stitch ⅛" (3 mm) from outer edge in light blue.

3. Stitch dart at center of top edge of back.

4. Right sides together, stitch fronts to back along shoulder seams. Then pin collar to neck edge, matching ends to center fronts.

5. Fold front facings to right side and pin in place. Stitch collar to fronts and back

6. Clip seams and fold facings to wrong side.

Back   Front

7. Press neck seam toward shirt body. Stitch edge in light blue ⅛" (3 mm) from seam through all layers.

11. Stitch side and underarm seams.

12. Press under ¼" (6 mm) twice along lower edge and top stitch hem in place using white thread.

10. Right sides together, ease sleeves to fit armhole edges and stitch seams.

Back   Front
Sleeve

8. Turn sleeve under ¼" twice along lower edge and stitch hem with white thread.

9. Make row of gathering stitches along top edges of sleeves.

13. Sew snaps to front edges.

14. Tie red ribbon into bow and sew it to center front of neck edge.

Nightshirt

He can be seen wearing his new red and white flannel nightshirt in the Baby Bear chapter. T.R. is reading him a story as they relax in a cradle with a doll's quilt made in the bear claw pattern.

Materials

¼ yard (22 cm) red-and-white checkered cotton flannel
Red and white thread
1½" (3.8 cm) square of red cotton flannel
1½" (3.8 cm) square of fusible bonding web
4 snap sets
Four ¼" diameter white buttons

Note: Patterns are shown reduced: One square equals 1 inch (6 mm)

1. Press under ⅛" (3 mm) along each center front, then stitch.

2. Trace heart from shirt front, cut fabric heart. Fuse to shirt front, then zigzag around edge in red thread.

3. Right sides together, stitch fronts to back at shoulder seams.

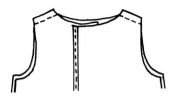

4. From red and white flannel, cut collar piece 10 x 1½" (25.5 x 3.8 cm). Fold collar lengthwise with right sides together and stitch seam at each end. Trim corners, turn right side out and baste open edges together.

5. Make a row of gathering stitches between dots along neck edge.

6. Mark edge of collar into 4 even lengths.

7. Right sides together, gather neck edge between dots evenly to collar. Match shoulder seams and back center to collar marks.

8. Fold center front edges to right side along fold. Stitch collar to shirt and clip corners. Turn facings to wrong side and baste in place at lower edge.

9. Turn under ¼" twice along lower edge of sleeve and stitch hem. Then make row of gathering stitches along top. Right sides together, ease sleeves to fit armhole edges, then stitch. Stitch fronts to back along side and underarm seams. Turn right side out.

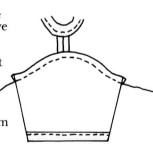

10. Turn under ¼" (6 mm) twice along lower edge and stitch hem. Then sew snaps where shown and sew buttons on left front over snaps.

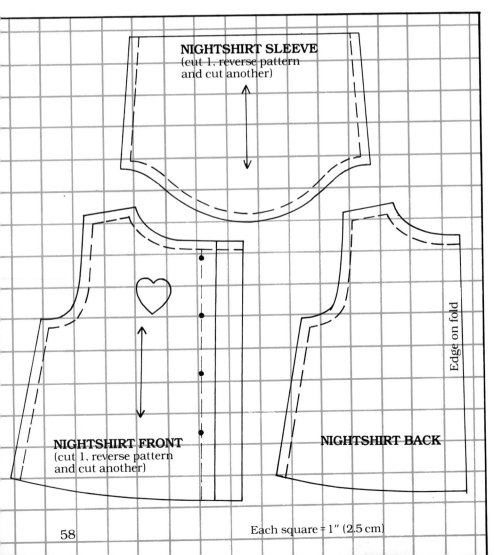

NIGHTSHIRT SLEEVE
(cut 1, reverse pattern and cut another)

NIGHTSHIRT FRONT
(cut 1, reverse pattern and cut another)

NIGHTSHIRT BACK

Edge on fold

Each square = 1" (2.5 cm)

BEARS OF A DIFFERENT CUT

Bearnice, Buddy, and T.R. (who always wears a bib to eat, even when it's just cookies) would like you to meet some of the other bear dolls you can make by following the instructions and patterns in this chapter. In the back row (left to right starting to Buddy's left), are one of the "Patchwork Pals," the corduroy "Hug-me Bear," and one of the "Cookie-Cutter Kids." The two "Country Bears," Zeke and Sara, are easy-to-make sock-dolls. To T.R.'s left are three more of the "Cookie-Cutter Kids": a grey velvet " Pillow Bear," a small denim "Hug-me Bear," and the ever-cheerful "Hi-there Bear." Seated to the left of Bearnice is "Sitting Bear," an exact reproduction of an antique animal doll; a pair of potholders from a later chapter entitled "Bears in the Kitchen".

The Cookie-Cutter Kids

The beauty of this group of patterns is their simplicity. Fronts, backs, heads, arms, and legs are all one piece: cut one for the front and an identical one for the back. Since they are so easy to make, they are fun for children to do and they can be cut and sewn in batches, like cookies, to sell at fairs, bazaars, and other money-raisers. Change sizes, fabrics, and facial expressions. Presto! You have created an infinite variety of friends to play with, of ways to decorate a bedroom, or of gifts to give.

The Boudoir Bear is made from the same pattern as Hi-there Bear, with minor changes. She is slightly smaller, 8¾" (13 cm) and holds both her arms at her sides. She is made in an elegant grey print with her features hand embroidered in pink silk, button eyes. She is every inch a lady with her lace choker and pink satin rose.

Pillow Bears can be made in any size. The three shown here are 14", 9½", and 5" (35.5, 24, 12.5 cm). The pattern makes comfortable pillows because the limbs are thick with very little space between them. Stuff them with foam, polyester fiber (which is washable), or down from an old bed pillow.

This Hi-there Bear with one hand up stands a bit less than a foot tall (30 cm) and is made out of a cotton chintz print. The mouth is embroidered and the felt eyes are stitched into place. You will also find him among the "Patchwork Pals," a few pages on, dressed in patchwork pieces.

Hug-me Bears have their arms out ready to hug someone back. They come in two sizes and are made of durable fabrics to hold up under lots of affection and to withstand being carried around by one arm. They range in height from 15" (38 cm) to 8" (20 cm).

A short course to demonstrate that bears of this cut are the easiest to make of all:

True, these bears aren't cut out from dough with cookie cutters, but their simple shapes resemble some of grandma's metal cutters. These cut-ups can be made in all shapes and sizes and decorated as simply or as elaborately as you wish. An ideal project for children or any beginning sewer, because all you need is a pattern, two pieces of fabric, some stuffing material, and scraps of this and that for decorating.

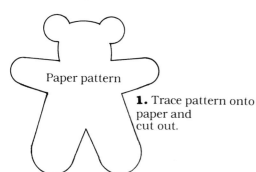

Paper pattern

1. Trace pattern onto paper and cut out.

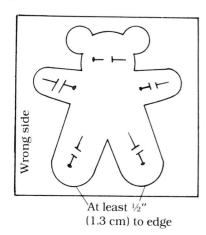

Wrong side

At least ½" (1.3 cm) to edge

2. Trace bear to wrong side of one fabric piece. For wool or any other fabrics where a pencil, chalk, or carbon will not show on fabric, hand-baste around pattern. For embroidery or applique, place pattern on right side in the same position as on wrong side. Hold fabric up to the light or, for opaque fabrics, place a few pins along seam line to determine placement.

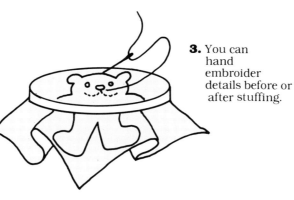

3. You can hand embroider details before or after stuffing.

or zig zag stitch around applique shapes before stuffing

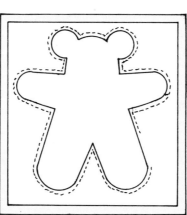

4. Place two fabric pieces together with right sides in, and pin along seam line. Stitch along the drawn line, leaving an opening for turning.

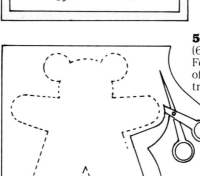

5. Trim away fabric ¼" (6 mm) from stitching. For smaller bears, made of firmly woven fabrics, trim fabric to ⅛" (3 mm) from stitching.

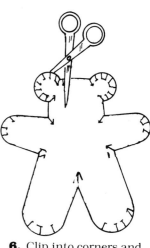

6. Clip into corners and clip seam allowance close to stitching.

7. Turn right side out and push in stuffing with pencil or stick

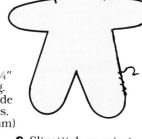

8. Slipstitch opening with tiny stitches.

9. Sew on buttons. Embroider mouth and nose.
10. Tie on a bow.

Cookie-Cutter bears with identical machine-embroidered features can be mass-produced for bazaars or party treats. Or, for that special gift, you can work each bear's features individually in hand embroidery. Check your sewing box for bits of fabric, lengths of ribbon, scraps of lace, and buttons to make each bear a bear of a definitely different cut.

Materials

Fabric scraps
Stuffing material
Embroidery floss
Ribbon, lace, buttons for decoration

If you are planning to make a lot of cookie-cutter bears of any one size, it's a good idea to transfer your tracing paper PATTERN to lightweight cardboard. A permanent cardboard pattern holds its shape well and will last a long time.

If you are not sure how to mark and cut patterns and fabric, look in the section of this book called "Momma Bear's Sewing Basket." Whenever you see this symbol ✂ in the instructions you will also find details about that procedure in "Momma Bear's Sewing Basket."

T.R.

Cutting, Marking and Decorating

There are four different pattern shapes in this family of cookie-cutter bears. They are all made the same way. A pattern is given here for each of the four shapes. As the photograph shows, the same pattern may be enlarged or reduced ✂ . By varying the type of fabric, the pattern printed on it, and the decorations and accessories you apply to it you can give the same shape many different personalities.

Cut out 2 rectangles of fabric at least ½″ (1.3 cm) longer and wider than the pattern for the front and back of each bear. The same pattern is used for both the front and the back.

Note: if you are going to decorate the bear with machine embroidery or appliqué, you must do it before stuffing. You can do decorative handwork either before or after stuffing. See the photographs and captions for ideas.

If you are going to decorate the bear with machine embroidery, handwork, or appliqué *before* stuffing, position pattern on *right* side of each fabric rectangle, transfer outline and other design details to fabric, then cut around outline.

If you are going to decorate the bear *after* it is stuffed position pattern on *wrong* side of each fabric rectangle, transfer outline only to fabric, and cut around it. Mark design details on right side of fabric.

To decorate bear using machine applique. Cut desired shapes from fabric. If you wish, cut fusible bonding web with which to back appliqués. Then baste or fuse appliqués onto fabric rectangle, using pattern markings as your guide for positioning. Zigzag stitch around appliqués.

To decorate with machine embroidery, select colors, designs, and stitches you wish to use and proceed.

Sewing and Stuffing

1. Right sides together, carefully baste front and back pieces together along outline of bear. With sewing machine set at 10 to 12 stitches per inch, stitch along outline, leaving an opening for stuffing.

2. Trim around the stitching with scissors, leaving a ½″ (1.3 cm) seam allowance. On a small bear, clip seam allowance all the way around to within ⅛″ (3 mm) from stitching. On a large bear, trim to ¼″ (6 mm). Carefully clip a bit farther along curves and into corners. Turn bear right side out, pulling fabric through stuffing hole.

3. Gently push out seam line all around, using eraser end of pencil. Insert small amounts of stuffing, starting with ears and paws, and push it into place with pencil. Continue until bear is fully and smoothly stuffed.

4. Turn under seam allowance along stuffing opening and slip-stitch edges together by hand. Embroider or appliqué features and other design details by hand now if you did not do so before stuffing.

5. If you wish to quilt along lines between ears and head, or arms and body, to give bear's shape greater definition, make row of tiny running stitches through both layers of fabric along lines.

6. Add that finishing touch—a bow, necktie, lace collar—and your cookie-cutter bear is ready to go out and cut up.

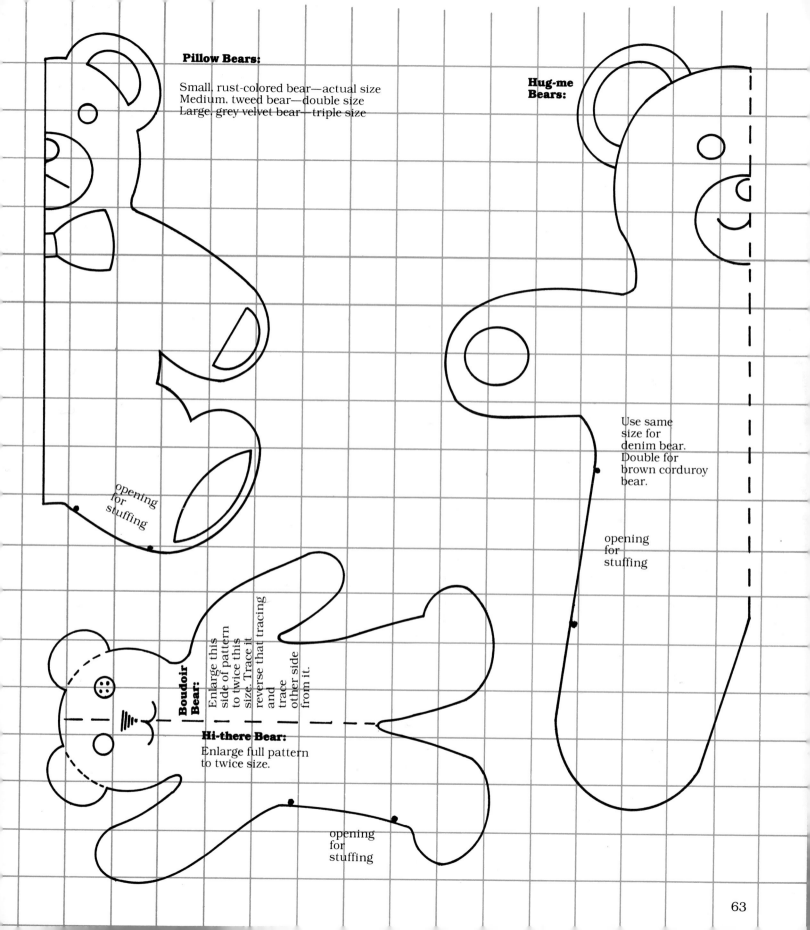

Pillow Bears:

Small, rust-colored bear—actual size
Medium, tweed bear—double size
Large, grey velvet bear—triple size

Hug-me Bears:

Use same size for denim bear. Double for brown corduroy bear.

opening for stuffing

opening for stuffing

Boudoir Bear:

Enlarge this side of pattern to twice this size. Trace it reverse that tracing and trace other side from it.

Hi-there Bear:
Enlarge full pattern to twice size.

opening for stuffing

Patchwork Pals

Patchwork was called "piecing" in the old days, when women found many creative ways to put valuable scraps of colorful fabric to good use. The three bears in this section are examples of that good art.

The first project is an easy-to-make, two-piece pattern for the "Hi-there" Bear found in the prior section. This time he has a patchwork skin, inside which he stands 13½" (34 cm) tall from the top of his friendly wave to the bottom of his turned-out toes.

"HI-THERE" BEAR
Materials
½ yard (44 cm) muslin
Scraps of assorted calico print, dotted, and/or solid-color fabrics
30 x 18" (76 x 44 cm) piece of quilt batting
Sewing and quilting thread to match fabrics
Quilting hoop about 12" (31 cm) in diameter
¼ pound (115 grams) polyester stuffing
Two ⁷⁄₁₆" (1.1 cm) buttons
½ yard (44 cm) embroidery floss
Cutting the Patterns and Fabric
Enlarge cookie-cutter bear pattern (shown in the "Cookie-cutter Kids" project which follows) so that ½" (1.25 cm) equals 1¼" (3.2 cm).

This cheerful fellow, made of patchwork calico fabrics, is about to make an unscheduled balloon ascent. With one arm raised he seems to be saying "Hi there!", so we call him the Hi-there Bear in the prior section on Cookie Cutter Kids where you will find his pattern.

If you plan to cut the bear on the diagonal, like the one pictured, you will need 1 piece of patchwork 9 by 18 squares.

If you plan to cut the bear parallel to the lines of the patchwork, you will need 2 pieces of patchwork each 8 x 9 squares.

If you prefer, the back can be cut from a single piece of solid or print fabric rather than from patchwork.

Making the Patchwork Fabric

1. Cut 2¼" (5.8 cm) squares from calico, dotted, and solid-color fabrics.

2. Arrange squares as desired and sew them together in strips, following instructions and illustrations for making patchwork fabric in the "Boss Tweed" project.

3. Trace bear shape onto right side of patchwork, then reverse pattern and trace again.

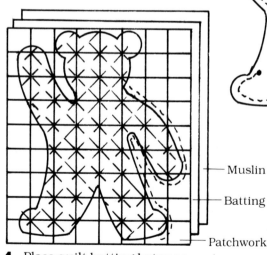

— Muslin

— Batting

— Patchwork

4. Place quilt batting between patchwork fabric and muslin with right sides out.

5. Baste layers together around outlines of bears.

6. Insert fabric in quilting hoop and quilt layers together within bear shapes.

7. Cut out bears, leaving a ½" (1.25 cm) seam allowance all around.

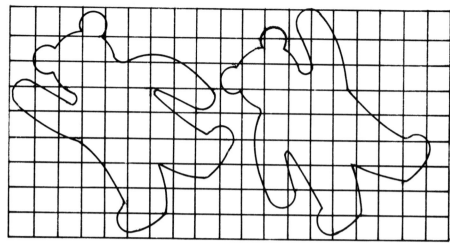

Bear on diagonal of patchwork

Making the Bear

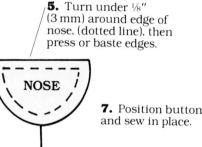

Wrong side

1. Right sides together, pin pieces together along basted outlines. Stitch seams, leaving a 4" (10.2 cm) opening.

2. Trim seams and turn bear right side out.

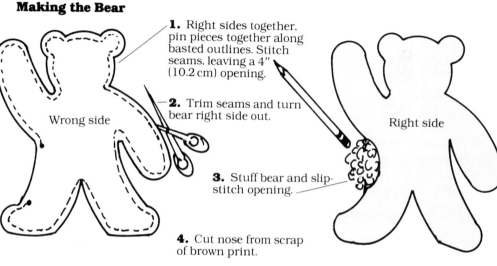

Right side

3. Stuff bear and slip-stitch opening.

4. Cut nose from scrap of brown print.

5. Turn under ⅛" (3 mm) around edge of nose, (dotted line), then press or baste edges.

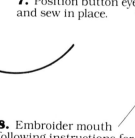

NOSE

AND MOUTH

6. Slip-stitch nose to face.

7. Position button eyes and sew in place.

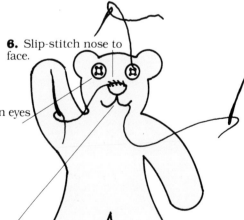

8. Embroider mouth following instructions for "Making the Face" in Heirloom Bear chapter.

65

Boss Tweed is a closet executive, a no-nonsense doer who won't stand for cluttered thinking. He is the top advisor to the firm's C.E.O. and the only member of the firm to have the C.E.O.'s ear 24 hours a day.

BOSS TWEED

Boss Tweed is made from scraps of wool suiting pieced together, then cut and sewn into a good-sized (27"/69 cm), dignified, durable bear, appropriate to an executive's study or to companionship in the very early years of a future mover and shaker.

So you see that the traditional teddy takes on totally new looks when cut from scraps of old patchwork or crazy quilts. If you don't want to cut up old quilts, we tell you how to make your own patchwork fabric from pieces of old wool; scraps of coordinated print and solid cottons; or leftover bits of velvet, silk, and satin. You can use any quilt pattern you desire. But since you'll be cutting bear shapes out of the fabric, and so losing some portions of the quilted design, it's best to select a fairly simple pattern—squares, triangles, or diamonds work very well.

Materials

24 x 48" (62 x 123 cm) piece of an old quilt top or scraps of wool suiting and solid wool at least 3" (7.6 cm) square

¾ yard (68.5 cm) muslin or other backing fabric

¼ yard (22 cm) brown velveteen

Scrap of red wool

4 x 7" (10.2 x 17.8 cm) scrap quilt batting

White, black, and red thread

1 pound (45 kg) polyester stuffing

Scrap of black felt

2 flat, black buttons ¾" (2 cm) diameter

1 yard (92 cm) ¾"-wide (2 cm) grosgrain ribbon

Making the Patchwork Fabric

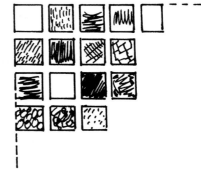

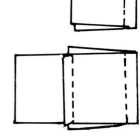

1. Cut 180 3" (7.6 cm) squares from wool suiting and solid wool fabrics.

2. Arrange squares as desired to make a quilted piece 10 squares by 18 squares.

3. Sew squares together in strips.

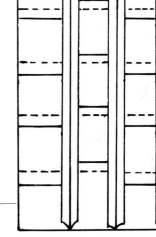

4. Press seams of first strip toward lower edge, those of second strip toward top edge, and so on until all strips are completed.

5. Stitch strips together, matching seam lines, and press seams open.

Cutting the Fabric

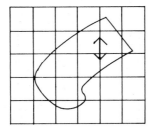

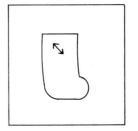

1. Position directional arrows on pattern pieces parallel to seams on old quilt top or patchwork fabric and cut out bear front, back, leg, and head front pieces.

2. Position pattern pieces on muslin with directional arrows diagonal to straight grain and cut out body parts.

3. Baste patchwork body pieces to corresponding muslin pieces along seam lines and stitch together.

Sewing the Bear

1. Right sides together, stitch head fronts together along short center edges.

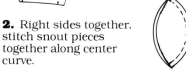

2. Right sides together, stitch snout pieces together along center curve.

3. With seams matching, stitch snout to head front.

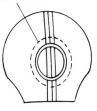

4. Baste quilt batting to wrong side of 2 velveteen front ear pieces. Right sides together, stitch each velveteen ear to a wool back ear piece along curved edge. Trim batting close to stitching and clip curves. Turn right side out and topstitch ¼″ (6 mm) from curved edge.

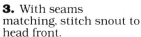

Batting
Velveteen
Wool

5. Right sides together, baste straight edge of ears to head front between dots.

6. Stitch head front to body front along neck edge.

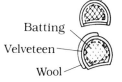

7. Right sides together, fold legs in half, matching edges. Stitch seam, leaving top end open. Clip curves and turn right side out. Stuff legs firmly.

8. Fold leg, fronts to backs along top edges, matching seam lines to center fold lines, and baste along top edge.

9. Stitch darts in back.

10. Pin, then stitch front to back, leaving straight lower edge open. Clip curves, then turn right side out.

11. Right sides together, matching raw edges, stitch legs to lower edge of front.

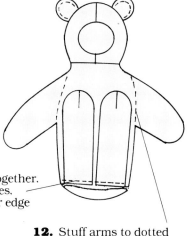

12. Stuff arms to dotted lines, then sew along line using quilting stitch. Stuff head and body firmly.

13. Pin back to front at lower edge, turning under ¼″ (6 mm) along seam line of legs and body. Slip-stitch edges together.

Like Joseph's coat of many colors, Boss Tweed's fabric is made of scraps of tweed and worsted saved from the good parts of old clothing.

14. Whip-stitch nose and mouth to snout. Sew buttons at positions indicated for eyes.

15. Press under ¼″ (6 mm) on heart. Position it on left side of body with small amount of stuffing under it. Slip-stitch edges to body.

16. Tie ribbon around neck and make bow.

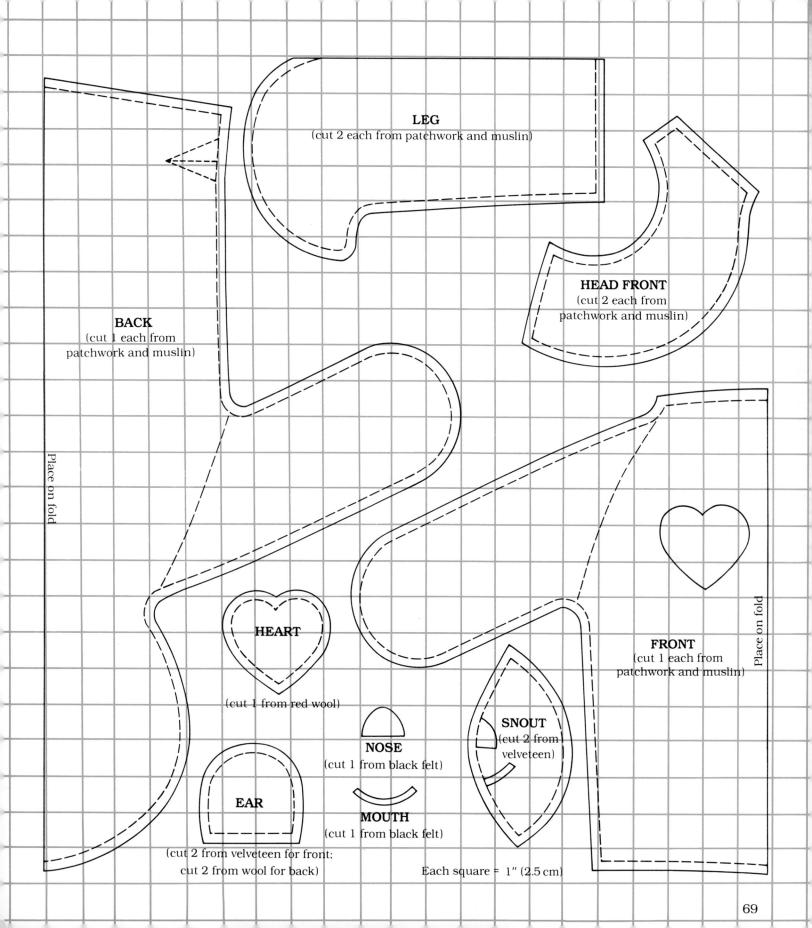

LEG
(cut 2 each from patchwork and muslin)

HEAD FRONT
(cut 2 each from
patchwork and muslin)

BACK
(cut 1 each from
patchwork and muslin)

Place on fold

Place on fold

FRONT
(cut 1 each from
patchwork and muslin)

HEART
(cut 1 from red wool)

NOSE
(cut 1 from black felt)

SNOUT
(cut 2 from
velveteen)

MOUTH
(cut 1 from black felt)

EAR
(cut 2 from velveteen for front;
cut 2 from wool for back)

Each square = 1" (2.5 cm)

Bavarian Bear

The most challenging project we call the Bavarian Bear, and he is as Victorian as satin ribbons. His arms and legs are jointed, his head is stuffed separately, and his body has the big belly and humped back of a pedigreed teddy bear in the best tradition of Fräulein Steiff of Giengen, Germany. The satin piecework, ribbons, and body construction make him too fragile, perhaps, to bear up under the unstinting energies of a two-year old, but he is a collector's item as precious as a rare stein. Fully extended, he measures 17″ (43 cm) in length.

The Bavarian Bear, in his Sunday satin ribbons, has just parked his Mercedes in the courtyard of the Schloss in the forest near Frankfurt. He is about to round off a perfect setting with a rich brew from an old stein. His crazy-quilt costume of satin-and-ribbon is typical of the Victorian era.

BAVARIAN BEAR

Materials

¾ yard (68.5 cm) 45"-wide (114 cm) muslin

Scraps of assorted velvet, satin, silk, and taffeta fabrics

Sewing thread

Ribbons: several feet each in assorted colors of ¹⁄₁₆"-wide (1.5 mm) satin ribbon; ½ yard (44 cm) 1¼"-wide (3.2 cm) taffeta ribbon for neck bow

¾ pound (345 grams) polyester stuffing

Tools and materials for 4 crown joints (see "How to Make a Crown Joint" in Heirloom Bear chapter)

Black 6-strand embroidery floss

Two ½" (1.25 cm) buttons

Cutting the Patterns and Fabric

The pattern pieces are shown in reduced dimension. Each square equals 1" (2.5 cm). All body parts are cut from muslin except for the pads and soles, which are cut from fabric scraps.

Making the Crazy-Quilt Fabric

1. Cut irregularly shaped patches from fabric scraps and begin placing them, one at a time, on muslin backing pieces.

2. Trim pieces even with edges of muslin.

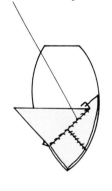

3. Turn under ¼" (6 mm) on all patch edges that overlap other patches.

4. Slip-stitch patches to muslin. Continue until all muslin pieces are covered with patches.

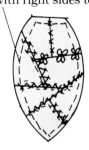

5. Using ¹⁄₁₆ (1.5 mm) ribbons embroider along edges of patches with any stitches that you like. See "Mama Bear's Sewing Basket" ✂ for embroidery instructions.

6. Baste around edges of each muslin piece. Note: unless otherwise indicated, stitch all body seams with right sides together.

Making the Bear

1. Stitch ears together in pairs along outer curves. Clip curves, turn ears right side out, and stuff lightly.

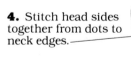

2. Turn under lower edges of ears and slip-stitch front to back, making a small pleat at center of each edge.

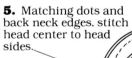

3. Stitch darts in head sides.

4. Stitch head sides together from dots to neck edges.

5. Matching dots and back neck edges, stitch head center to head sides.

6. Turn head right side out. Turn under ¼" (6 mm) along neck edge and baste.

7. Stuff head firmly.

8. Slip-stitch ears to head along lines marked on pattern.

9. Stitch fronts together along center.

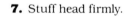
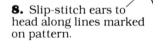

10. Stitch backs together, leaving a 4" (10.2 cm) opening in seam between dots.

11. Stitch front to back, leaving neck edge open.

12. Turn under ¼" (6 mm) along neck edge and back opening and baste. Turn right side out.

13. Stitch pads to inner arms.

14. Stitch inner arms to outer arms, leaving a 4" (10.2 cm) opening along shoulder edge between dots. Turn arms right side out.

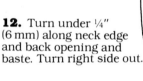
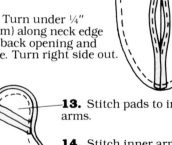

15. Stitch legs together in pairs, leaving a 4" (10.2 cm) opening at upper back edge between dots, and leaving lower edge open.

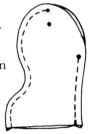

71

16. Stitch soles to lower edges of legs. matching dots to seams. Turn legs right side out.

17. Attach arms and legs to body with crown joints. See instructions on "How to Make a Crown Joint" in Heirloom Bear chapter.

18. Stuff arms and legs firmly.

19. Slip-stitch body openings together.

20. Stuff body firmly.

21. Pin head to body, then slip-stitch head to body until about 2" (5.1 cm) of seam remains open. Push in as much stuffing as possible to make the neck sturdy. then finish slip-stitching the seam.

22. Stitch buttons in position for eyes.

23. Using 3 strands of black embroidery floss. first embroider nose in satin stitch. Then do mouth in back stitch.

24. Tie ribbon around bear's neck and make bow.

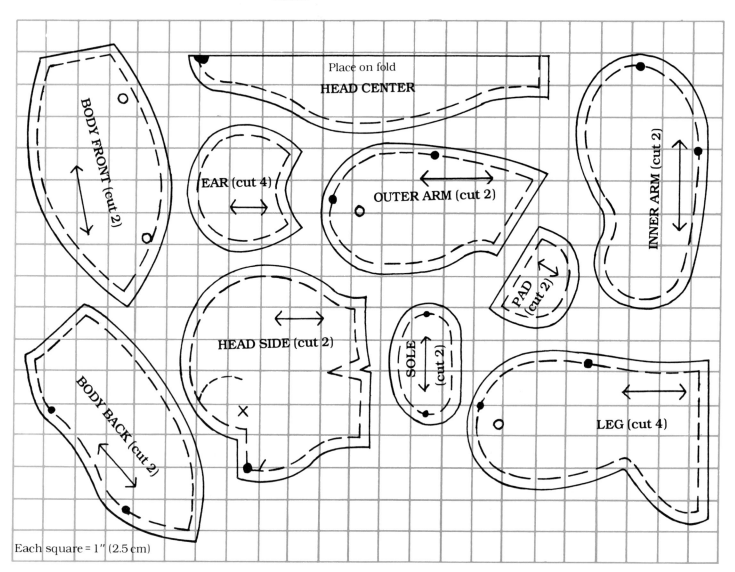

BODY FRONT (cut 2)

BODY BACK (cut 2)

EAR (cut 4)

HEAD SIDE (cut 2)

Place on fold
HEAD CENTER

OUTER ARM (cut 2)

SOLE (cut 2)

PAD (cut 2)

INNER ARM (cut 2)

LEG (cut 4)

Each square = 1" (2.5 cm)

Cousins Huggable

Stitch up four big huggable bears—two of velvet and two of corduroy—and give them party-going expressions. Then dress them to the hilt—one girl bear resplendent in a Victorian velveteen frock, the other in a checkered gingham dress; a checkered gingham shirt and corduroy knickers for one boy bear, a plaid flannel shirt and corduroy pants complete with suspenders for the other. These bears will have such active social lives you'll have to reserve hugging time in advance. Some folks may also have to stand on tip-toes to get in their hugs—the larger bear measures approximately 23 inches (56 cm) from top of ears to toes, the smaller bear is approximately 18 inches (44 cm) tall.

These upright citizens are not really blood cousins, but they are such close friends they have chosen, without ever really saying so out loud, to call each other "cousin." The dark brown corduroy couple made that lovely, burgundy velvet dress, with the lace trim, for their friend's birthday. It was so elegant that she invited them to a formal tea so she could wear it and have their picture taken together. (They are not usually that stiff.)

Materials for Making Bears

45"-wide (114 cm) velvet or corduroy:
  ½ yard (44 cm) for small bear; ¾
  yard (68 cm) for large bear. Our
  large bears are made of velvet, the
  smaller of corduroy.
Matching thread
Polyester stuffing: 1½ pounds
  (1.2 kg) for large bear; 1 pound
  (460 g) for small bear
½ yard (44 cm) black embroidery
  floss
Scraps of black felt
2 black buttons: ¾" (2 cm) for large
  bear; ½" (1.25 cm) for small bear

Patterns

The patterns for the bears are
shown in reduced dimension. For
the large bear, each square equals
1¼" (3.2 cm). For the small bear,
each square equals 1" (2.5 cm).

Legs and Arms

1. Right sides together, stitch legs together in pairs, leaving top and bottom edges open.

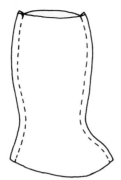

2. Stitch foot pads to bottom edges of legs, matching large and small dots. Clip curves, then turn legs right side out.

3. Stuff legs firmly until close to top. Add a small amount of stuffing at top, then fold legs in half lengthwise, matching seam lines at center front and back. Baste along top edges.

4. Right sides together, stitch arms together in pairs, leaving straight end open. Clip curves. Turn arms right side out.

5. Stuff arms firmly until close to top. Add a small amount of stuffing at top. With seams at sides, baste top edges together along seam line.

Body

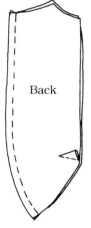

Back

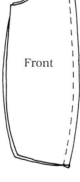

Front

1. Stitch darts in body backs. Right sides together, first stitch fronts and then backs together along center lines.

2. Right sides together, stitch fronts to backs at shoulders and at sides below dots. Clip curves along shoulders. Turn body right side out.

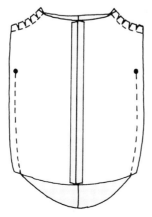

3. Turn under seam allowances around neck, armholes, and lower edges of body; then baste.

4. Position arms in armholes. Slip-stitch arms to body.

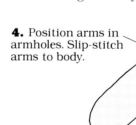

5. Position legs at lower edge of body so seam allowances overlap slightly. Slip-stitch legs to body.

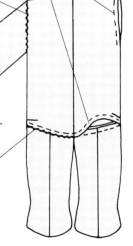
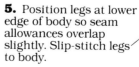

6. Stuff body, pressing stuffing in firmly through neck opening.

Head

1. Right sides together, stitch ears together in pairs along outer curves. Leave bottom edge open. Clip curves. Turn ears right side out and baste lower edges together.

2. Right sides together, stitch head fronts and then head backs together along center lines.

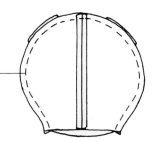

Front   Back

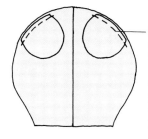

3. Position ears in place on head front between dots and baste.

4. Right sides together, stitch head front to back, leaving straight bottom edge open. Clip curves. Turn head right side out and stuff firmly.

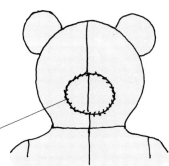

As you may know, in an effort to be helpful to beginners—and to those of us who occasionally need our memories jogged—I persuaded my mother (who is one of the greatest home-sewers of all time) to explain a few of the finer points, such as **MITERING**, in Mama Bear's Sewing Basket, a section at the end of this book.

T.R.

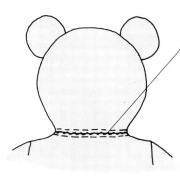

5. Position head in neck opening of body and slip-stitch edges securely together.

6. Stitch snout pieces together along center straight lines. Clip curves. Turn under ¼" (6 mm) all around edge and baste along fold. Pin snout to head front, following markings on pattern. Slip-stitch in place.

Features

1. Thread needle with embroidery floss and knot end. Insert needle in nose area and bring it out at center of lower edge of nose; then stitch mouth, using pattern markings as your guide. Allow stitches to lay loosely along lines of smile. Fasten thread in nose area.

2. With 1 or 2 strands of floss, tack curve of smile in place at ¼" (6 mm) intervals.

3. Cut nose from black felt and sew in place on snout using tiny whip stitches.

4. Attach 2 black button eyes and your bears are ready for their first wardrobe fittings.

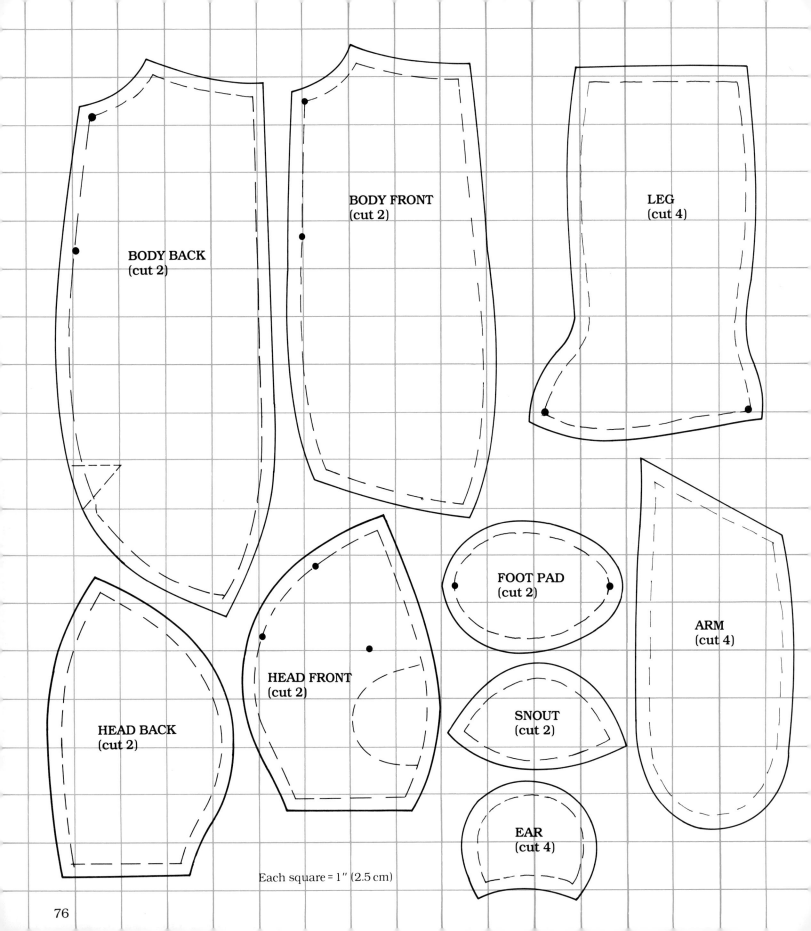

BODY BACK
(cut 2)

BODY FRONT
(cut 2)

LEG
(cut 4)

HEAD BACK
(cut 2)

HEAD FRONT
(cut 2)

FOOT PAD
(cut 2)

ARM
(cut 4)

SNOUT
(cut 2)

EAR
(cut 4)

Each square = 1″ (2.5 cm)

76

MAKING THE BROWN VELVET DRESS

Materials

¾ yard (68 cm) brown velvet
  with white dots
Brown and off-white thread
1 yard (92 cm) ½"-wide (1.25 cm)
  lace edging
¾ yard (68 cm) 1½"-wide (3.8 cm)
  Cluny lace threaded with ribbon
⅝ yard (56 cm) off-white satin
  ribbon
1¾ yards (160 cm) ¾"-wide (2 cm)
  lace edging
3 snap sets

Cutting Out Patterns and Fabric

1. The patterns are shown in
reduced dimensions. Each square
represents 1" (2.5 cm). Enlarge and
cut out patterns, then cut out fabric
pieces.

2. In addition, cut out the following
fabric pieces:
1 collar piece 15 x 1¾" (38 x 4.5 cm)
1 skirt piece 36 x 10" (92 x 25.4 cm)
2 ruffle strips:
  44 x 4½" (110 x 11.5 cm)
  18 x 4½" (46 x 11.5 cm)

Top

1. Zigzag or overcast
center edges of both back
pieces.

2. With right sides
together, stitch front to
backs at shoulders.

3. Fold collar in half
lengthwise with right
sides together. Turn
under ¼" (6 mm) and
stitch. Clip corners and
turn right side out.

4. Baste long edges of
collar together, then pin
collar to right side of
neck edge between fold
lines. Fold back edges to
right side along fold lines
and stitch neckline seam.
Zigzag or overcast seam
allowance. Fold back
facings to wrong side.

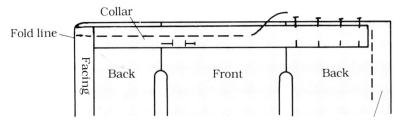

5. Stitch ½"-wide
(1.25 cm) lace edging
along collar, turning
ends under. Use off-white
thread.

6. Stitch Cluny lace onto
bodice along lines shown
on pattern, mitering
point at center front. Use
off-white thread. Tie bow
of off-white ribbon and
tack at point of lace.

7. Zigzag or overcast
lower edges of sleeves.
Fold ¾" (2 cm) hems to
wrong side, then baste in
place. Sew ½"-wide
(1.25 cm) lace edging
around lower edges of
sleeves

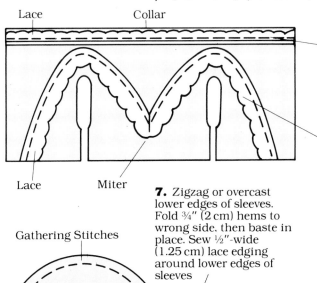

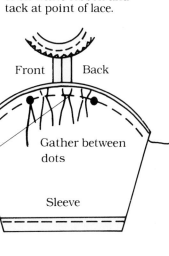

8. Make row of
gathering stitches along
top curved edges. Gather
sleeves to armholes
between dots. Stitch
seams. Stitch front to
backs along underarms
and sides.

Skirt

1. Right sides together, stitch ends of 2 ruffle strips together, making 1 long strip. Overcast 1 long edge of ruffle.

2. Turn under 1″ (2.5 cm) for hem and baste in place. Stitch ¾″-wide (2 cm) lace edging to right side of ruffle, ⅛″ (3 mm) from lower edge, using off-white thread.

3. Make rows of gathering stitches ¼″ (6 mm) and ½″ (1.25 cm) from top edge of ruffle. Right sides together, gather ruffle to lower edge of skirt and stitch a ½″ (1.25 cm) seam.

4. Run gathering stitches and gather skirt to bodice beginning ½″ (1.25 cm) from edge of facings. Stitch a ½″ (1.25 cm) seam.

5. Beginning 3½″ (9 cm) below waistline seam, stitch skirt and ruffle together at center back.

6. Fold facings to inside and stitch to seam allowance. Sew snaps on back at positions indicated by dots.

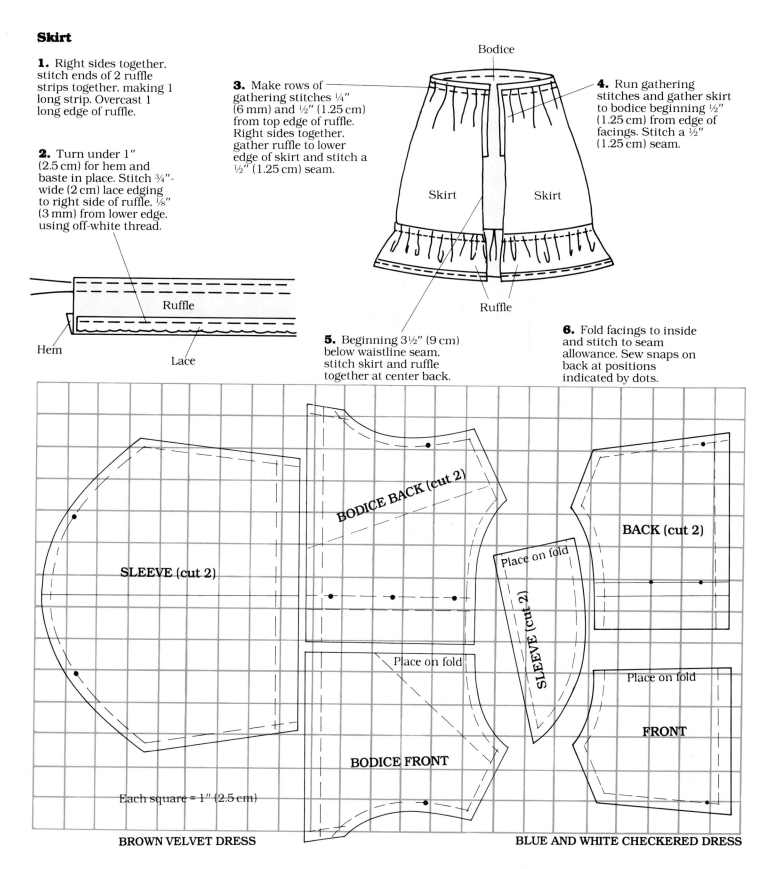

Bodice

Skirt   Skirt

Ruffle

Ruffle

Hem

Lace

SLEEVE (cut 2)

BODICE BACK (cut 2)

Place on fold

SLEEVE (cut 2)

BACK (cut 2)

Place on fold

Place on fold

BODICE FRONT

FRONT

Each square = 1″ (2.5 cm)

BROWN VELVET DRESS

BLUE AND WHITE CHECKERED DRESS

78

MAKING THE BLUE-AND-WHITE CHECKERED DRESS

Materials

½ yard (46 cm) light blue-and-white gingham with ⅛" (3 mm) check

⅜ yard (34 cm) ruffled quilt binding with ½" (1.25 cm) ruffle or ⅜ yard (34 cm) ½"-wide (1.25 cm) eyelet ruffling and ¾ yard (68 cm) white bias tape

¾ yard (68 cm) ½"-wide (1.25 cm) eyelet edging

1 yard (92 cm) 2"-wide (5.1 cm) eyelet ruffling

White thread

2 snap sets

1 hook and eye

1½ yards (136 cm) ⅝"-wide (1.5 cm) light blue velvet ribbon

Sprig of small artificial flowers

Cutting Out Patterns and Fabric

1. The patterns are shown in reduced dimensions. Each square equals 1" (2.5 cm). Enlarge and cut out patterns, then cut out fabric pieces.

2. In addition, cut 1 skirt piece 35 x 9¼" (89.4 x 22.6 cm).

Top

1. Press under ¼" (6 mm), then ¾" (2 cm) along center edges of back pieces. Stitch in place. Right sides together, stitch front to backs at shoulders.

3. Right sides together, stitch opposite edge of 1 length of bias tape along neck edge. Clip curves.

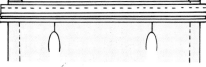

5. Turn under ¼" (6 mm) twice and hem bottom of bodice.

6. Press under ¼" (6 mm) on straight edges of sleeves for hems. Stitch ½"-wide (1.25 cm) eyelet edging onto hems.

7. Make row of gathering stitches along curved edges of sleeves.

2. To make collar, stitch ruffled quilt binding to neck edge. Or stitch ½"-wide (1.25 cm) eyelet ruffling between edges of 2 lengths of bias tape with right sides out.

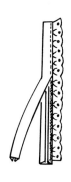

4. Position edge of other length of bias tape on inside over seam line and slip-stitch to neck edge. Trim ends of collar to ½" (1.25 cm) from center back.

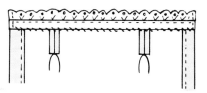

8. Right sides together, gather fabric and eyelet to sides between dots, then stitch seams. Stitch side seams below dots.

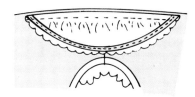

Skirt

1. Beginning 3½" (9 cm) from 1 edge, stitch sides of skirt pieces together using a ½" (1.25 cm) seam allowance. Press seam open. Press under ½" (1.25 cm) on edges of 3½" (9 cm) opening. Fold under ¼" (6 mm) on seam allowances of opening and stitch.

2. Press under ¼" (6 mm) on lower edge of skirt.

3. Cut a 34" (86 cm) length of 2"-wide (5.1 cm) eyelet ruffling and stitch ends together ¼" (6 mm) from edge. Zigzag or overcast seam allowance.

4. Right sides together, stitch eyelet to lower edge of skirt. Turn under a 1" (2.6 cm) hem and slip-stitch in place.

5. Make 2 rows of gathering stitches ¼" (6 mm) and ½" (1.25 cm) from top edge of skirt.

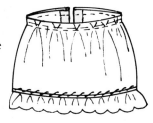

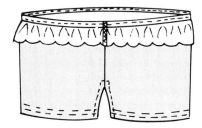

6. Right sides together, gather skirt evenly to lower edge of bodice and stitch a ½" (1.25 cm) seam. Trim and press seam toward bodice, then top-stitch ⅛" (3 mm) above seam.

Finishing

1. Sew snaps on back at positions indicated by dots. Sew hook and eye to center back of collar.

2. Wrap a 41" (105 cm) length of light blue velvet ribbon around dress waist to make sash, then tie a bow.

3. Tie a small bow of remaining ribbon around sprig of flowers, then pin or sew bow to ear.

MAKING THE SHIRTS
Materials
For large shirt: ⅜ yard (35 cm) plaid flannel

For small shirt: ¼ yard (22 cm) light blue-and-white gingham, with ⅛" (3 mm) check

Matching thread

3 snap sets

5 buttons: ⁷⁄₁₆" (1.1 cm) diameter for large shirt; ⅜" (1 cm) diameter for small shirt

Patterns
The patterns are shown in reduced dimension. For large shirt, enlarge pattern pieces so each square equals 1¼" (3.2 cm). For small shirt, enlarge pieces so each square equals 1" (2.5 cm).

1. Right sides together, stitch collar pieces together along ends and outer edge, using ¼" (6 mm) seam allowance. Clip corners, then turn right side out.

2. Top-stitch ⅛" (3 mm) from finished edges.

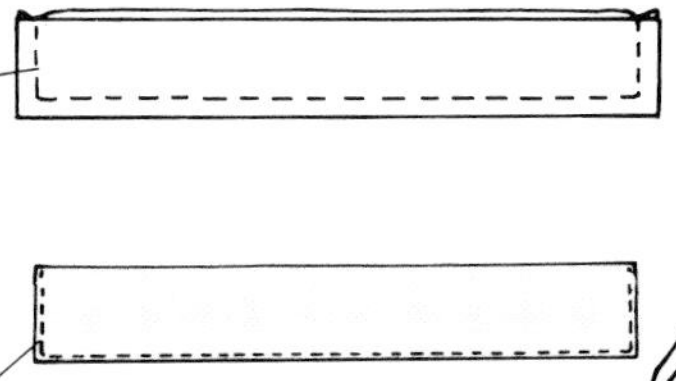

3. Stitch fronts to back at shoulder seams.

4. Stitch collar to right side of neck edge between center fronts.

5. Press ¼" (6 mm) to wrong side on center front edges.

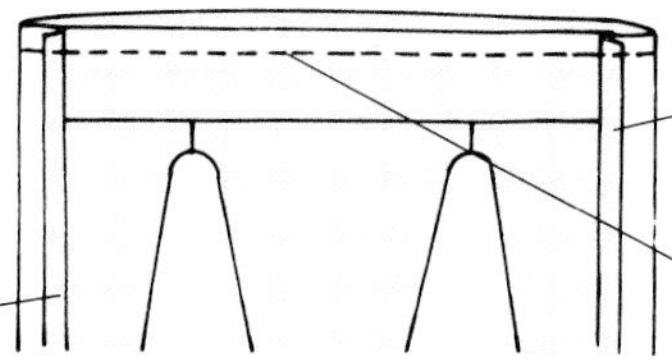

6. Fold facings to front along fold lines.

7. Stitch collar and facings to neck edge. Press facings and seam allowances to wrong side.

8. Stitch along inner edge of facings and ⅛" (3 mm) from fold line.

9. Stitch along seam allowance of collar ⅛" (3 mm) from seam.

10. Fold pleats on lower edges of sleeves.

11. Baste along seam line.

12. Stitch 1 long edge of cuff to wrong side of lower sleeve edges.

13. Turn under ¼" (6 mm) on other long edge and fold to right side over seam.

15. Make gathering rows along top edges of sleeves. Right sides together, ease sleeves to fit armhole edges and stitch seams.

14. Top-stitch along each long edge of cuff. Fold pleat in cuff. Top stitch ⅛" (3 mm) from front fold.

16. Right sides together, stitch back to fronts along sides and underarms.

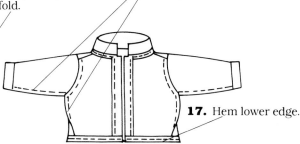

17. Hem lower edge.

Finishing
With left front overlapping right, sew snaps at positions indicated by dots. Sew buttons to right side of left front at dots. Sew buttons to cuffs at dots, stitching through all layers.

Bow Tie
From a scrap of blue velveteen, cut a 7 x 3" (17.8 x 7.6 cm) piece for bow and a 1¼ x 2¼" (3.2 x 5.8 cm) piece for center.

1. Fold bow in half lengthwise with right sides together, then stitch along long edge ¼" (6 mm) from edge. Turn right side out with seam centered on 1 side.

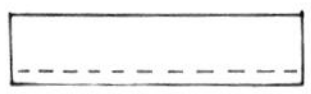

2. With seam inside, fold ends to center and whip stitch together.

3. Fold under ¼" (6 mm) on 2¼" (5.8 cm) edges of center. Wrap around middle of bow piece, overlapping ends in back. Whip-stitch edges together. Pin or sew to shirt collar.

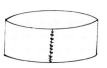

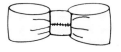

Knotted Tie

From a scrap of brown corduroy, cut a 6 x 4½" (15.2 x 11.5 cm) bias piece for tie and a 4 x 3" (10.2 x 7.6 cm) bias piece for knot.

1. Fold tie in half lengthwise with right sides together, then stitch along long edge and 1 end, using a ¼" (6 mm) seam allowance. Turn right side out. Fold down 1" (2.5 cm) on unfinished end for top.

2. Fold knot in half lengthwise and stitch along long edge. Turn right side out.

3. Center knot across right side of top edge of tie.

4. Fold ends to back of tie, turning under top corners to resemble a knot. Sew ends to each other and to tie. Pin or sew to shirt collar.

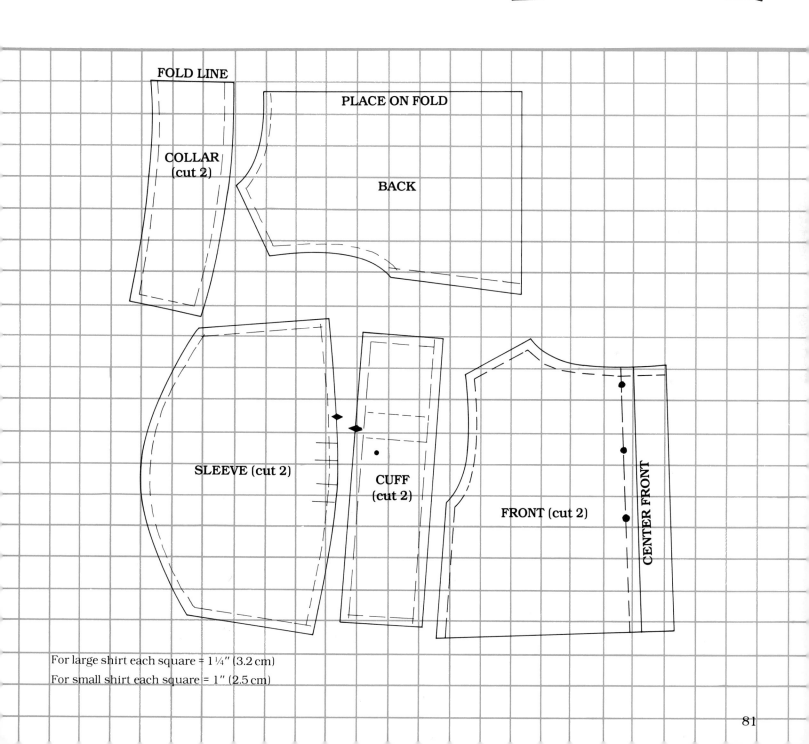

FOLD LINE

COLLAR (cut 2)

PLACE ON FOLD

BACK

SLEEVE (cut 2)

CUFF (cut 2)

FRONT (cut 2)

CENTER FRONT

For large shirt each square = 1¼" (3.2 cm)

For small shirt each square = 1" (2.5 cm)

MAKING THE KNICKERS

Materials
⅜ yard (34 cm) blue velvet
Blue thread
Five ⁷⁄₁₆″ (13.8 cm) blue buttons
1 hook and eye set

Cutting Patterns and Fabric
The patterns are shown in reduced dimension. Each square equals 1″ (2.5 cm). Enlarge and cut out pattern pieces, then cut out fabric. In addition, cut out the following fabric pieces:
2 cuffs 10¼ x 2″ (26 x 5.1 cm)
1 waistband 19½ x 2″ (48 x 5.1 cm)
2 suspender straps 12½ x 2½″ (32 x 6.4 cm)

1. Stitch darts in back pieces.

2. Right sides together, stitch backs together along center lines.

3. Zigzag or overcast edges of fly facing.

4. Right sides together, stitch fronts together below dots.

5. On left front, fold facing to wrong side along fold line. Top-stitch along line of fly.

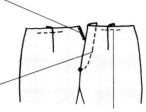

6. Fold pleats in fronts and baste along seam line.

7. Right sides together, stitch front to back along inner leg seam and side seams above dots.

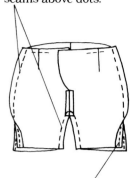

8. Press under seam allowance below dots.

9. Make row of gathering stitches along bottom edge of each leg. Right sides together, gather lower edge of leg to 1 long edge of cuff, leaving ¼″ (6 mm) extension at each end of cuff. Stitch leg to cuff using ¼″ (6 mm) seam allowance.

10. Press under ¼″ (6 mm) along other cuff edge.

11. Right sides together, fold cuffs in half lengthwise and stitch ends. Turn other cuff edges to inside of lower legs and slip-stitch along seam lines. Top-stitch ⅛″ (3 mm) from edges of cuffs.

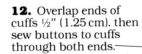

12. Overlap ends of cuffs ½″ (1.25 cm), then sew buttons to cuffs through both ends.

13. Right sides together, stitch 1 edge of waistband to knickers, leaving ¼″ (6 mm) of band extending on each side.

15. Sew hook and eye at center fronts.

16. Sew button on left side of waistband.

14. Fold waistband in half lengthwise, right sides together, and stitch ends. Turn other waistband edge to inside of knickers and slip-stitch along seam line. Top-stitch all around waistband ⅛″ (3 mm) from edges.

17. Right sides together, fold suspender straps in half lengthwise. Then stitch along 1 end and long edge.

18. Turn right side out. Top-stitch all the way around straps ⅛″ (3 mm) from finished edges.

19. Put knickers on bear and pin finished strap ends to waistband above pleats. Then cross straps in back and pin ends under waistband. Remove knickers and stitch suspenders in place. Sew buttons to suspenders through waistband.

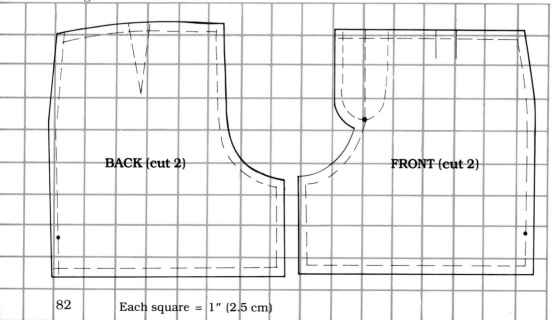

BACK (cut 2)

FRONT (cut 2)

82   Each square = 1″ (2.5 cm)

MAKING THE TROUSERS

Materials
½ yard (44 cm) brown wide-wale corduroy
Brown thread
1 hook and eye

Cutting Patterns and Fabric
The patterns are shown in reduced dimension. Each square equals 1″ (2.5 cm). Enlarge and cut out pattern pieces, then cut out fabric. In addition, cut 1 waistband 23 x 2¾″ (56 x 7 cm)

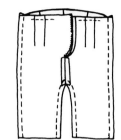

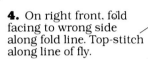

1. Stitch darts in back pieces. Right sides together, stitch backs together along center lines.

2. Zigzag or overcast edges of fly facing.

3. Stitch fronts together below dots.

4. On right front, fold facing to wrong side along fold line. Top-stitch along line of fly.

5. Fold pleats in fronts and baste along seam lines.

6. Right sides together, stitch front to back along side and inner leg seams.

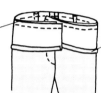

7. Right sides together, stitch waistband to trousers, leaving ¼″ (6 mm) of band extending on each end.

8. Press under ¼″ (6 mm) along opposite edge of band.

9. Right sides together, fold waistband in half lengthwise and stitch ends. Turn waistband right side out.

10. Slip-stitch edge to seam line on inside.

11. Top-stitch ⅛″ (3 mm) from edges. Sew hook and eye on waistband ends.

12. Zigzag or overcast lower edges of legs. Turn under ¾″ (2 cm) and stitch hem.

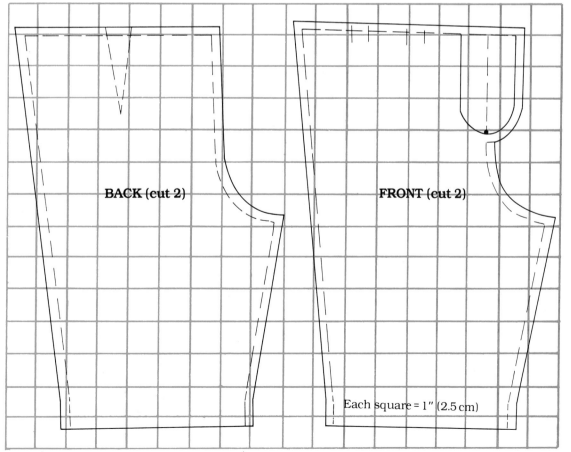

BACK (cut 2)

FRONT (cut 2)

Each square = 1″ (2.5 cm)

Each square = 1″ (2.5 cm)

Small children love this seated bear because it, too, has to be lifted up all the time to take a seat in a big person's world. Like the child, it is expected to sit quietly until the time suddenly comes to be lifted down, taken by the hand, and moved to another oversized experience.

Sitting Bear

The pattern for this bear, made in a permanently seated position, is at least a century old. Very likely, children in Colonial America had similar animal dolls. The blue overalls form the fabric of the body and the features of the face are painted onto the velveteen. Dolls of this design seem to become one of the vivid memories of early childhood. Perhaps for this reason they tend to be passed down through the generations.

Materials

⅜ yard (35 cm) tan upholstery velvet or cotton velveteen
¼ yard (22 cm) blue cotton with white pinstripes
¾ pound (345 grams) polyester stuffing
Acrylic paint: white, blue, pink, and black
Size 0 paintbrush for acrylic paint
Two white buttons, ½" (1.25 cm) in diameter

Cutting the pieces

Cut the following from tan velvet, placing patterns with arrows parallel to straight grain of fabric and nap running in the direction of arrows: two head sides, one head center, four ears, four arms, two paw fronts, two paw backs, one body back, and two chest pieces.

Cut the following from blue-and-white cotton, placing arrows parallel to stripes: two romper fronts, one romper back, two back legs, and two 1½"-by-7" (1.25-by-17.8 cm) straps. Transfer placement of dots and darts to wrong side; transfer facial features to right side. Use ⅜" (1 cm) seams unless otherwise indicated.

Front

1. With right sides together, stitch chest pieces along front center seam. Stitch romper fronts along center front seam from top to dot, also with right sides together. Stay-stitch curved sides and top edges of romper front. Along the curve, clip fabric to the stitches. Press under the seam allowance along stay-stitches.

2. Lap romper front over chest, matching seam lines. Using white thread, top-stitch along the top edges of romper.

3. Stitch ankle seam of paw to lower edge of romper fronts, keeping right sides together.

4. Press seam allowance toward romper; with white thread, top-stitch along edge of romper.

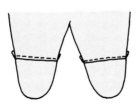

Back

5. Fold straps in half lengthwise, with right sides together. Stitch down the long edge and one of the short ones using a ¼" (6 mm) seam. Press seams open; turn right side out. A knitting needle or unbent wire coat hanger can help accomplish this. Top-stitch along long edges and the stitched end.

With raw ends at bottom, place straps obliquely along marked lines on right side of body back and baste. The straps should cross.

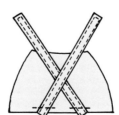

6. Stitch leg backs along back center seam from top to dots, keeping right sides together.

Matching curved edges, stitch paw backs to leg backs with right sides together.

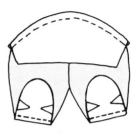

7. Fold foot and stitch darts. Slash fabric at center of dart; press open.

8. With right sides together, stitch arm halves along curved sides, leaving short edge open. Trim seam allowance to ¼" (6 mm); clip seam allowance along curves.

9. Stuff arm; baste along seam line of open edge. Matching squares and raw edges, baste arms to right side of body back.

Joining back to front

10. With right sides together and arms sandwiched between, pin, then baste fronts to backs, matching dots and leaving neck open. Be sure that the shoulder straps do not get caught in the seams. Stitch the front to the back; use thread that matches each section of fabric you pass through. Clip seam allowance along the curves of the feet and body sides. Turn right side out.

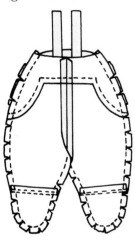

11. Bring straps to front; tack to top of romper. Sew a button over end of each strap. Turn under seam allowance along the neck edge and baste it in place. Stuff body and legs firmly but allow legs to flex where they join body.

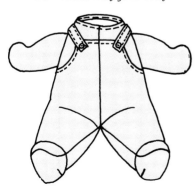

Ears

12. With right sides together, stitch ear halves along curved edge. Trim seam to ⅛″ (3 mm) and clip seam allowance at curves. Turn right side out.

Head

13. Stay-stitch dart lines in head center and top dart lines of head side. Slash dart center, leaving ¼″ (6 mm) near inside of angle. With right sides together and stay-stitches aligning, stitch each head side to center between darts and nose. With ear on right side of fabric, baste it to stay-stitches of the dart *fronts* of the head center and head sides; match large and small dots.

14. Right sides together, stitch each head side to head center behind the darts. Stitch across each ear-holding dart; make sure you catch the ears securely.

15. Stitch up lower dart on each side of head. Right sides still together, stitch center seam from nose to neck.

16. Turn head right side out. By hand, beginning at center back, make a row of gathering stitches along the neck seam line. Stuff the head firmly.

17. Insert the head into the body and pin it in place. With the thread doubled in the needle, slip-stitch the head to the body using tiny stitches. Before seam is completed, push in as much stuffing as possible to fill neck completely.

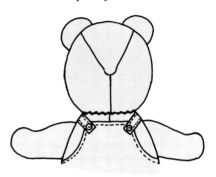

Features

With acrylic paint, color the eyes white, the nose and pupils blue, the tongue pink, and outline the eyes, mouth, and lashes with black.

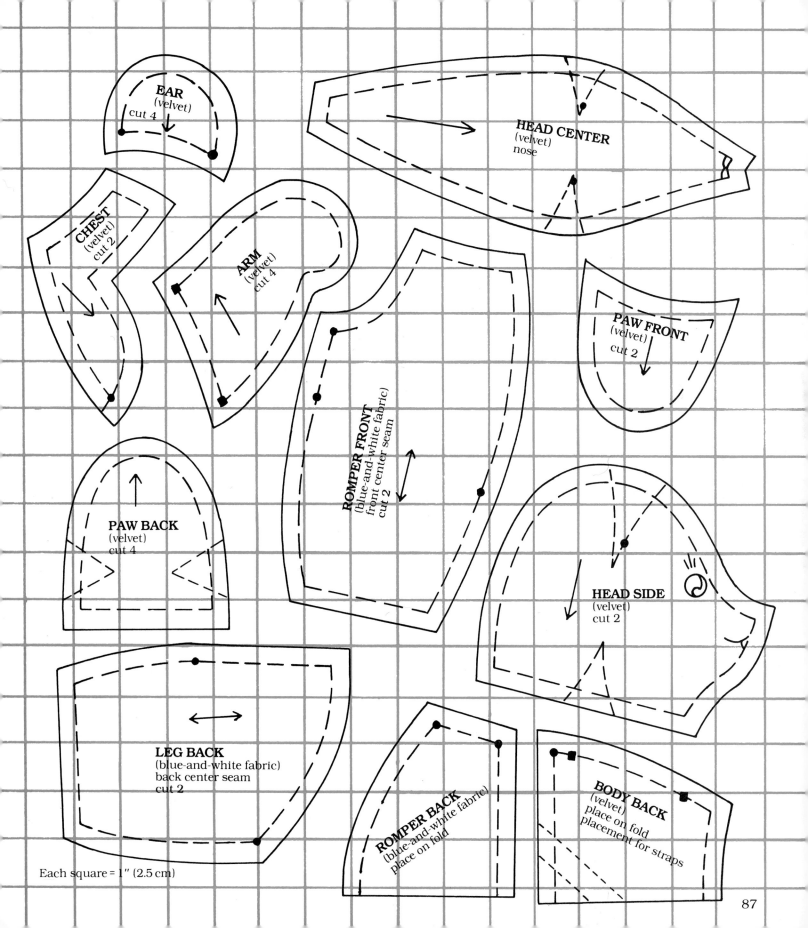

EAR
(velvet)
cut 4

HEAD CENTER
(velvet)
nose

CHEST
(velvet)
cut 2

ARM
(velvet)
cut 4

PAW FRONT
(velvet)
cut 2

ROMPER FRONT
(blue-and-white fabric)
front center seam
cut 2

PAW BACK
(velvet)
cut 4

HEAD SIDE
(velvet)
cut 2

LEG BACK
(blue-and-white fabric)
back center seam
cut 2

ROMPER BACK
(blue-and-white fabric)
place on fold

BODY BACK
(velvet)
place on fold
placement for straps

Each square = 1″ (2.5 cm)

87

Country Bears

Country bears are as homey and unpretentious as a pair of socks, which is what they are. Their identical bodies are extremely easy to sew from a new pair of cotton socks. The fun part is embroidering their expressions and making clothes for them.

Sadie and Zeke, who are made from identical patterns, stand 14½" (37 cm) high not counting Zeke's flat-crowned straw hat. It is cut from a woven straw placemat and goes together in just a few minutes.

As a practical note, if you use polyester stuffing and colorfast yarn for the facial features, sock bears like these are good gifts for little children—who will want to take them *everywhere*—because their mothers can simply throw the dolls into the washing machine and dryer with the rest of the family wash.

Materials

For one bear
1 pair men's tan cotton socks with knitted-in heel
½ pound (460 grams) polyester stuffing
Tan and dark-brown sewing thread
Small scraps of brown and white felt
½ yard (44 cm) red six-strand embroidery floss
White glue or white sewing thread

For Sadie's clothes
½ yard (44 cm) 45"-wide (1.14 m-wide) yellow-print calico
¼ yard (22 cm) red fabric with white dots
⅜ yard (35 cm) off-white cotton muslin
10" (25.5 cm) -piece of ¼" (6 mm) elastic
9¼" (22.6 cm) piece eyelet ruffling
2 yards (1.84 m) red baby rick-rack
2½" x 10" (6.3 x 25.5 cm) piece

medium-weight interfacing
red, off-white, and yellow sewing thread
2 sets of snaps

For Zeke's clothes
¼ yard (22 cm) red-and-white striped cotton fabric
⅜ yard (35 cm) blue denim
3" x 11" strip (7.6 x 28 cm) red fabric with white dots
Five ⁵⁄₁₆"-diameter (9 mm-diameter) red buttons
Two ½"-diameter (1.25 cm-diameter) white buttons
Red, white, and blue thread
3 snap sets
1 hook-and-eye set
Lightweight woven straw placemat or old straw hat

To make the bodies

Head

1. The top of your bear's head should be flat, so start by turning one sock inside out and flattening it along the toe. Stitch across toe ½" (1.25 cm) from edge by hand or machine. Turn sock right side out.

2. By hand, make a row of gathering stitches around sock about 4½" (11.45 cm) from top seam. Roll a ball of stuffing and insert it into the head. Draw up the gathers below the stuffing to a diameter of about 2½" (6.3 cm). Knot the thread securely and, using the needle, bury the ends in the stuffing.

Body Stuff the rest of the foot so it is firm and full. The heel forms the bear's bottom. Pin the sock evenly where the foot meets the cuff and make a row of running stitches.

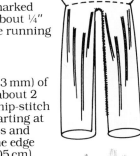

Legs

1. Count the ribs in the cuff and mark the midpoint front and back. Cut along the marked ribs, stopping about ¼" (6 mm) from the running stitches.

2. Turn in ⅛" (3 mm) of the raw edges (about 2 stitches) and whip-stitch the outsides, starting at running stitches and going toward the edge about 7½" (19.05 cm). Stuff the legs firmly. Trim the ends so only ½" (1.25 cm) is left.

3. For each paw turn in ⅛" (3 mm) to ¼" (6 mm) of the raw edges so the paw is rounded and whip-stitch the outsides together.

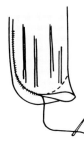

4. Bend the paw forward. Slip-stitch the edges of the fold together to form a dart.

Ears

1. Cut 4 ears from foot section of second sock. Right sides in, stitch ears together in pairs along outer curve. Trim seam allowance to ⅛" (3 mm). Turn right side out.

2. Fold in ¼" (6 mm) along remaining edge; slip-stitch edges together. Pin ears to head as shown and slip-stitch along front and back to head.

Muzzle. Cut off the end of toe of the remaining sock to make a 2¼" x 3" (5.8 x 7.6 cm) muzzle. Turn in edges ¼" (6 mm); baste them in place. Center muzzle on your bear's face about ½" (1.25 cm) from neck stitching; slip-stitch to attach.

Nose. Cut nose from brown felt. With brown thread, make a row of gathering stitches ⅛" (3 mm) from edge. Roll a small ball of stuffing, place it on the nose, and gather edge over it. Knot thread securely and slip-stitch nose to top of muzzle.

Arms

1. Cut the cuff from the second sock, find the midpoint of the front and back. Cut the cuff in half vertically along the ribs. With right sides in, fold the arms in half lengthwise and trim one end so it is round.

3. With seam along back side of the bear turn under ends with the side of arm that is closer to the body about ½" (1.25 cm) shorter at the top. Pin sides together so shoulder is rounded tucking in ends of seam and slip-stitch them together. Slip-stitch shoulder to sides of bear ¾" (17.8 cm) from neck stitching.

2. By hand, back-stitch the rounded end and long edge together about ¼" (6 mm) from the edge until the arm is about 7" long. Turn right side out; stuff arm firmly.

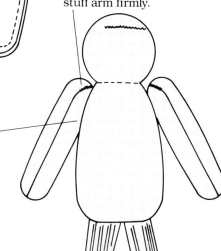

Eyes. Cut large circles from white felt, small ones from brown felt. Glue or stitch the brown circles to the white ones, and attach them to the face. Make sure Sadie and Zeke are looking sideways at each other!

Mouth. Using red floss, bury the knot in the muzzle, and embroider lines of mouth with three straight stitches. Bring needle out just above nose, take a stitch to knot the thread, and bury the end in the muzzle stuffing.

Any calico will suit Sadie but she has a sunny disposition and favors yellow. You can see by the way she keeps an eye on Zeke that she thinks the world of him. He wears everyday overalls to work the farm, but has his best pair on now because they are on their way to a square dance and picnic at the county fairgrounds.

Sadie's clothes

Dress. From yellow calico, cut patterns given plus two 7"x 9" (17.8 x 22 cm) sleeves and a 2½" x 40" (6.3 x 102 cm) ruffle. Follow instructions for Bearnice's Dress on page 54, steps 1-4.

5. Press under ¼" (6 mm) along neck edge. Make a row of gathering stitches along this edge. Gather the neckline between center backs to 9" around with most of the gathers close to the center front and back. Follow steps 6 and 7 on page 54.

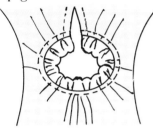

8. Narrow-hem the 9" (22 cm) cuff edge of each sleeve. Cut elastic in half, stretch it out, and stitch across wrong side of sleeve ¾" (2 cm) from finished edge. Make a row of gathering stitches on top edge of sleeve. Gather sleeve so it matches the sleeve edge of dress, and with right sides together, stitch seam. Follow steps 9 and 10 on page 54.

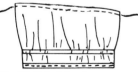

11. Right sides in, sew ends of bottom ruffle together. Narrow-hem one long edge. Make two rows of gathering stitches, one ¼" (6 mm) and one ½" (1.25 cm) from raw edge. With right sides together, gather ruffle and stitch it to bottom edge of dress; using ½" (1.25 cm) seam allowance. Follow step 12 on page 54.

Apron. From off-white muslin, cut a bib, a 7¼"x 10½" (18.4 x 27 cm) skirt, two 1½"x6½" (3.8 x 16.45 cm) straps, and a 1½"x 25" (3.8 cm x 64.5 cm) waistband.

Follow step 1 for Bearnice's Apron on page 55, omitting top-stitching. Sew rick-rack across bib ¼" (6 mm) below fold. Cut heart from red fabric with white dots. Machine-applique heart to center of bib ¼" (6 mm) below rick-rack. Follow step 2-4 on page 55 omitting eyelet and sewing rick-rack to center of straps.

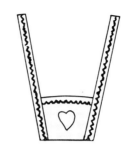

5. Press under ½" (1.25 cm) on 7½" (19.05 cm) sides of skirt; sew rick rack ¼" (6 mm) from fold. Press under ½" (1.25 cm) at bottom. Stitch rick-rack to lower edge ¼" (6 mm) from fold, leaving ¼" (6 mm) extending at each end. Fold rick-rack around to wrong side; tack ends in place by hand.

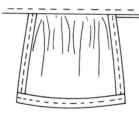

6. Make a row of gathering stitches ¼" (6 mm) from remaining raw edge. Gather skirt so it measures 4¼" (108.2 cm) across. Center skirt on one long edge of waistband and stitch ¼" (6 mm) seam. Fold waistband in half with right sides together. Stitch edges of waistband together, on either side of skirt. Turn right side out.

7. Tuck seam allowance into waistband and stitch it in place.

8. Lap center of waistband ¼" (6 mm) over lower edge of bib; stitch along top edge of waistband. Place apron on bear. Pin straps under waistband at back; sew in place on wrong side of waistband. Fold ends of ties diagonally and tack in place.

Bonnet. From red fabric with white dots, cut one crown, two brims, and two 1¼"-by-8" (3.2 x 20 cm) ties. Cut one brim from interfacing.

1. Press under ¼" (6 mm) along straight edge of crown. With right sides together, turn up folded edge to dot and stitch between dot and edge. Clip corner at dot; turn right side out. Make a row of gathering stitches to attach folded edge and back of crown.

2. Clip in ¼" (6 mm) at squares; press under ¼" (6 mm) between clips for ear holes. Make a row of gathering stitches ⅛" (3 mm) from fold. Gather each section to 2" (5.1 cm); secure along gathers using a regular-length stitch. Make gathering stitches along remaining sections of crown.

3. Fuse or baste interfacing to one brim piece.

4. Right sides in, stitch brim pieces together along curved edge. Clip seam allowance; turn right side out. With right sides together, match dots and squares, or keep area between ears at center. Gather crown to match brim length and stitch to interfaced side. Fold under seam allowance of remaining edge along seam; top stitch in place. Gather hemmed edge to fit head of bear; secure along gathers with a regular stitch length.

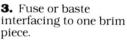

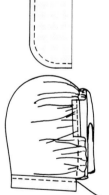

5. For ties, fold pieces in half lengthwise and stitch seam along edges. Turn right side out; trim one end diagonally. Tack other end to lower corner of bonnet between brim and ruffle.

Zeke's clothes

Shirt. Follow instructions for Cousins Huggable Shirt on page 80.

Pants. See instructions for Cousins Huggable Trousers on page 83 for steps 1-4 and 6.

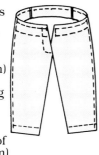

7. Turn under ¾″ (2 cm) along top edge; stitch along broken lines using red thread, making two red lines ½″ (1.25 cm) apart. Press up ½″ (1.25 cm) at lower edge of legs; top-stitch ¼″ (6 mm) from fold.

8. For suspenders, cut red fabric with white dots in half lengthwise. Fold each piece in half lengthwise with right sides together; stitch long edges together. Turn right side out. Turn under ¼″ (6 mm) then ½″ (1.25 cm) on one end for front. Place clothes on bear. Bring suspenders over shoulders; pin raw ends to inside of pant back at an angle so they cross in back; sew to inside of pants. Make a thread loop at other end of each suspender. Sew a button at center of the top seam on each side of pant front.

Hat

1. From lightweight straw, cut a 5″ (12.7 cm) circle; cut a 3″ (7.6 cm) circle from center of that circle to make both brim and crown. Cut a strip for sides 1″-by-10¾″ (2.5 x 27.5 cm). Using matching thread, zigzag stitch around edges of all pieces to prevent fraying.

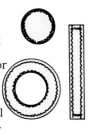

2. With thread doubled in needle, overcast-stitch side to brim. Stitch ends of side together. Stitch crown to side. Cut a 1 by 11″ (2.5 x 28 cm) piece of denim. Press under ¼″ (6 mm) on each long edge. Top-stitch along edges with red thread. Glue strip around lower edge of side.

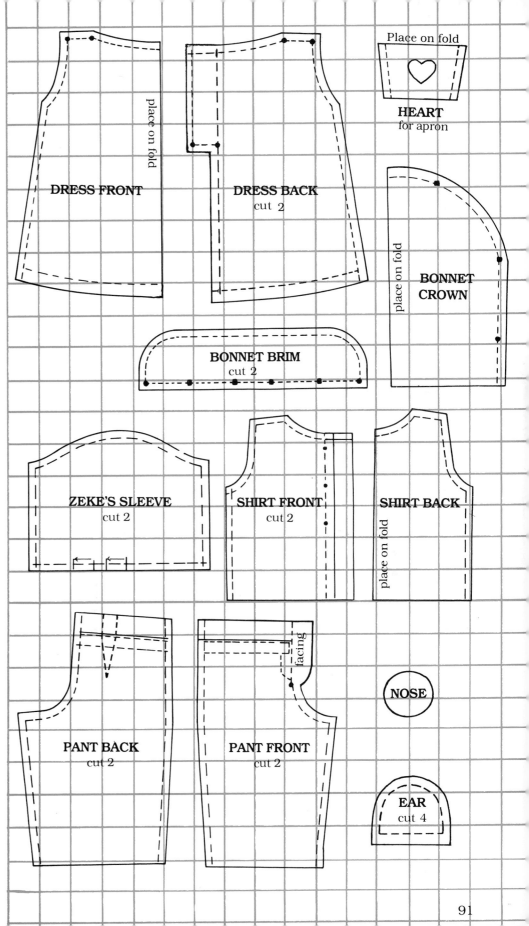

DRESS FRONT

place on fold

DRESS BACK
cut 2

Place on fold

HEART
for apron

place on fold

BONNET CROWN

BONNET BRIM
cut 2

ZEKE'S SLEEVE
cut 2

SHIRT FRONT
cut 2

SHIRT BACK

place on fold

PANT BACK
cut 2

PANT FRONT
cut 2

facing

NOSE

EAR
cut 4

Christine Crochet

Her name is Christine Crochet, but very close friends may call her Crystal. She is a with-it lady of "a certain age," and she prefers lavenders, pinks, lilacs, and mauves over acid punk colors. The lightly floral scent she wears is so delicate it almost isn't there—until she smiles at you.

Abbreviations:

Ch = chain stitch
sc = single crochet
sl st = slip stitch
inc = increase
dec = decrease
MC = main color
CC = contrasting color
rnd = round
[ ] = repeat directions in brackets the number of times given

Note:

To increase 1 st, work 2 sc in same st.

To decrease 1 st, draw up a loop in each of next 2 sts, yarn over hook, draw it through all three loops on hook.

Size:
About 18″ high, standing.

Materials:
2, 3½-oz. balls brown knitting worsted (MC)
scraps of Lt. Rose (CC), black, and white knitting worsted
Crochet hook size F (4.00 mm)
Yarn needle
About 6 oz. stuffing
30″ of ¾″-wide pink satin ribbon
Small bunch of fake flowers

Gauge:
4 sc = 1″.

Head
Front: Starting at center with MC, ch 2.

Rnd 1 (right side): Make 6 sc in 2nd ch from hook. Mark beginning of rnds. All rnds are worked with right side facing you.

Rnd 2: 2 sc in each sc—you have 12 sc around.

Rnd 3: [Sc in next sc, 2 sc in following sc] 6 times—18 sc.

Rnd 4: [Sc in next 2 sc, 2 sc in following sc] 6 times—24 sc.

Rnd 5: [Sc in next 3 sc, 2 sc in next sc] 6 times—30 sc.

Rnd 6: [Sc in next 4 sc, 2 sc in next sc] 6 times—36 sc.

Rnd 7: [Sc in next 5 sc, 2 sc in next sc] 6 times—42 sc.

Rnd 8: [Sc in next 6 sc, 2 sc in next sc] 6 times—48 sc.

Rnd 9: [Sc in next 7 sc, 2 sc in next sc] 6 times—54 sc.

Rnd 10: [Sc in next 8 sc, 2 sc in next sc] 6 times—60 sc.

Rnd 11: Sc in next 9 sc, 2 sc in next sc, sc in 18 sc, 2 sc in next sc, sc in 31 sc—62 sc.

Rnd 12: Sc in next 10 sc, 2 sc in next sc, sc in 20 sc (mark this section with yarn or safety pin for bottom of head), 2 sc in next sc, sc in next 30 sc—64 sc. Sl st in next sc. Fasten off.

Back of Head: Work as for front.
Assemble Head: With right sides of work held together, bottom edges of front and back matching, mark off 12 stitches each on center bottom of back and front for neck opening. With MC and yarn needle, sew the rest of the back and front for neck opening. With MC and yarn needle, sew the rest of the back and front together with a whip-stitch in each stitch through both thicknesses. Fasten off. Turn right side out. (Muzzle is made later).

Body:

Rnd 1: Starting in one corner of neck opening, work 14 sc along each neck edge, working an sc in each sc already sewn at each joining—28 sc. Mark beginning of rnds.

Rnd 2: Work 2 sc in each of first 2 sc, sc in next 10 sc, 2 sc in each of next 4 sc, sc in next 10 sc, 2 sc in each of last 2 sc—36 sc.

Rnd 3: 2 sc in each of next 3 sc, sc in 12 sc, 2 sc in each of next 6 sc, sc in 12 sc, 2 sc in each of last 3 sc—48 sc.

Rnd 4: Sc in next 4 sc, 2 sc in next sc, sc in next 14 sc, 2 sc in next sc, sc in 8 sc, 2 sc in next sc, sc in next 14 sc, 2 sc in next sc, sc in last 4 sc—52 sc.

Rnds 5 through 13: Sc in each sc around.

Rnd 14: Sc in next 10 sc, [2 sc in next sc, sc in next sc] 4 times, sc in 34 sc—56 sc.

Rnd 15: Sc in next 98 sc, [2 sc in next sc, sc in next 3 sc] 4 times, sc in 31 sc—60 sc.

Rnds 16 through 31: Sc in each sc around.

Rnd 32: *Sc in next 2 sc, dec over next 2 sc; repeat from * around—45 sc.

Rnd 33: *Sc in next sc, dec over next 2 sc; repeat from * around—30 sc.

Rnd 34: Repeat Rnd 33—20 sc. Fasten off.

Muzzle:

Starting at center, with MC ch 5.

Rnd 1: Sc in 2nd ch from hook and next 2 ch, 3 sc in last ch, working on opposite side of chain, sc in next 2 ch, 2 sc in last ch—10 sc. Mark beginning of rnds.

Rnd 2: 2 sc in first sc, sc in next 2 sc, 2 sc in next sc, sc in next sc, 2 sc in next sc, sc in next 2 sc, 2 sc in next sc, sc in last sc—14 sc.

Rnd 3: 2 sc in first sc, sc in next 4 sc, 2 sc in next sc, sc in next 2 sc, 2 sc in next sc, sc in next 4 sc, 2 sc in last sc—18 sc. (Beginning of rnd is top of muzzle.)

Rnd 4: Sc in first sc, 2 sc in next sc, [sc in next 4 sc, 2 sc in next sc] 3 times, sc in last sc—22 sc.

Rnd 5: Sc in first sc, 2 sc in next sc, [sc in next 5 sc, 2 sc in next sc] 3 times, sc in 2 sc—26 sc.

Rnd 6: Sc in first 2 sc, 2 sc in next sc, [sc in next 6 sc, 2 sc in next sc] 3 times, sc in last 2 sc—30 sc.

Rnds 7 and 8: Sc in each sc around. Sl st in first sc and fasten off, leaving long end for sewing.

Legs (make 2):

Starting at toes, with MC ch 8.

Rnd 1: 2 sc in 2nd ch from hook, sc in next 5 ch, 3 sc in last ch; working on other side of ch, sc in next 6 ch—16 sc. Mark beginning of rnds;

Rnd 2: Sc in first sc, 2 sc in next sc, sc in next 5 sc, 2 sc in next sc, sc in 8 sc—18 sc.

Rnd 3: Sc in first sc, [2 sc in next sc] twice, sc in next 5 sc, [2 sc in next sc] twice, sc in 8 sc—22 sc.

Rnds 4 through 8: Sc in each sc around.

Rnd 9: Sc in 6 sc, [dec over next 2 sts] twice (heel), [sc in 5 sc, 2 sc in next sc] twice—22 sc.

Rnd 10: Sc in 4 sc, dec 1 sc, sc in 3 sc, dec 1 sc, sc in 3 sc, 2 sc in next sc, sc in 6 sc, inc 1 sc—22 sc.

Rnds 11 through 19: Sc in each sc around.

Rnd 20: Sc in 4 sc, 2 sc in next sc, sc in 9 sc, 2 sc in next sc, sc in 7 sc—24 sc.

Rnds 21 through 29: Sc in each sc around.

Rnd 30: Sc in 4 sc, 2 sc in next sc, sc in 10 sc, 2 sc in next sc, sc in 8 sc—26 sc.

Rnds 31 and 32: Sc in each sc around. Fasten off, leaving long end for sewing.

Left Arm:

Starting at lower end, with MC ch 8.

Rnd 1: 2 sc in 2nd ch from hook, sc in next 5 ch, 3 sc in last ch: working on opposite side of ch, sc in 6 ch—16 sc. Mark beginning of rnds.

Rnd 2: 2 sc in first sc, sc in next 6 sc, [2 sc in next sc] twice, sc in 6 sc, 2 sc in last sc—20 sc.

Rnds 3 through 7: Sc in each sc around.

Rnd 8: Dec 1 sc, [sc in 3 sc, dec 1 sc] twice, sc in 8 sc—17 sc.

Rnd 9: Sc in each sc around.

Rnd 10: 2 sc in first sc (mark this inc with safety pin), sc in next 7 sc, dec 1 sc (mark dec with scrap yarn), sc in 7 sc—17 sc.

Rnd 11: Sc in each sc around.

Rnd 12: Sc around, working an increase over first marker and a decrease over 2nd marker—17 sc.

Rnds 13 through 18: Repeat Rnds 11 and 12, 3 times.

Rnd 19: Sc around.

Rnd 20: Sc around, increasing 1 sc over *2nd* marker—18 sc.

Rnd 21: Sc in 18 sc.

Rnd 22: Repeat Rnd 20-19 sc.

Rnds 23 and 24: Sc in 19 sc each rnd.

Rnd 25: Sc around, increasing 1 sc over first *and* 2nd markers—21 sc.

Rnds 26 through 28: Sc in 21 sc each rnd.

Rnd 30: [Dec 1 sc, sc in next sc] 7 times—14 sc. Fasten off, leaving long end for sewing.

Right Arm:
Work as for left arm through Rnd 7.

Rnd 8: Dec 1 sc, sc in 8 sc, [dec 1 sc, sc in 3 sc] twice—17 sc. Complete as for left arm.

Ears:
Outer Ear (make 2): Starting at center, with MC, work as for head. Through Rnd 2.

Rnd 3: Sc in 3 sc, 2 sc in next sc, [sc in next sc, 2 sc in next sc] 4 times—17 sc.

Rnd 4: Sc in 4 sc (mark these sc for bottom of ear), 2 sc in next sc, [sc in 2 sc, 2 sc in next sc] 4 times—22 sc. Fasten off.

Inner Ear (make 2): With CC, work 3 rnds as for outer ear, completing last st with MC. Fasten off CC. Work Rnd 4 as for outer ear with MC; do not fasten off.

Join Inner and Outer Ear: Holding one inner and one outer ear with wrong sides together and bottoms matching, sc in each sc through both thicknesses. Fasten off. Push together to cup forward as shown.

Assembly:
Stuff head and body, pushing out jowels and tummy as shown and making sure neck is firmly stuffed and does not wrinkle in back. (Do not stretch too much or stuffing will show through: however it will show through slightly.) Sew back and front lower edge of body closed with whipstitch, working in matching stitches. Stuff muzzle and sew to

lower part of face with lower edge about 3 rows from neck; stretch all edges out to form smooth contour with head. Tack any gaps where stuffing shows around neck closed. Stuff legs. Sew top of legs closed. Bend foot forward and sew 7th row to 9th row on front to bend foot forward. Sew rear legs to body along lower seam (and slightly beyond at sides) and meeting at center; stitch along back and front of leg seam for firm joining. Stuff front legs: sew top closed and sew to shoulders on slight angle; tack top of inner arm to body.

Nose:
With black yarn, ch 2.

Rnd 1: 6 sc in 2nd ch from hook.

Rnd 2: 2 sc in each of next 3 sc, sl st in next sc; do not complete rnd. Fasten off, leaving end for sewing. Sew nose to muzzle as shown.

Embroider eyes with black straight stitches, work 1 white straight stitch in center of each eye. Embroider mouth with lt. rose straight stitches.

Paw Pads (make 4):
With CC, work 3 rnds as for head—18 sc.

Rnd 4: Work 1 more sc in same sc as last st, sc in next 3 sc, 3 sc in next sc, sl st in next sc. Fasten off leaving long end for sewing. Sew a pad to bottom of each paw with wide end forward.

Tie bow around bear's neck, insert flowers with knot.

Pierre Bear

"Eh bien, le journal, le croissant, le patriotisme, C'est l'homme français. I stand here with dignity only 41 cm (16") tall, and perhaps you think that I am too short to interest you, but as all Frenchwomen know, it is not one's size, but one's esprit that counts finalement."

Size:
15" high not counting ears

Materials:
Knitting worsted. About 1½ oz. brown, 1 oz. blue, and ½ oz. each white and red (we used Brunswick's Cinnamon, Tornado, Christmas Red, and White), scrap black; knitting needles size 4, or size to give gauge; about 4 oz. stuffing; yarn needle

Gauge:
11 sts = 2".

Head:
Starting at top of head with brown, cast on 19 sts. Working in stockinette stitch (knit one row, purl one row), inc 1 stitch at each end of Rows 3, 9, 13, and 19—27 sts. Work 5 rows. Dec 1 stitch at each end of next row—25 sts. Purl 1 row. Dec 1 stitch at each end of following row—23 sts. Purl 1 row.

Neck:
Next row: K 2 tog, * k 1, k 2 tog; repeat from * across—15 stitches. Purl 1 row.

Body:
Join red, cut brown. Continuing in stockinette st, cast on 7 sts at beginning of next 2 rows—29 sts. Join white, carry red up side edge. Working 2 rows white, 2 rows red for stripe pattern, work even until there are 5 red stripes. Inc 1 st at each end of next row (white)—31 sts. Work until there are 8 red stripes from beginning. Join blue, cut red and white.

Pants:
Work 2 rows even, then inc 1 stitch at each end of next row—33 sts. Work 15 rows even (or until pants measure 2" from beginning), end with purl row. Dec 1 stitch at each end of next row—31 sts. P 1 row.

Legs:
Next row: K 15 for first leg, join 2nd ball of blue, k 2 tog, k 14 for 2nd leg—15 sts on each leg. Working each leg with a separate ball, work 11 rows even. * Dec 1 st at outer edge of each leg on next row—14 sts each side. P 1 row. Dec 1 st at inner edge of each leg on next row *—13 sts each side. Work 7 rows even. Repeat from * to * once—11 sts each side. Work 3 rows even.

Feet:
First Foot: Join brown, cut blue. With brown, cast on 6 sts at beginning of next row, k across—17 sts. P 1 row. * Inc 1 st at each end of next row—19 sts. Work 7 rows even. Dec 1 st at each end of next row—17 sts. P 1 row. Bind off. Second Foot: Join brown, cut blue. K across, cast on 6 sts at end of row. P 1 row. Work to correspond to first foot, starting at *.

Back:
Make same as front.

Arms:
Starting at tip of paw with brown, cast on 16 stitches. P 1 row.
Next Row: Inc 1 st in first st, k 6, inc in each of next 2 sts, k 6, inc 1 st in last st—20 sts. P 1 row.
Next Row: Inc 1, k 8, inc 1 in each of next 2 sts, k 8, inc 1—24 sts. Work 7 rows even.

Next Row: K 2 tog, k 8, k 2 tog, skip 1, k 1, psso, k 8, k 2 tog—20 sts. P 1 row. Join red, cut brown. Working stripe pattern of 2 rows red, 2 rows white, inc 1 st at each end of rows 7 and 15—24 sts. Work until first row of 7th red stripe is completed. Bind off as to purl.

Finishing:
Sew back and front together, matching colors (use only 1 color for stripes) (either weave seams with wrong sides together or backstitch them with right sides together). Leave an opening between legs for stuffing. Stuff, filling out jowls and tummy; sew opening closed. Fold arms in half lengthwise and sew closed, leaving top edge open. Stuff. Sew top closed. With seam at underarm, sew to sides as shown.

Ears (make 2):
Starting at lower edge with brown, cast on 12 stitches. Work 2 rows even. Inc 1 st at each end of next row—14 sts. Work 3 rows even. Dec 1 st at each end of next row. Work 1 row even. Dec 1 st at each end of next 2 rows—8 sts. Work 1 row even. Inc 1 st at each end of next 2 rows. Work 1 row even. Inc 1 st at each end of next row—14 sts. Work 3 rows even. Dec 1 st at each end of next row. Work 1 row. Bind off. Fold ear in half, wrong side out. Sew sides, taking up one stitch on each side. Turn right side out. Sew lower edge closed and sew to head, slightly behind top seam.

Face:
With yarn needle, embroider black nose and eyes, red straight stitch mouth.

Abbreviations:
k = knit
p = purl
st(s) = stitch(es)
psso = pass the slipped st over
inc = increase (To increase: k or p in back and front of same st)
dec = decrease (To decrease: k or p 2 together)
tog = together

Digger Koala

Materials

⅓ (31 cm) or ⅜ (35 cm) yard 54"-wide (136 cm) light brown, long-pile, fur fabric

⅜ yard (35 cm) or a 10 x 21" (25.5 x 53.5 cm) piece of long-pile, white, fur fabric

6 x 10" (15.2 x 25.5 cm) piece of white fleece or velour fabric

5" (12.7 cm) square stiff interfacing

5" (12.7 cm) square black velveteen

1 pound (460 grams) polyester stuffing

Two ⅝" (1.5 cm) diameter black shank buttons

3 yards (276 cm) black yarn

Tools and materials for 2 crown joints (see "How to Make a Crown Joint" in Heirloom Bear chapter)

Light brown, white, and black thread

Light brown carpet thread and buttonhole twist

Making the Bear

1. Right sides together, stitch pads to inner arms. With fingers, firmly press ¼" (6 mm) seam allowances toward inner arm pieces.

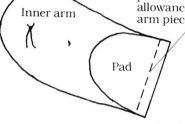

2. Matching dots, and with right sides together, stretch and pin inner arms to outer arms.

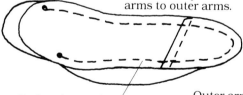

3. Stitch together, leaving ends between dots open for stuffing.

Outer arm

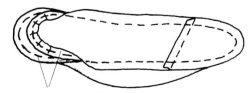

4. Turn under ¼" (6 mm) along edges of openings, then baste. Turn arms right side out.

"Digger" just stepped off the airplane after a long flight from his homeland—the "outback" of Australia. And sure enough, he's brought along a supply of those yummy eucalyptus leaves. After you've made your Koala bear, bring in a bushel of leaves and get ready for a big hug because he has the softest fur of all the bears in the book. Digger's no tiny sprout at 14½" (37 cm) tall, and his arms are joined for really good cuddling. P.S. Don't believe all that baloney about Koala bears being shy—beneath Digger's meek smile lies a very friendly heart. Incidentally, Koala bears do not have tails although their bone structure indicates that their evolutionary ancestors once did. So go ahead and add a tail if you like.

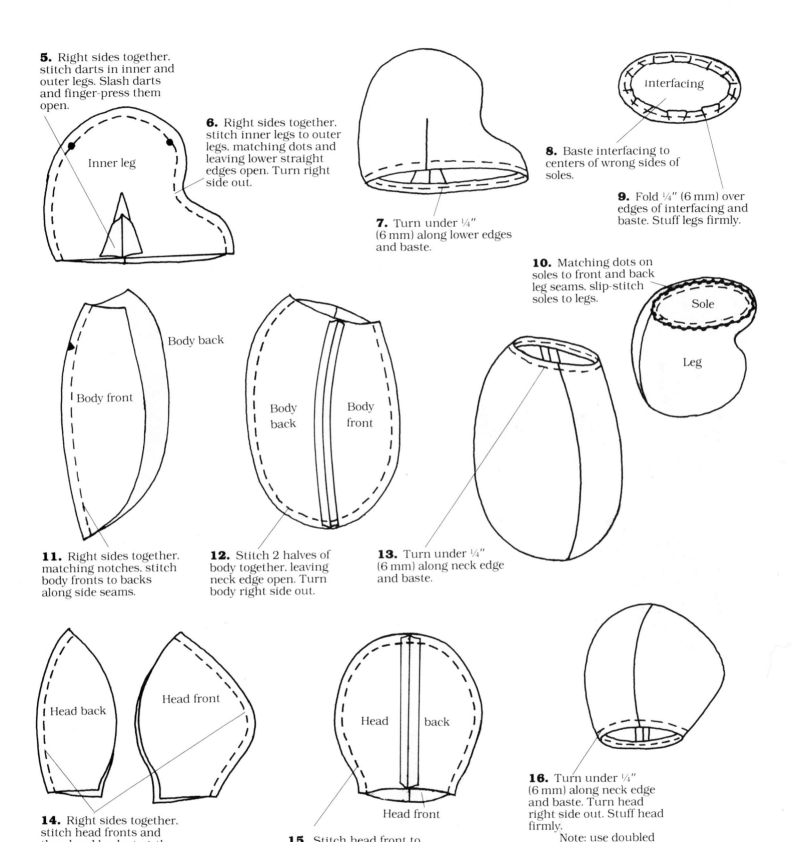

5. Right sides together, stitch darts in inner and outer legs. Slash darts and finger-press them open.

Inner leg

6. Right sides together, stitch inner legs to outer legs, matching dots and leaving lower straight edges open. Turn right side out.

7. Turn under ¼" (6 mm) along lower edges and baste.

Interfacing

8. Baste interfacing to centers of wrong sides of soles.

9. Fold ¼" (6 mm) over edges of interfacing and baste. Stuff legs firmly.

10. Matching dots on soles to front and back leg seams, slip-stitch soles to legs.

Sole

Leg

Body back

Body front

11. Right sides together, matching notches, stitch body fronts to backs along side seams.

Body back

Body front

12. Stitch 2 halves of body together, leaving neck edge open. Turn body right side out.

13. Turn under ¼" (6 mm) along neck edge and baste.

Head back

Head front

14. Right sides together, stitch head fronts and then head backs together along centers (edges without dots).

Head   back

Head front

15. Stitch head front to back leaving straight neck edge open.

16. Turn under ¼" (6 mm) along neck edge and baste. Turn head right side out. Stuff head firmly.

Note: use doubled carpet thread for all hand sewing.

17. Attach arms to body at X's with crown joints. See instructions on "How to Make a Crown Joint" In Heirloom Bear chapter.

18. Stuff body and arms firmly.

19. Slip-stitch arm openings.

20. Pin head to body, matching center front and back seams. Slip-stitch head to neck leaving a 2" (5.1 cm) opening.

21. Stuff neck area as firmly as possible, then finish slip-stitching seam.

22. Pin inner legs to sides of body, following placement lines on pattern. Slip-stitch legs to body.

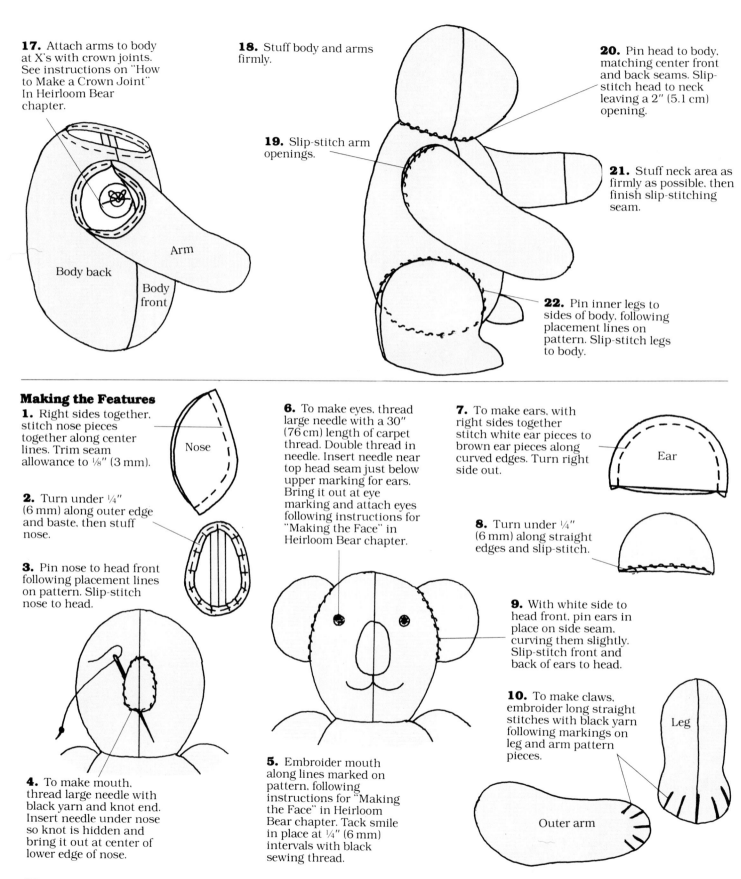

Arm

Body back

Body front

Making the Features

1. Right sides together, stitch nose pieces together along center lines. Trim seam allowance to ⅛" (3 mm).

2. Turn under ¼" (6 mm) along outer edge and baste, then stuff nose.

3. Pin nose to head front following placement lines on pattern. Slip-stitch nose to head.

4. To make mouth, thread large needle with black yarn and knot end. Insert needle under nose so knot is hidden and bring it out at center of lower edge of nose.

5. Embroider mouth along lines marked on pattern, following instructions for "Making the Face" in Heirloom Bear chapter. Tack smile in place at ¼" (6 mm) intervals with black sewing thread.

6. To make eyes, thread large needle with a 30" (76 cm) length of carpet thread. Double thread in needle. Insert needle near top head seam just below upper marking for ears. Bring it out at eye marking and attach eyes following instructions for "Making the Face" in Heirloom Bear chapter.

7. To make ears, with right sides together stitch white ear pieces to brown ear pieces along curved edges. Turn right side out.

8. Turn under ¼" (6 mm) along straight edges and slip-stitch.

9. With white side to head front, pin ears in place on side seam, curving them slightly. Slip-stitch front and back of ears to head.

10. To make claws, embroider long straight stitches with black yarn following markings on leg and arm pattern pieces.

Nose

Ear

Leg

Outer arm

98

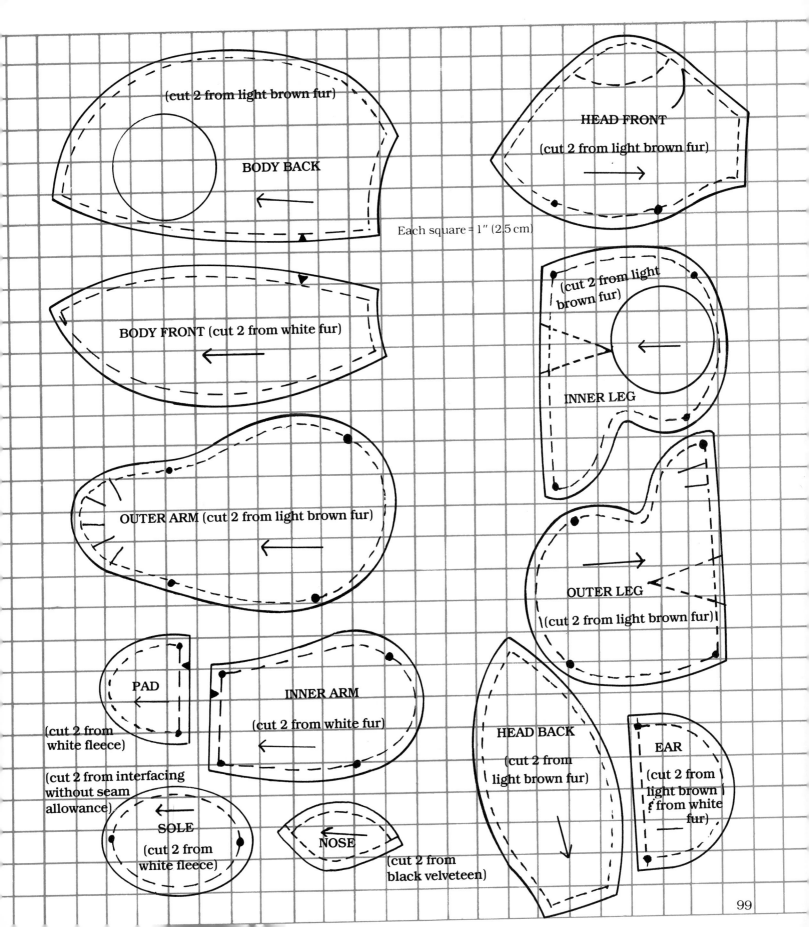

(cut 2 from light brown fur)

BODY BACK

HEAD FRONT

(cut 2 from light brown fur)

Each square = 1″ (2.5 cm)

BODY FRONT (cut 2 from white fur)

(cut 2 from light brown fur)

INNER LEG

OUTER ARM (cut 2 from light brown fur)

OUTER LEG

(cut 2 from light brown fur)

PAD

INNER ARM

(cut 2 from white fur)

(cut 2 from white fleece)

(cut 2 from interfacing without seam allowance)

SOLE

(cut 2 from white fleece)

NOSE

(cut 2 from black velveteen)

HEAD BACK

(cut 2 from light brown fur)

EAR

(cut 2 from light brown & from white fur)

99

BABY BEAR

"A full-blooded teddy bear," said T.R., "knows a secret that other toys don't; it can grow up with the child. Have you ever noticed that a teddy who is around to look after a baby is usually still a friend in memory, if not in fur, when that same baby has grown up to be a sophisticated young woman or man?"

"Absolutely!" replied Bearnice. "And a teddy is known by the company it keeps. 'To thine own bear be true,' I tell young children, 'and it will follow you night and day so you can't be false to anyone.'"

"Polonius said that first," said T.R., "I heard him."

"Well then, if he did, he got it in just before me," replied Bearnice.

Buddy, shown here modeling the Lickin' Good Bib, doesn't really wear bibs now that he is a grownup, of course. When he was young he wore one whenever he ate, even cookies. His parents insisted. So would you if you ever had to brush crumbs or wash honey out of the fur of a six month old, 110 pound (50 kg) bear cub.

100

Lickin' Good Bib

Materials

- 8"x 20" (20 x 51 cm) piece beige fabric with white dots
- 8"x 10" (20 x 25.5 cm) piece white cotton fabric
- 8"x 10" (20 x 25.5 cm) piece quilt batting
- 3½"x 24" (9 x 62 cm) piece blue-and-white gingham with ⅛" (3 mm) checks
- Scraps of pink print fabric and dark-brown fabric with white dots
- Dark-brown, pink, and white sewing thread
- 4" (10.2 cm) square fusible bonding web

Cutting the Pieces

Trace pattern from book onto tracing paper; add ¼" seam allowance all around. Make separate patterns for nose, tongue center of ears and pupil and white of eyes. Cut these pieces from fusible bonding web. Cut 2 bib pieces from beige fabric and one from white fabric; transfer all markings to one beige piece. From pink fabric, cut tongue and 2 ear centers. Cut eye whites from white fabric, nose and eye pupils from dark-brown dotted fabric. From blue-and-white gingham, cut 2 ties 1"x 12" (2.5 x 30.6 cm) and a bow 2½" x 20½" (6.3 x 52.25 cm).

Front

Fuse ear centers, eye pieces, nose, and tongue to indicated positions on right side of front. With wrong sides together baste front to white bib piece along edges. Zigzag-stitch around eyes and nose with brown thread. Hand-stitch eyelashes using a single long running stitch for each lash. Zigzag-stitch outer edges of tongue and ear centers with pink thread.

Stuffing and Finishing Edges

Place batting between bib pieces with right sides out. Pin layers together and baste along outer edges and along lines of mouth and snout. Trim batting as close to stitching as

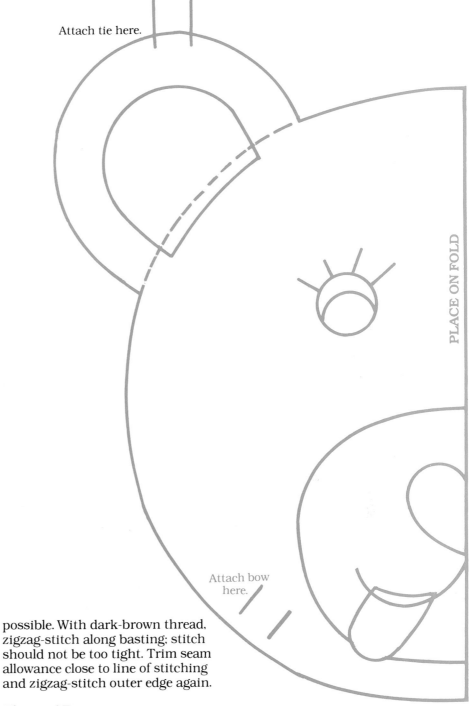

Attach tie here.

PLACE ON FOLD

Attach bow here.

Pattern shown full size.

possible. With dark-brown thread, zigzag-stitch along basting; stitch should not be too tight. Trim seam allowance close to line of stitching and zigzag-stitch outer edge again.

Ties and Bow

Use a ¼" (6 mm) seam allowance. Fold ties in half lengthwise; stitch, leaving one end open. Clip corners of seam allowance. Turn right side out (a knitting needle or unbent wire coat hanger can help accomplish this). Turn under ¼" (6 mm) on raw ends of ties and sew to back side of ears between markings.

Fold bow piece in half lengthwise. Trim ends diagonally from fold out to edges. Stitch, leaving an opening at center; turn right side out. Tie a bow and tack to lower edge of bib at markings.

Bear-Paw Cradle Quilt

At 19½" (50 cm) square, this quilt is just the right size for a cradle. The traditional four-toed "bear-paw" quilt blocks are stitched together on your sewing machine, and then quilted by hand. The border and heart motifs are also hand-quilted. When your baby graduates to a crib, pass along the quilt to a teddy bear friend, or use it as a wall hanging in baby's room.

Materials

½ yard (44 cm) pink floral print
¼ yard (22 cm) each blue-green and off-white fabric
⅛ yard (11.25 cm) or scraps of beige fabric with white dots
20" (51 cm) square backing fabric
20" (51 cm) square quilt batting
Off-white sewing thread
Off-white and dull-green quilting thread
Small quilting hoop

Cutting the Pieces

From pink floral print: cut four 2" x 21" (5.1 x 56.1 cm) strips, and four 4½" (11.45 cm) squares. From off-white fabric: cut four 6½" x 2½" (16.45 x 6.3 cm) strips, four 2½" (6.3 cm) squares, and eight 3" (7.6 cm) squares. Cut the 3" (7.6 cm) squares in half diagonally to make right triangles. From beige fabric with white dots: cut one 2½" (6.3 cm) square and eight 3" (7.6 cm) squares. Cut the 3" (7.6 cm) squares in half diagonally to form right triangles. From blue-green fabric, cut two 14½" x 3¼" (37.85 x 8.3 cm) strips and two 20" x 3¼" (51 x 8.3 cm) strips.

The geometric shapes defined by the darker fabric in the four panels of this pieced quilt are a traditional pattern called "bear claw." T.R. is reading a bedtime story to Quite A. Small-Bear who gets to go to bed early because he is so small.

"There are two major advantages to going to bed earlier than bigger people or bears," he maintains. "you get stories read to you and you get out of doing the dishes."

Piecing the Quilt Top

Stitch pieces together, following numbered diagrams. Stitch all seams with right sides together, using ¼" (6 mm) seam allowance. Press seams open as you work to insure perfectly square corners.

Quilting

Trace quilting motifs on right side of blue-green border. Transfer curved line by placing pattern at midpoint of each border strip, tracing it, flopping it, and tracing it again. Transfer heart to corners with points facing out.

Place batting between quilt top and backing; right sides should face out. Pin layers together. Baste from center of quilt top to midpoint of sides. Baste ⅜" (1 cm) from edges. Insert quilt in hoop and quilt ⅛" (3 mm) inside all seams, and along border, quilting motifs (as shown in drawing of completed quilt top).

Binding

With wrong sides together stitch short ends of pink floral print strips together. With wrong sides together stitch strip to quilt top ⅜" (1 cm) from the edge, mitering corners. Fold binding over, turn under edge ⅜" (1 cm), and slip-stitch to backing.

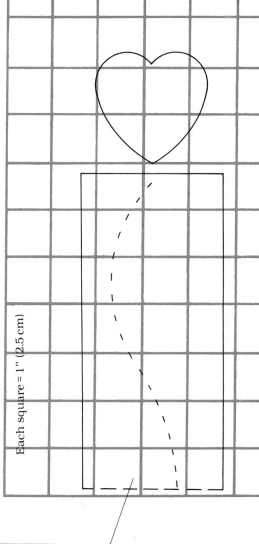

Each square = 1" (2.5 cm)

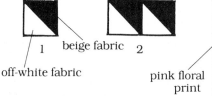

1   beige fabric   2

off-white fabric

pink floral print

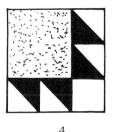
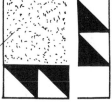

3

4

off-white fabric

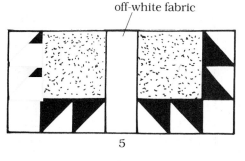

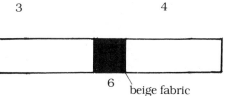

5

6   beige fabric

blue-green fabric

dotted lines represent quilting

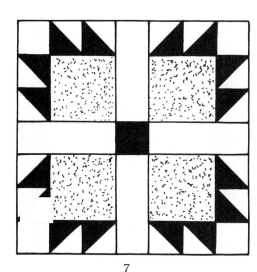

7

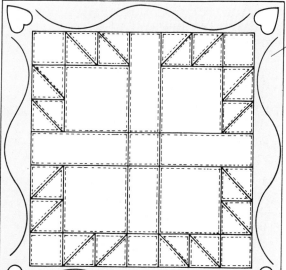

8

103

Crib  Mobile

This sunny mobile will hold a baby's attention for hours, and the soft, friendly pieces invite him to reach and stand. The individual bears are decorated with hand- and machine-embroidery before being stuffed with batting.

Enlarge pattern pieces following instructions on page 166. Unless instructions say otherwise, all pieces are traced onto fabric first, and then cut out adding a ¼" (6 mm) seam allowance all around. Use matching thread for all stitching unless otherwise indicated. *T.R.*

Materials

Cotton fabrics:
   scraps of white, brown, honey-gold, honeybee-yellow, sunshine-yellow
Single-fold bias tape:
   1 yard (92 cm) red: ¾ yard (68.5 cm) each orange and yellow: ⅝ yard (55 cm) each green and blue: ½ yard (44 cm) purple
Sewing thread to match each fabric and bias tape, plus dark-brown thread
Off-white quilting thread (to string mobile)
12" (30.6 cm) square of muslin
8" x 11" (20 x 28 cm) piece lightweight cardboard
Scraps of quilt batting
Scraps of fusible bonding web
Two or three handfuls of polyester stuffing
Embroidery floss:
   2 to 3 yards (1.84 to 2.76 m) dark brown, white, and red: 1 yard (92 cm) blue
Embroidery hoop and needle

Making the Sun

Cut out 2 suns from honeybee-yellow fabric. Cut out 2 sun centers each from sunshine-yellow fabric and fusible bonding web: don't add seam allowances. Fuse a center to the middle of each sun piece. Zigzag-stitch around centers.

   Cut 2 sun pieces from batting and 1 from cardboard. Trim ⅛" (3 mm) from all sides of cardboard piece. Place cardboard between batting pieces with fabric pieces on each side. Right sides should face out. Match points of rays and hand-baste over traced line. Stitch over basting with sewing machine and zigzag-stitch over machine stitching. (Use stitches that are not too close together.) Trim fabric close to zigzag stitching, and zigzag-stitch around shape again for a neat finish.

Making the Rainbow

Cut out 2 rainbows from muslin. Cut bias tape as follows:
red—two 14" (35.5 cm) pieces:
orange—two 13" (33 cm) pieces:
yellow—two 12" (30.5 cm) pieces:

green—two 11" (28 cm) pieces; blue—two 10" (25.5 cm) pieces; and purple two 9" (23 cm) pieces.

Press open both folds of red bias tape. Press into the curve of the upper edge of each rainbow piece. Center tape on area of red stripe, and baste along line where fold was. Press open one edge of orange bias tape. With folded edge at top, press into curve of second section of rainbow, overlapping red tape. Stitch along upper edge. Continue for each stripe of each rainbow side.

Cut 2 rainbows from quilt batting and 1 from cardboard. Trim ⅛" (3 mm) from all sides of cardboard piece. Baste, stitch, and zigzag-stitch layers together as for sun.

Making the Clouds

With cloud patterns facing up, trace and cut out 1 cloud of each type from white fabric. Flop patterns, and trace and cut out other sides. Trace and cut out 2 facings for each cloud from white fabric.

With wrong sides together, stitch facings to clouds between dots along traced line. Finish edges with zigzag stitching as for sun. Stitch clouds together, with right sides out, along remaining edges, leaving faced edges open. Finish as above. Stuff clouds lightly. Place clouds on rainbow, matching dots. Sew in place by hand with white thread and whip stitches that will blend into zigzag stitching.

Making the Honey Pot

Trace and cut out 2 pots from honey-gold fabric, and 2 lids from white fabric. Trace 2 label shapes on white fabric, but don't cut them out. Embroider the word "HONEY" on labels with 3 strands of red floss and straight stitches. Cut out labels along traced lines. Cut 2 labels and 2 lids from fusible bonding web; don't add seam allowances. Fuse labels and lids to honey pots. Zigzag-stitch around the lids with red, and around the labels with blue. Zigzag-stitch a blue band on the lids as well.

With wrong sides together, stitch the 2 pieces of the honey pot together along traced line, leaving a small opening. Stuff pot lightly, and stitch opening closed. Finish as for sun. Sew to one side of rainbow.

Making the Bees

Trace 3 bees on honeybee-yellow fabric. Embroider eyes with white straight stitches: make a brown French knot for each pupil. Back-stitch stripes with brown thread. Cut out bees and fold in half along center with right sides together. Stitch ⅛" (3 mm) from edge, leaving tail end open. Turn right side out; stuff body. Turn under edges of opening and slip-stitch closed.

Trace 3 sets of wings on white fabric. Don't cut them out. With right sides facing out, place batting between fabric with tracings, and plain white fabric. Using dark-brown thread, stitch along traced line. Finish as for sun. Sew wings to backs of bees with white thread.

Making the Bears

Trace 3 bears on brown fabric. Don't cut them out. Transfer all markings. Embroider eyes and nose in satin stitch, using white and blue floss for eyes, and brown floss for nose. Back-stitch mouths and hearts in red. Cut bears apart, making sure not to cut into seam allowances. Place batting between bears and pieces of plain brown fabric. Stitch and zigzag-stitch on tracing lines, leaving openings between dots. Trim as close to stitching as possible. Insert a little stuffing behind batting to pad bears. Stitch openings closed and zigzag-stitch over stitching. Finish with more zigzag stitching around entire shape.

To make bows, cut 2½" (6.3 cm) scraps of bias tape. Fold ends in towards center, right sides facing out. Tack down ends. Cut a ¾" (1 cm) strip of same color tape for bow center. Trim off one fold, and fold raw edge under. Fold center around bow and tack ends together in back. Sew bows to necks of bears at squares.

Assembling the Mobile

Attach pieces to one another with quilting thread. Refer to illustration for length of threads and position of pieces. Connection points are indicated on each piece by x's. When connecting pieces, take several tiny stitches on each piece to anchor thread. If desired, use felt-tip pens in colors to match each piece to camouflage quilting thread. Attach a long thread to the top of the sun and hang from a skyhook.

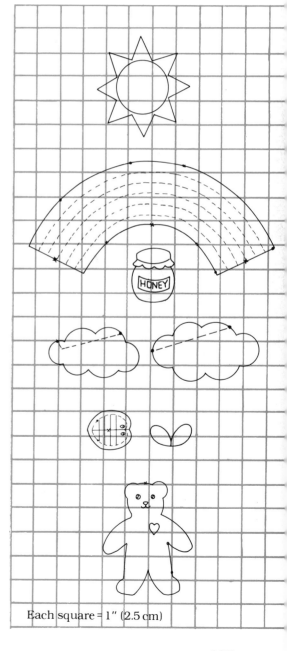

Each square = 1" (2.5 cm)

105

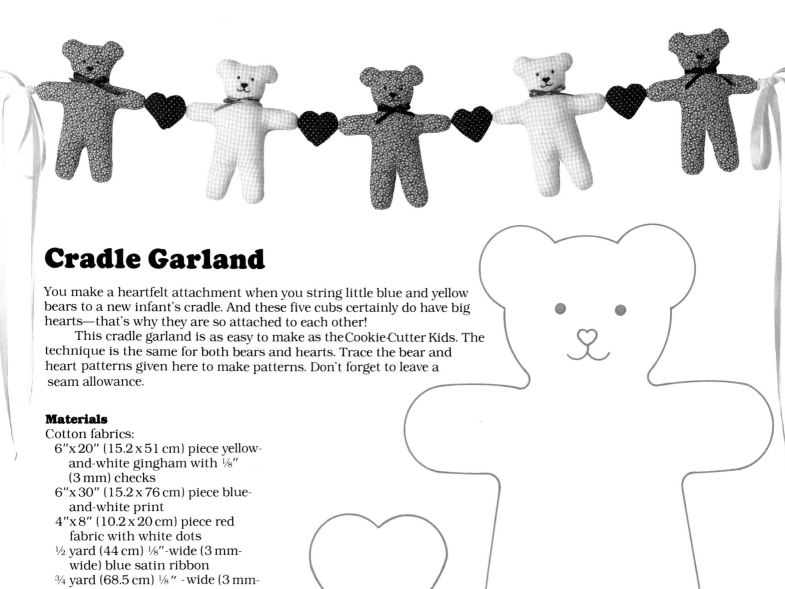

Cradle Garland

You make a heartfelt attachment when you string little blue and yellow bears to a new infant's cradle. And these five cubs certainly do have big hearts—that's why they are so attached to each other!

This cradle garland is as easy to make as the Cookie-Cutter Kids. The technique is the same for both bears and hearts. Trace the bear and heart patterns given here to make patterns. Don't forget to leave a seam allowance.

Materials
Cotton fabrics:
 6"x 20" (15.2 x 51 cm) piece yellow-and-white gingham with ⅛" (3 mm) checks
 6"x 30" (15.2 x 76 cm) piece blue-and-white print
 4"x 8" (10.2 x 20 cm) piece red fabric with white dots
 ½ yard (44 cm) ⅛"-wide (3 mm-wide) blue satin ribbon
 ¾ yard (68.5 cm) ⅛" -wide (3 mm-wide) red satin ribbon
 1 yard (92 cm) each red and brown embroidery floss
 2¼ yards (2.06 m) ⅜" (1 cm) white grosgrain ribbon
Three or four handfuls of polyester stuffing
Red, blue, and white sewing thread

These are full-size patterns

Making the Bears and Hearts
Cut and sew 3 bears from blue-and-white print and 2 bears from yellow-and-white gingham. Separate embroidery floss and use only 2 strands at a time. Work eyes and nose in brown floss and satin stitch, and mouth in red floss and tiny back-stitches. Cut and sew 4 hearts from red fabric with white dots.

Assembling the Tie
Pin hearts between bear's paws, alternating blue and yellow bears. From back side, using a doubled thread, sew bears and hearts together securely with tiny stitches. Cut white ribbon in half. Fold each piece in half and sew center to outer paws of end bears. To reinforce ties, stitch ribbon together ⅛" (3 mm) from center. Trim ends diagonally. Cut blue and red ribbons into 9" (22 cm) lengths. Tie blue ribbons around necks of yellow bears and red ribbons around necks of blue bears. Tie bows and clip off extra ribbon. Tack to necks of bears using matching thread.

The following pages give instructions and patterns for these three accessories for a child's room. The ruffled pillow, left, with appliquéd bears, is a companion piece to the large "Story Quilt" later in this chapter. The fabric frame is decorated with crewel embroidery on linen, and the pillow on the right, with the eyelet lace ruffle, is embroidered in counted-cross-stitch from charts provided with the instructions.

Happy-Stitch Pillow

Can't sleep? Count threads, not sheep, and you will end up with a pillow and a message...for anyone who has ever hugged a teddy, be he four or eighty-four. Use a counted-thread cross-stitch technique on aida cloth; trim with an off-white eyelet ruffle. Finished size is 9″ x 11½″ (23 x 29 cm) plus 1½″ (4 cm) for the ruffle.

Materials
½ yard (44 cm) aida cloth, 14 stitches to the inch (about 28 stitches to 5 cm)
Embroidery floss (DMC numbers): 5 yards (4.60 m) brown (433)
2 yards (1.84 m) each light brown (840), rose (961), light-blue (809)
1 yard (92 cm) each light green (996), yellow (445), lavender (554), pink (3689), peach (353), beige (442), light gold (435) and black
Embroidery needle
Embroidery hoop or frame
Off-white and light-blue sewing thread
1½ yards (1.36 m) off-white eyelet ruffling, 1½″ (3.8 cm) wide
1¼ yards (1.14 m) light-blue bias tape
1¼ yards (1.14 m) cotton cord for piping
12″ (30.6 cm) zipper
¼ pound (115 grams) polyester stuffing
Two 10″ x 12″ (25.5 x 30.6 cm) pieces of muslin

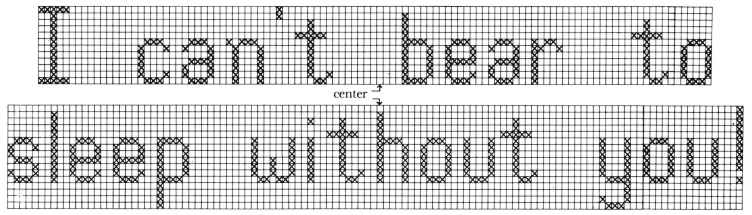

center

Pillow Top

Cut a 14" x 16" (35.6 x 40 cm) piece of aida cloth. Zig-zag or overcast edges. With fabric held horizontally, measure a horizontal rectangle 9" x 11½" (23 x 29 cm) in center of fabric marking corners and edges with pins. Using light-blue thread, baste along outer edge of rectangle through holes between woven squares in fabric. In the same way, mark the vertical and horizontal center with basting stitches. The vertical center is in the center of a stitch worked to one side of the basting thread. The horizontal center falls between two stitches. Insert fabric in embroidery hoop or frame. Separate floss and use 2 strands for stitching.

For cross-stitch directions, see embroidery stitches in Mama Bear's Sewing Basket. Work the bed design in cross-stitch from the chart so that the basting threads correspond to centers marked on chart. Outline the sheet and pillow case with backstitches worked between the holes in the aida cloth. Work the bears' features in black straight stitches on top of cross-stitching. To embroider words above bed, count 7 rows from top of bed design. Beginning at center of lower edge of top chart, stitch "I can't bear to" matching vertical center of chart to basting. There are 6 blank rows between bed design and words above and below bed. In same manner, count 7 rows below bed design. Beginning at center of top edge of bottom chart, stitch "sleep without you!" matching vertical center of chart to basting. When embroidery is complete remove center basting threads. Press embroidery on wrong side. Trim the fabric to ½" from outer edge of pillow which is marked by basting threads.

For piping, press folds of bias tape open. Fold it in half lengthwise and insert cotton cord along fold. With a zipper foot, stitch along edge of cord. Beginning at lower edge near corner, baste piping to seamline of pillow; stitch again with zipper foot.

Raw edges should extend out. Clip seam allowance to piping when turning corners. Overlap blue fabric and join ends neatly. Right sides together, baste eyelet ruffling around pillow behind piping cord, making a ½" (1.25 cm) pleat on both sides of each corner to add fullness.

Pillow Case

Cut two 12¼" x 6" (31.2 x 15.2 cm) pieces from aida cloth for the pillow back. Press under ¼" (6 mm) on long edge of one piece. Stitch pressed edge along one side of the zipper a scant ⅛" (3 mm) from teeth. Press under ¾" (2 cm) on long edge of second piece. Lap over zipper, covering stitching line of first piece. Stitch to other side of zipper tape about ½" (1.25 cm) from fold. Baste across ends of zipper at seamline.

Open zipper a few inches. Right sides in, pin pillow back to front; stitch along seamline. Turn pillow right side out.

Inner Pillow

Leaving an opening for turning, stitch muslin pieces together with a ¼" (6 mm) seam allowance. Turn right side out and stuff pillow with polyester fiber so it is smooth and soft. Slip-stitch opening. Insert into pillow case.

eyelet ruffling

piping

stitch

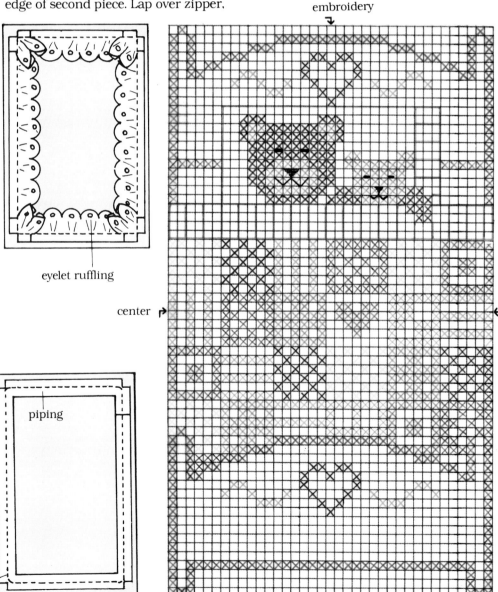

embroidery

center

center

Ruffled Pillow

This pillow is a warm-up for the Story Quilt on the following pages. Or you can use your scraps from the quilt to put these two pin-dot cotton bears back-to-back on a matching appliqué pillow. Finished size is 13½" x 10½" (34 x 27 cm), with a 2½" (6 cm) ruffle of flowered muslin.

Materials

*¼ yard (22 cm) each off-white fabric and off-white print on blue background
*⅝ yard (55 cm) blue print on off-white background
12"x 15" (30.6 x 38.1 cm) piece quilt batting
12"x 15" (30.6 x 38.1 cm) off-white fabric for backing
  *Scraps of brown fabric with white dots, beige fabric with white dots, red fabric with white dots, blue fabric, and pink fabric
1 yard (92 cm) green embroidery floss
14" (35.6 cm) zipper
  Two 12"x 15" (30.6 x 38.1 cm) pieces of fabric for inner pillow Polyester stuffing.

Cutting the pieces

From off-white fabric, cut a 10½"x 7½" (26.75 x 18.05 cm) piece for background. From off-white print on blue background, cut two border strips 10½"x 2½" (26.75 x 6.3 cm) and two strips 12" by 2½" (30.6 x 6.3 cm). From blue print on off-white fabric, cut two 6½"x 15" (16.45 x 38.1 cm) pieces for pillow back and enough 5½"-wide (13.95 cm-wide) strips to make a ruffle 9 feet (2.76 m) long.

Applique

Enlarge pattern for pillow. Following instructions for making quilt blocks in the "Story Quilt" project, make appliqué pieces for bears' bodies, heads, bows, and heart. Cut pieces from fabrics and machine-appliqué them to off-white background. Transfer lines for flower and grass onto background. Machine

embroider lines of bodies and ears. Hand-embroider eyes, noses, mouths, and claws in dark brown; grass, stem, and leaf in green; and flower in yellow.

Pillow case and inner pillow

Stitch shorter border strips to top and bottom of background. Using ¼" (6 mm) seams, stitch longer border strips to sides. Place batting between top and muslin; pin

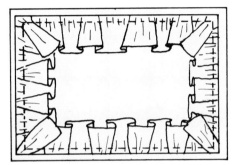

layers together. Baste ½" (1.25 cm) from outer edges. Insert into quilting hoop. Quilt around bears in off-white; quilt ³⁄₁₆" (4.5 mm) from outer edge of background using three strands of pink floss. Stitch ends of ruffle together to form a continuous strip. Fold in half lengthwise with right sides outside. Make rows of gathering stitches ¼" (6 mm) and ½" (1.25 cm) from raw edges. Place ruffle on right side of embroidery with raw edges together and gather ruffle evenly around top with a little more fullness at corners. Baste ½" (1.25 cm) from edge.

Make back of pillow case and entire inner pillow according to the instructions given with the cross-stitch pillow project in this chapter.

These materials are leftover from the "Story Quilt" project in this chapter, so save your scraps if you make it!

Each square = 1" (2.5 cm)

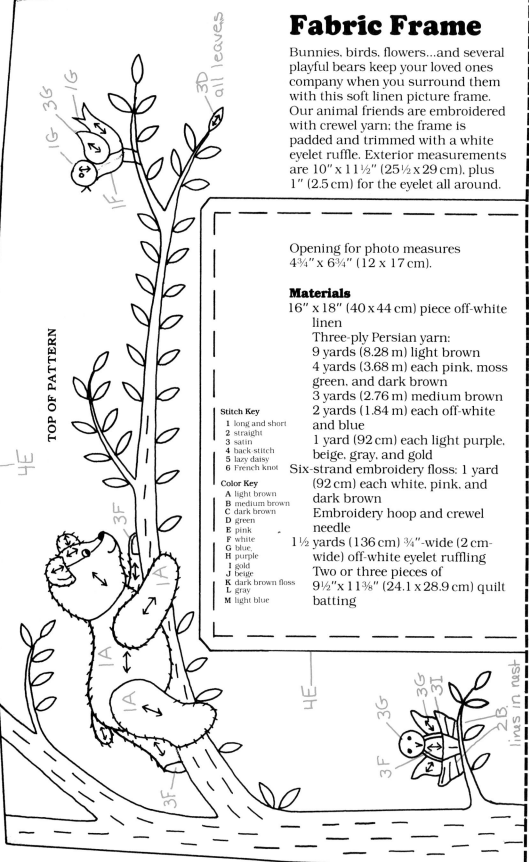

Fabric Frame

Bunnies, birds, flowers...and several playful bears keep your loved ones company when you surround them with this soft linen picture frame. Our animal friends are embroidered with crewel yarn; the frame is padded and trimmed with a white eyelet ruffle. Exterior measurements are 10" x 11½" (25½ x 29 cm), plus 1" (2.5 cm) for the eyelet all around.

Opening for photo measures 4¾" x 6¾" (12 x 17 cm).

Materials

16" x 18" (40 x 44 cm) piece off-white linen
  Three-ply Persian yarn:
  9 yards (8.28 m) light brown
  4 yards (3.68 m) each pink, moss green, and dark brown
  3 yards (2.76 m) medium brown
  2 yards (1.84 m) each off-white and blue
  1 yard (92 cm) each light purple, beige, gray, and gold
Six-strand embroidery floss: 1 yard (92 cm) each white, pink, and dark brown
Embroidery hoop and crewel needle
1½ yards (136 cm) ¾"-wide (2 cm-wide) off-white eyelet ruffling
Two or three pieces of 9½"x 11⅜" (24.1 x 28.9 cm) quilt batting

Stitch Key
1 long and short
2 straight
3 satin
4 back-stitch
5 lazy daisy
6 French knot

Color Key
A light brown
B medium brown
C dark brown
D green
E pink
F white
G blue
H purple
I gold
J beige
K dark brown floss
L gray
M light blue

Off-white sewing thread
7"x 9" (17.8 x 22.9 cm) piece off-white or other cotton fabric.
Heavy cardboard: one 9½" x 11⅜" (24.1 x 28.9 cm) piece and one 11" x 13" (27.9 x 33 cm) piece
½ yard (44 cm) solid pink or pink-print fabric
White glue
30"-long (76 cm-long) strong string
Optional: fusible bonding web

Embroidery

Zigzag or overcast edges of linen. Trace embroidery design from book onto tracing paper, assembling pieces to make frame shape. Transfer design to linen. For bears, trace the outline of body (there is no need to trace the tiny lines of fur).

See embroidery stitches in "Mama Bear's Sewing Basket." Insert fabric into frame or hoop and work embroidery, using stitches and colors indicated on pattern. Cut yarn into 18" (44 cm) lengths. Separate yarn and use one-ply for all stitches. Separate floss and use three strands for all stitches. Work long-and-short stitch and satin stitch in direction of arrows. On bears, work tiny lines for fur indicated on pattern using medium straight stitches and brown thread. Use embroidery floss for the features of the animals. For bears' eyes, use white and brown thread and satin stitch; for nose, use brown thread and satin stitch; and for mouth, use pink back-stitch. For features of bunny, work eyes using brown thread and straight stitch, nose in pink thread and satin stitch, and mouth in pink thread and back stitch.

Assembling the frame

1. When needlework is complete, steam-press embroidery on wrong side. Draw a 4⅜" x 6¼" (11.1 x 15.8 cm) rectangle in center of the off-white muslin. Pin muslin to right side of linen along matching inner rectangle. Baste, then stitch along lines, using between 12 and 15 stitches per inch (5 or 6 stitches

Connect top to bottom along dotted line.

per cm). Cut center out of both linen and muslin ½" (1.25 cm) from stitching; clip to corners. Turn all fabric in through rectangle; press to wrong side.

2. Sew eyelet around outer edge of embroidery ¼" (6 mm) outside pink back stitches; miter corners so there will be just enough fullness to turn corner when eyelet is folded outward. Stitch ends of eyelet together; zigzag seam allowance. Trim edge 1¼" (3.2 cm) from eyelet; trim corners diagonally. Press under ¼" (6 mm) on all edges except corners.

3. Cut a 4⅜"x 6¼" (11.1 x 15.8 cm) opening in center of smaller cardboard piece. Cut two or three pieces of quilt batting using cardboard frame as pattern. Place frame between linen and muslin; attach muslin to back of frame with glue or strips of fusible web. Place batting between cardboard and embroidery.

4. Fold ends of linen to back side of frame; eyelet should run around edge of cardboard frame. Miter corners; hold edges in place on wrong side with pins. Glue or sew linen to edge of cotton fabric.

For back, round the corners of larger cardboard rectangle. Cut a 12½"x 14½" (31.7 x 36.8 cm) piece of pink fabric. Center large cardboard on back of frame; fold edges of pink fabric over cardboard, clipping at corners; fuse or glue in place. Cut a 10¾"x 12½" (27.3 x 31.7 cm) piece of pink fabric; round corners. Glue or fuse edges in place on the other side of the cardboard.

Punch tiny holes through the covered cardboard at each top corner of the frame, about 3" (7.6 cm) from the top edge. (Use something sharp and pointed, such as the tip of a pair of scissors.) Make second holes ¼" (6 mm) below the first. From back, stitch through holes on one side, then the other. Tie ends in back so string is taut.

STEP 1

STEP 2

STEP 3

STEP 4

Place a line of glue around edge of back of top, bottom, and one side of embroidered frame just inside eyelet; place another line about 1½" (3.8 cm) inside the first one. One side stays open so picture may be inserted. Center frame on covered cardboard and press down. Allow glue to dry before placing a photo of your favorite cub inside.

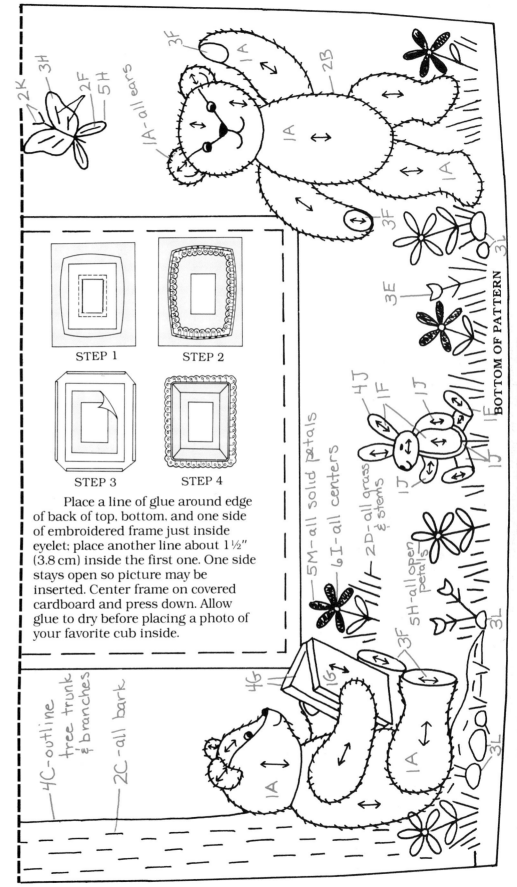

Once upon a time there was a loving grandmother who made a magic quilt just big enough for her grandchild's crib. In it, she sewed nine stories about teddy bears so that her grandchild's mother and father could tell the child a different one each night at bedtime.

After a while, the child would ask to be told a special favorite story and the characters in the story would come visit the child's dreams.

(cont'd on page 116)

Story Quilt

From a morning in the park, to naps in the dark, scenes of bear cubs at play become an inspiration for bedtime stories when they are stitched into a quilt. The border is pink and white floral to match the ruffled applique pillow on the prior pages. The binding is blue and white. Each square measures 9" (22 cm) and the quilt, at 45" (1.14 m) square, is perfect for a baby's crib.

Materials
Cotton fabrics, 45" (1.14 m) wide:
    1 yard (92 cm) off-white
    1 yard (92 cm) off-white print on blue background
    1½ yard (1.36 m) pink print on off-white background
    ⅛ yard (11.5 cm) pink print with white hearts
    3 yards (2.76 m) blue print on off-white background (for sky and quilt backing)
    ¼ yard (22 cm) each dusty green, white print on green, yellow print, white, beige-and-white stripe, white dot on navy, white dot on beige, green print on off-white
    Scraps of other colors for appliques (see photograph)
  1 yard (92 cm) fusible bonding web
    Sewing thread to match fabrics
    Embroidery floss: a few yards (about two meters) each grey, red, black, brown, pink, yellow, and rose
    Embroidery hoop and needle
  52" (130 cm) square quilt batting
    Quilting frame or hoop
    Off-white, navy, and light green quilting thread

General guidelines for the appliqué blocks

Background
1. From off-white fabric, cut nine 10" (25.5 cm) squares. Enlarge design for each block following instructions in "Mama Bear's Sewing Basket." Add ½" (1.25 cm) seam allowance to outer edges of blocks.

Make pattern for upper part of background (sky or wall) by tracing top portion of each block; add ¼" (6 mm) to lower edge (continue horizontal lines behind figures); also make pattern for lower part of background (earth or floor). Cut pieces from fabrics suggested on pattern. Pin upper part of background to muslin block; lap lower part over bottom edge of the upper part already in place. By hand, baste the overlap.

Cutting the pieces
2. Work on one block at a time. From each enlarged drawing of the pattern block, make patterns for all appliqué pieces by tracing the shape onto tracing paper. Look at the photograph and notice which pieces seem to overlap others. Where the shapes come together, extend the part of the one that appears to go under the other by ⅛" to ¼" (3 to 6 mm) so they both can be finished by a single row of zigzag stitching. In the first block, for example, the cloud goes over the sun, so extend the edge of the sun. The sun will go on the background first, then the cloud.

3. It is easier to work with big pieces than small ones, so simplify shapes that seem interrupted by other shapes. In the first block, for example, you can cut a single piece for most of the bear's body; just connect his legs, back, and neck. The rompers will then fit over his whole body. The bear's right arm, which overlaps the romper, has to be cut separately and sewed on last.
    Cut all the applique pieces following suggestions in the photograph, or choose your own

colors. Back each piece with fusible web. To do this, place a piece of scrap paper on your ironing board and put a piece of web on it. Arrange the appliqué pieces right side up on the web and with the steam off. Touch the very tip of your iron to the pieces for just a second in a few places to tack them down. Gently pull the web away from the paper and cut out the shapes.
    When all the pieces have been cut out and backed, arrange them on the block. Turn on steam on iron and fuse pieces in place. Zig zag around each shape using matching or contrasting thread. Draw or transfer additional shapes indicated on pattern for machine embroidery and stitch. Draw and hand-embroider features and other details on blocks. Separate floss: for most embroidery, use three strands; for claws and tiny bears, use two.

The appliqué blocks
Block 1. Make patterns for path, cloud, sun, large bear's body, rompers, arm, wagon top, wagon side, small bear's body, small arm, and bow. Machine-embroider wagon wheels, sun's rays, pocket, and wagon handle. Hand-embroider eyes, nose, mouth, heart on pocket, button, and claws.

Block 2. Make patterns for table, chairs, hats, bows, dresses, sleeve of dress on left, cups and saucers, tea pot, arms, ear, heads, legs, and paws. Machine-embroider tea pot spout, handle, and knob, hat bands, and waistbands of dresses. Hand-embroider folds of dress on left, flower on hat, eyes, noses, mouths, and claws.

Block 3. Make patterns for cloud, bird, hat, head, arms, collar, sailor suit, sleeve, handle bars, bike frame, fender, bike seat and wheels. Machine-embroider wings, spokes of wheels, pedals, and waistband of sailor suit. Hand-embroider, eyes, nose, mouth, center of ears, ties on hat and suit, bird's beak, and claws.

Block 4. Make patterns for tree trunk, bird, nest, leaves, stars, head, ears, eye "patch," paws, legs, night shirt, sleeve, entire toy panda, and face and chest of toy. Machine-embroider wing, lines of night shirt and eye "patch" of toy panda. Hand-embroider eyes, noses, mouths, bow, buttons of shirt and bird's beak.

Block 5. Make patterns for butterfly wings, cloud, head, arms, legs, small teddy bear, dress, and doll carriage. Machine-embroider butterfly body, detail of dress, carriage wheels, details of carriage, and carriage handles. Hand-embroider eyes, noses, and mouths, inside of ears, butterfly's antennae, bow, and claws.

Block 6. Make patterns for tree trunk, bird, nest, leaves, moon, head, night shirt, sleeve, hands, small bear, and legs. Machine-embroider wing, shirt placket, and details of ears. Hand-embroider eyes, noses, mouths, bird's beak, buttons, bow, and claws.

Block 7. Make patterns for cloud, bird, bear's head and torso, arm, legs, pinafore, wheels, frame of scooter (2 pieces), and handle of scooter. Machine-embroider spokes of wheels, details of pinafore, ears, and wings. Hand-embroider eyes, nose, mouth, bird's beak, and claws.

Block 8. Make patterns for chair, pillow, head, sweater, book, legs, foot pads, and paws. Machine-embroider details of chair, pillow, and pages and spine of book. Hand-embroider eyes, nose, mouth, spectacles, and claws.

Block 9. Make patterns for tree trunks, leaves, bird, head, center of ears, arms, paw pad, legs, T-shirt and shorts. Machine-embroider suspenders, thin branches of trees and wings. Hand-embroider eyes, nose, mouth, claws, and bird's beak.

Heart block. Cut sixteen 2¾" (7 cm) squares from off-white fabric. Cut sixteen hearts from pink heart print. Tack hearts to fusible web and cut them out. Fuse hearts to center of squares; zigzag around hearts.

Assembly

Trim appliqué blocks to measure 9½" (23.25 cm) square.

From off-white print on blue background, cut 24 lattice strips 9½" x 2¾" (23.25 x 7 cm) and cut bias strips to make a binding 200" (5 m) long. From pink print on off-white background, cut two border strips 37"x 7" (94.5 x 17.8 cm) and two border strips 51"x 7" (128.5 x 17.8 cm). For backing, from blue print on off-white, cut one length 52" (130 cm) by width of fabric and one length 52"x 9" (130 x 22 cm). Remove selvages from backing pieces. Right sides in, stitch them together along one 52" (130 cm) edge.

Use ¼" (6 mm) seam allowance for joining quilt top. Following piecing diagram, with right sides together, join appliqué blocks 1, 4, and 7 vertically with lattice strips; stitch a lattice strip to top and bottom. Join blocks 2, 5, and 8, and then 3, 6, and 9 in the same manner. Then make four strips alternating four heart blocks and three lattice strips. Press all seams toward lattice

strips. Matching corners of appliqué blocks and heart blocks, stitch appliqué strips and heart strips together alternately. Press seams open. Stitch short border strips to top and bottom; if necessary, trim ends of border even with patchwork. Stitch long border strips to sides of patchwork.

Place batting between patchwork and backing with right sides out. Pin layers together. Baste from center of quilt to corners and from center to midpoint of each side. Baste edges together. Insert quilt in frame or hoop. Quilt along edges of lattice strips and around pink hearts. For appliqué blocks, use matching thread and quilt along the horizontal line of background and over top of bears. In Block 8, quilt over top of chair. Quilt around clouds, along tree trunks and branches, and around the sleeping bears on the ground. Quilt around border 2¾" (7 cm) from edge of lattice strips. Baste around border 5½" (13.95 cm) from lattice strips. Trim quilt a scant ½" (1.25 cm) from basting. Stitch ends of bias strips

1

together with right sides together on straight grain; press seams open. Place binding on right side of quilt and with raw edges together, stitch binding to quilt, mitering corners. Fold binding toward underside along stitching. Turn raw edge in and slip-stitch binding to underside.

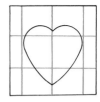

2

3

4

5

Each square = 1″ (2.5 cm)

6

7

8

9

At first the child's favorite was the story about the panda that fell asleep one night in the wild bamboo forests of China, and woke up in a natural-habitat zoo the child had visited.

As the child with the magic quilt grew up, so did the stories about the bears in its squares (like the story about the young bear in the upper right corner who made friends with a red bird that told the little bear secrets about life that only grown-ups were supposed to know).

And do you know another magic thing about that quilt? It never grew too small for the child. As the child grew bigger, somehow that quilt always fit nicely on the bed somewhere. When the child grew up and moved into his own house, he tucked the magic story quilt around his own baby and told it some of the same stories, and some new ones because the nine applique squares in that magic quilt never ran out of interesting stories to tell at bedtime.

Bear Cub Pull Toy

Do you think life is just a drag for this furry cub? Not when he is being tugged along on a red ribbon by the most natural energy source there is—kid power. This traditional brown bear stands 6½" (16.5 cm) high from paw to head; the platform measures 5" x 9" (12.5 x 23 cm).

Bearnice is having a hard time persuading this lovably stubborn toy, mounted on a wooden platform and wheels, to follow her. Typically, she came up with an old saying appropriate to the situation—"A rolling bear lathers no boss."

Materials

¼ yard (23 cm) 54"-wide (1.36 m-wide) "fur" fabric
Scrap of sturdy brown cotton fabric
Two ⅜" (10 mm) safety eyes
Brown sewing thread
1 pound (460 grams) polyester stuffing
Brown carpet or buttonhole thread
2 yards (1.84 m) black yarn
9" x 5" x 1" (22 x 12.7 x 2.5 cm) piece pine for base
Four 1¼" x 1" x ¾" (3.2 x 2.5 x 2 cm) pine blocks
Four 2⅜"-diameter (6.1 cm) wheels cut from 1" (2.5 cm) pine
8" (20 cm) wooden dowel, ⁵⁄₁₆" (.75 cm) diameter
Two round toothpicks
Dull gold paint
One round wooden bead 1¼" (3.2 cm) diameter
1¾ yards (1.60 m) red dotted Swiss grosgrain ribbon
White glue
Four 1½" (3.8 cm) screws

Tools

Drill
Screw driver
Awl or knitting needle
Paintbrush
Sandpaper
Saw

Cutting. Read T.R.'s instructions for cutting and marking fur fabric on page 18. From fur fabric, cut 2 backs, 2 undersides, 2 head sides, 1 head center, 2 tails and 4 ears. From brown fabric, cut 4 paw pads. Use ¼" (6 mm) seams. For all hand sewing, use carpet thread.

Body

1. Right sides together matching dots, stitch backs to undersides, leaving straight lower edge of legs open. Turn right sides out.

2. Right sides in, stitch undersides together along center seam, and backs together between open dots. Turn under seam allowance on lower edge of legs and baste.

3. Right sides in, stitch tail pieces together leaving straight end open. Turn right side out. Place tiny bit of stuffing in tail. Insert tail in back opening of body; slip-stitch in place.

4. Turn under seam allowance on paw pads; baste in place. On the 1¼"x ¾" (3.2 cm x 2 cm) face of each wooden

block, drill a ⅛"-diameter (3 mm-diameter), ¾"-deep (2 cm-deep) hole. Stuff body and legs of bear very firmly. Holding bear upside down, insert wooden blocks in feet with hole side up, so blocks are even with lower edge. Place stuffing around sides of block but not on top.

5. Pin paw pads to lower edge of legs, easing fur fabric to fit. Slip-stitch pads to legs. Using two strands of black yarn, embroider claws with long straight stitches.

Make a row of gathering stitches along seam line of neck. Gather so neck opening is about 2¼" (5.8 cm) in diameter from seam line to seam line; knot thread securely.

6. Stitch darts in head sides. Right sides in, stitch head sides together along center front edge. Stitch head sides to head center along curved edges. Turn right side out. Turn under ¼" (6 mm) along neck edge; baste edge in place. Insert safety eyes; T.R. explains on page 27. Stuff head firmly.

7. Pin head to neck edge of body; slip-stitch securely in place. Embroider nose and mouth following instructions in Heirloom Bears.

8. Stitch ears together in pairs along curved edge. Turn right side out. Turn under ¼" (6 mm) along lower edge; slip-stitch lower edges together. Pin ear to head in a curve between x's; slip-stitch ears to head along front and back.

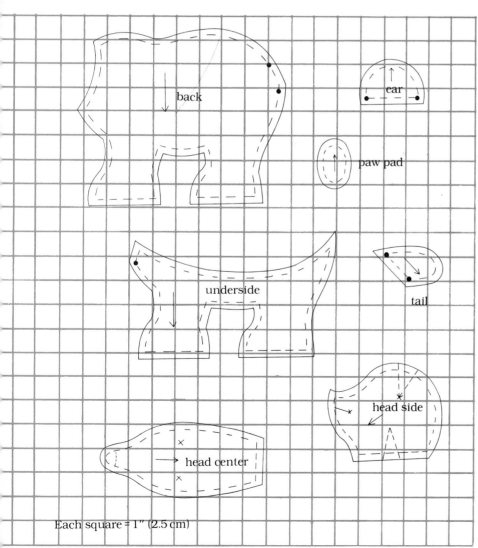

Each square = 1" (2.5 cm)

Platform assembly.
Drill a ⅜"-diameter (1 cm-diameter) hole in center of each wheel. Sand wheels and base. Cut four 1½" (3.8 cm) lengths of dowel for axles. (To avoid splintering, wrap masking tape around dowel below cutting mark before sawing.) Drill a 3/32"-diameter (2 mm-diameter) hole through

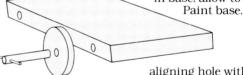

Attaching bear to base.
Drill two ⅛"-diameter (3 mm-diameter) holes in base 1⅛" (2.8 cm) from side edges and 2¾" (7 cm) from front end. Drill two ⅛"-diameter (3 mm-diameter) holes 1⅛" (2.8 cm) from side edges and 4" (10.2 cm) behind first two holes. Working from bottom, insert a screw in each hole until it just shows on top of base. Using an awl or the point of scissors, pierce fabric of paw pads over drilled hole in block. Hold block in bear's paw firmly against base,

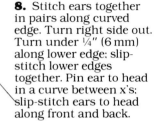

each axle ⅛" (3 mm) from end. Cut four ¾" (2 cm) lengths from the widest part of toothpicks and glue one through hole in each axle. On each side of base, drill two ⅜"-diameter (1 cm-diameter), ½"-deep (1.25 cm-deep) holes, one 1½" (3.8 cm) from front edge and one 1½" (3.8 cm) from back. Insert axles through wheels and glue in place in holes in base; allow to dry. Paint base.

aligning hole with screw. Twist screw into block until it is flush with lower edge of base.

To finish.
Drill a hole through the base ½" (1.25 cm) from edge at center. Cut a 33" (84 cm) length of ribbon. Insert it through hole; knot end several times below base. Insert free end through hole in bead. Fold end back over head to wrong side of ribbon; turn under ¼" (6 mm) on end and sew securely. Tie a bow around bear's neck with the remaining ribbon. Trim ends of ribbon diagonally.

BEARS IN THE KITCHEN

"That's the place for me," said Buddy.

"Or very nearby," said Quite A. Small-Bear, "so you can tell when there are spoons ripe for licking and still be elsewhere when you hear the dirty pots hit the sink."

"It's fun to put on an apron and experiment using the tools, and equipment like stoves, pots, whisks, thermometers, measuring cups, and laboratory-stuff like that. Cooking makes me feel good; there's just something about a kitchen. You take a few berries, a little honey, a few nuts, a little more honey, some, uh, some, uh, well, maybe just a little more honey . . ."

"You may love to cook, Buddy—I cook for love. And that's all there is to it," interrupted Bearnice.

Teddy-Tote

It is designed for carrying groceries to your car, ice to your boat, bears to your picnic...and for dragging things a dozen other places. The sturdy canvas wears well and can handle a load. It is big enough at 5½"x 15"x 17" (14 x 38 x 43 cm) to do the whole job. And the appliqued dishtowel is as cute as a bear's ear.

Materials

5/8 yard (55 cm) bright yellow canvas, or ¾ yard (68.5 cm) if the fabric is 45" (1.14 m) wide
10½"x 12½" (26.75 x 31.85 cm) piece blue-and-white windowpane-check dishtowel fabric with border along 10½" (31.85 cm) edge
10"x 12" (25.5 x 30.6 cm) piece brown canvas or denim
Scraps of red, dark-brown, and white cotton fabric
Dark-brown, red, yellow, and blue sewing thread
10"x 12" (25.5 x 30.6 cm) piece fusible bonding web

Cutting and fusing

Enlarge the pattern for applique panel following instructions in "Mama Bear's Sewing Basket." Cut one pattern piece for the bear's head, body, and legs combined, and a separate one for each of the bear's arms. Also make patterns for the smaller pieces. Cut bear body and arms from brown. Cut bow, jar lid, and tongue from red. Cut nose from dark brown; honey and honey drops from bright yellow. Cut label and top portion of jar from white. Transfer markings to applique pieces for machine embroidery of mouth, ears, eyes, label, lines of jar and lid, paws, and paw pads.

Cut fusible web to fit behind applique pieces. Place scrap paper on ironing board. Put a piece of fusible web on the paper and arrange the applique pieces right side up on it. Be sure the steam is off, then touch the tip of your iron to the pieces for just a second in a few places to tack

them down. Tack the larger appliques just around the edge of the shape; cut away the unfused webbing at the center so it forms a ¼"-band (6 mm-band) around outer edge. Gently pull the webbing away from the paper. Cut out the shapes. Press under ¼" (6 mm) on edge of dishtowel piece. Fuse pieces in place on right side of towel; the border should be at bottom.

From yellow canvas, cut two 21"x 22½" (53 x 57.35 cm) pieces for the bag's front and back and two 4"x 15½" (10.2 x 39.25 cm) handles.

Assembly

1. With right sides together, and using a ½" (1.25 cm) seam allowance, stitch front to back along sides and bottom edge. Zigzag-stitch seam allowance.

4. Trim seam to ½" (1.25 cm) and zigzag-stitch seam. Do this for each side, then turn bag right side out.

7. Fold each in half lengthwise with right sides out. Top-stitch ⅛" (3 mm) from long edges; zigzag or overcast ends.

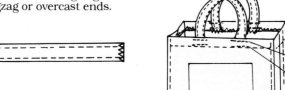

2. Zigzag-stitch along top edge. Along top edge, press 1" (2.5 cm) to wrong side; stitch hem in place. Press side seams to bag front and bottom seam to back.

5. Fold bag into a box using bottom corners as a guide. Press folds along edges; front and back should be 15"x 17" (38 x 43 cm) and bottom 5½"x 15" (13.95 x 38 cm). Top-stitch along each fold ⅛" (3 mm) from edge. At bottom corners begin and end stitching ⅛" (3 mm) from ends of fold.

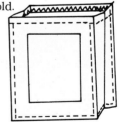

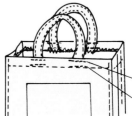

Arranging the applique pieces

Center appliqued towel horizontally on right side of front panel 6" (15.2 cm) from lower edge; baste in place along edges. Zigzag-stitch edge with red thread. With dark-brown thread, zigzag-stitch around bear's body, head, arms, and nose, and along details of eyes, paws and paw pads. With red, zigzag-stitch edges and lines of bow, jar lid, ears, and mouth. With yellow, zigzag lines of jar and honey drops. With blue, zigzag edge of label and the word HONEY.

3. To box bottom, pinch bottom corners at bottom and side seams and diagonally match seamlines (bag should still be inside out). Mark a point 2¾" (7 cm) in from corner stitching and through it, draw a 5½" (13.95 cm) line perpendicular to seamline. Stitch along line.

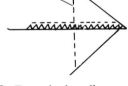

6. To make handles, press down 1" (2.5 cm) to wrong side of each long edge of the 4"x 15½" (10.2 x 39.25 cm) strips.

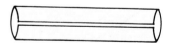

8. Place handles inside top edge of front and back of bag so ends are even with hemline; handle ends should be 4" (10.2 cm) apart and centered at top of bag. Make sure handles are in the same place on each side. Stitch them once ⅛" (3 mm) from top edge of bag, and again along hemline.

Hot Potholders

If you enjoy cooking and like to be kissed (or know someone who likes both), take a look at this super-easy project. The potholders are machine-appliquéd corduroy padded with terrycloth. Embroider the message on before you sew the pieces together.

Materials

⅜ yard (35 cm) beige pinwale corduroy
  Scraps of beige, white, and gold cotton fabric
  Scraps of red fabric with white pin dots
  Scraps of fusible bonding web
  Red, beige, green, brown, and gold sewing thread
2 yards (1.84 m) each green, red, and black six-strand embroidery floss.
⅜ yard (35 cm) terrycloth
  Small embroidery hoop

Making the Potholders

Enlarge the patterns for the potholders following the instructions in "Mama Bear's Sewing Basket." Make separate patterns for the hats, aprons, ears, nose, paw pads, spoons, bow ties, and hearts. Cut 2 bear outlines from corduroy. Transfer markings for appliqués and embroidery to one of each bear piece; these pieces become the fronts. Transfer aprons to white

Each square = 1" (2.5 cm)

fabric. Place aprons in embroidery hoop and, using three strands of floss each time, back-stitch words on his apron with red thread and hers with green thread. Now cut out aprons. Cut beige ears, nose, and feet; white hats; gold spoons; and red hearts and ties.

Cut fusible web to go behind appliqué pieces. Fuse pieces to position on front pieces. Zigzag-stitch around inner edges of his apron and hat with green thread and her apron and hat with red thread. Straight stitch along lines in both hats and her apron to make "gathers." Zigzag-stitch around edges of other appliqué pieces with matching thread.

With brown thread, zigzag along inner lines of arms, feet, legs, and chins. Using three strands of floss, satin stitch eyes and nose with black thread and mouth with red thread. Cut a single layer of terrycloth padding 1/8" (3 mm) smaller all around than the potholder shapes; baste to wrong side of front piece. With right sides out, baste front to back along seamline. With matching thread, zigzag along seamline; stitches should not be too close together. Trim away seam allowance and zigzag around edge a second time. Machine quilt along chin of heads with brown thread. To make loops to hang the potholders with, cut two 2½" x 2" (6.3 x 5.1 cm) corduroy rectangles. Fold each in half lengthwise with wrong sides together. Make two rows of zigzag stitches with dark-brown thread ¼" (6 mm) apart; trim fabric close to outer edges of stitching. Stitch edges a second time.

Fold each strip in half. Keeping the folded edge just below the top of the bear's head, center the strip on the back of the head and slip-stitch the ends of the loop to the fabric.

Aprons

Decorate aprons for you and your bears using the design shown above. Enlarge the design on a ½" (1.25 cm) grid for bears, a ¾" (2 cm) grid for children, and a 1" (2.5 cm) grid for adults. Appliqué the brown fabric bear and the red fabric bowl. Use fusible web to hold the pieces in place and zigzag stitch around the edges. For the embroidery, use as many strands of embroidery floss as necessary depending on the size of your apron. Embroider the words and mouth in red back-stitch, the eyes and nose in brown satin stitch, and the fork and spoon with yellow satin and straight stitch.

Cross-Stitched Hand Towels

There is no reason to be cross about cross-stitch. The pattern is simple and the embroidery done on cotton or cotton-linen blend dishtowels printed with a country-kitchen windowpane check. It looks almost as if the embroidered bears are on the other side of a bright window looking in at you.

Before you begin. See "Mama Bear's Sewing Basket" for cross-stitch and embroidery directions.

Separate six-strand embroidery floss and use four strands for embroidering dishtowels. In one corner of your towel, plan how many threads you must stitch over to obtain a fairly even cross-stitch with about seven stitches to the inch (about 14 stitches in 5 cm); on the towels shown here, the stitches were worked over four threads horizontally and five vertically. The stitches are not as even as they would be on Aida cloth, but are close. Don't forget to remove your sample stitches.

Bears-and-flowers design

Materials

One 20"x 30" (51 x 76 cm) cotton or
   cotton-linen blend red-and-white
   windowpane-check dishtowel
Embroidery floss:
   2 skeins brown
   2 yards (1.84 m) blue
   1 yard (92 cm) each light green,
black, red, and yellow
Embroidery hoop and needle

If you would like the center of your flowers to fall on the intersection of windowpane stripes, figure out if the spacing between motifs needs to be adjusted to accomodate the pattern on your piece of fabric.

Start with brown thread one thread above the border—or about 2" (5.1 cm) from the 20" (51 cm) end—with the left toe of the center bear. Continue stitching each row of bear according to the chart. Next,

work flower and leaves in the same position on each side of bear. Repeat bear and flower on each side of center embroidery.

Following features diagram, embroider eyes and nose on each bear with black thread and satin-stitch and mouth with red thread and satin stitch. On center bear, stitch loops of bow with lazy daisy stitch and yellow thread; use straight stitch for ends and center. Stitch blue bows on side bears in the same manner.

Bears-and-hearts design

Materials

One 20"x 30" (51 x 76 cm) cotton or
   cotton-linen blend blue-and-white
   windowpane-check dishtowel
Embroidery floss:
   1 skein each brown and red
   1 yard (92 cm) each blue and black
Embroidery hoop and needle.

If you wish to center hearts on windowpane check, figure out if the spacing between the motifs needs to be adjusted to fit your piece of fabric.

Start one thread above border—or about 2" (5.1 cm) from 20" (51 cm) end of towel—with the right foot of the bear on the left. Continue stitching bear according to chart. Stitch the second bear to the right of the first one. Embroider hearts with red thread on either side of the bears.

Following features diagram, embroider eyes and nose on each bear with satin stitch and black

thread and mouth with satin stitch and red thread. With blue thread, stitch loops of bows with lazy daisy stitch. Stitch ends and center of bow with straight stitch.

Cookie Hugger

Buy a cotton dish towel. Cover a standard two-pound coffee can with it. Make a cookie-cutter bear whose 11" (28 cm) arms wrap around the can. Pad the lid and trim it with eyelet ruffle. Finally, sew a label-holder on the tin so people will know what kind of cookie you baked for them this time.

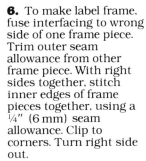

Cutting the pieces. Enlarge patterns following instructions in "Mama Bear's Sewing Basket." From the gingham dish towel cut two circles, each with a diameter 2" (5 cm) greater than the diameter of your can. Figure dimensions of the side pieces this way: width should be two times plus 2½" (6.3 cm) the height of your can; the length should be the circumference plus ½" (1.25 cm); cut the piece from gingham. From quilt batting, cut one circle the same size as the gingham circles and one rectangle as long but only half as wide as the gingham rectangle.

Cut two label frames from solid red fabric. Also cut a frame from interfacing but this time omit seam allowance. For lid, cut one quilt-batting circle with a diameter 1" (2.5 cm) greater than the diameter of your can and one white cotton circle with a diameter 2" (5 cm) greater than that of your can. For bear, from both brown dotted fabric and batting, cut one front, two backs, four arms, and four legs. Transfer markings for features to front of bear. From the markings on the front, make patterns for nose and ear appliqués. Use a ¼" (6 mm) seam allowance and cut nose and two ears from solid red fabric. Cut fusible bonding web to go behind ear and nose appliqué pieces.

Materials

Materials

- 2-pound (1 kg) coffee can with plastic lid
- ⅝ yard (55 cm) 18"-wide (44 cm-wide) blue-and-white gingham dishtowel or towel fabric
- ⅜ yard (35 cm) brown cotton fabric with white pin dots
- 6½" (16.45 cm) square of white cotton fabric
- Scraps of solid red cotton fabric
- 2" (5.1 cm) square fusible bonding web
- 2"x3" (5.1 x 7.6 cm) piece fusible interfacing
- 20"x 40" (15 x 30 cm) piece quilt batting
- ½ yard (44 cm) red baby rick rack
- ¾ yard (68.5 cm) ⅜"-wide (1 cm-wide) blue grosgrain ribbon
- ½ yard (44 cm) ¾"-wide (2 cm-wide) pleated or ruffled eyelet edging
- Two ⁷⁄₁₆"-diameter (1.1 cm-diameter) black buttons
- Polyester stuffing
- Red, brown, black, and white sewing thread
- 1½"x 2½" (3.8 x 6.3 cm) piece white lightweight cardboard

Can cover

1. Baste quilt batting to wrong side of one bottom circle. Trim batting close to stitching. With right sides in, stitch bottom circles together, leaving a 2" (5 cm) opening for turning. Clip seam allowance; turn right side out. Slip-stitch edges of opening together. Press circle flat.

2. Place one piece of quilt batting on half of wrong side of side piece. Baste along raw edges; overcast inside edge of batting to fabric.

3. With right sides in, fold side piece in half along inside edge of batting. Stitch around inside and raw edges, leaving an opening for turning on the raw-edge side. Trim batting close to stitching on the outside of the seam. Clip corners; turn right side out. Slip-stitch edges of opening.

4. Slip-stitch short edges together to form a tube.

5. Slip-stitch bottom to seamed end of tube.

6. To make label frame, fuse interfacing to wrong side of one frame piece. Trim outer seam allowance from other frame piece. With right sides together, stitch inner edges of frame pieces together, using a ¼" (6 mm) seam allowance. Clip to corners. Turn right side out.

7. Fold seam allowance back and press to wrong side of frame. Overcast edges on wrong side.

8. Pin frame horizontally on can cover directly opposite seam and 1¼" (3.2 cm) from top edge; slip-stitch side and bottom edges to cover. Insert can.

Lid cover

1. Baste white fabric to batting. Stitch binding of eyelet edging over raw edge of white fabric circle using a widely spaced zigzag stitch. Stitch ends of eyelet together and finish seam allowance.

2. Pin edges of circle around lid and pin in place. With thread doubled in needle, sew edge of fabric to side of lid with ¼"-long (6 mm-long) running stitches.

3. Sew red baby rick rack over binding of eyelet.

Bear

1. Fuse nose and ear pieces in place on front panel of bear. Using red thread zigzag around edges of appliqué pieces and along lines of mouth.

2. Baste batting to front, backs, arms, and legs. Stitch backs together along center seam; clip seam allowance. Make a row of gathering stitches along bottom edge of back panel; start and stop at side seam lines. With right sides together, stitch front to backs leaving lower edge open. Clip seam allowance; turn right side out.

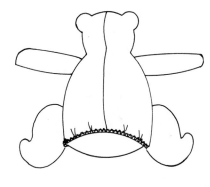

3. By hand, stitch through all layers along broken line at bottom of ears. Stuff the bear, but let it stay flat and soft.

4. Turn under lower edge along seamline and gather back evenly so it fits the front. Slip-stitch edges together.

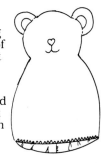

5. Stitch pairs of arm and leg pieces with right sides together; leave short, straight edges open. Clip seam allowance along curves. Turn right side out.

6. Stuff arms and legs but let them remain flat. Turn under seam allowance on ends; slip-stitch edges together. Stitch arms and legs to sides of body as indicated by dots. Sew buttons in place for eyes.

7. Matching center front of bear to center back of fabric cover, pin lower edge of body plus about 1¼" (3.2 cm) of legs to bottom of cover; slip-stitch edges together.

8. Stitch sides of bear's tummy to can, about ½" (1.25 cm) from side seam. Pin arms to fabric cover as shown in photo and slip-stitch paws to edge of frame. Tie blue ribbon around bear's neck. Write the cookie name on a cardboard rectangle and slip it into the label frame.

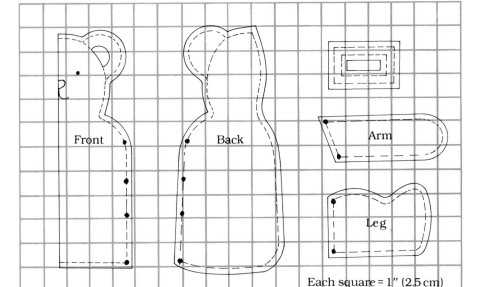

Front

Back

Arm

Leg

Each square = 1" (2.5 cm)

Beehive Tea Cozy

Those who take their tea the proper way will brew it in a pot and keep the pot cozy so the second cup will still be hot. This old-fashioned cozy, decorated and quilted to look like a beehive, will snuggle a pot 13" (33 cm) wide (including spout) by 9½" (24 cm) high.

Materials

Cotton fabrics:
⅜ yard (35 cm) gold-and-white print
⅜ yard (35 cm) solid gold for lining
Scraps of red with white dots, green-and-white print, brown print, and solid brown
1" (2.5 cm) square gold felt
Brown embroidery floss or quilting thread
Gold, green, red, and brown sewing thread
16" x 24" (41 x 61 cm) quilt batting
Small amount of polyester stuffing
Small scrap of fusible bonding web

Patterns

Enlarge pattern pieces following instructions in "Mama Bear's Sewing Basket." From enlarged patterns, make separate pattern piece for door frame and door opening. Add ⅛" to outer edge of door opening; also make a pattern for flower center.

Hive

Cut 2 beehive pieces from both gold-and-white-print, solid gold, and quilt batting.

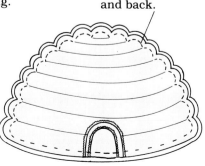

1. Transfer outline of door to one piece of gold-and-white print; this becomes front of hive. Trace quilting lines to both front and back pieces. Cut door frame from solid brown and opening from brown print. Cut fusible web to go behind frame and opening. Fuse opening, then frame, in place on front. Using brown thread, zigzag along edges of frame. Baste quilt batting to wrong side of both front and back.

2. With right sides together, stitch one piece of gold fabric to hive front and one to back for lining, leaving an opening at bottom edge between dots. Trim batting close to stitching. Clip seam allowance along curves with one clip at points between the curves. Turn right side out.

3. Turn under seam allowance of opening; slip-stitch edges together. Press scallops in place along side and top edges. Pin layers together along horizontal quilting lines. Quilt along lines using 3 strands of brown embroidery floss or 1 strand of quilting thread. With 2 strands of gold sewing thread, quilt ⅛" (3 mm) outside outer edge of door frame.

126

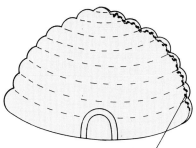

4. Starting above first scallop on each side, pin front to back. Slip-stitch edges together.

8. With 2 strands of red thread, quilt along broken lines. Cut centers from gold felt; whip stitch to right sides of flowers.

Leaves

Trace 4 leaves to scraps of green-and-white print fabric, leaving room for seam allowance. With right sides together, pin traced pieces to other scraps of green print. Stitch along outline leaving an opening between dots. Trim seam allowance to ⅛″ (3 mm) turn right side out. Stuff leaves with a little stuffing. Turn under seam allowance along

opening; slip-stitch edges. Quilt along center line of leaves with green thread. Place two leaves next to each other on wrong side of flowers; slip-stitch flowers. Sew flowers to cozy as shown in photo.

Flowers

5. Trace 2 flowers to wrong side of scraps of red fabric with white dots, leaving room for seam allowances. With right sides together, pin traced pieces to other red scraps; stitch around edges.

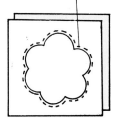

6. Trim seam allowance to ⅛″ (3 mm); clip along curves and to points between petals.

7. Make a 1″ (2.5 cm) slash at center of one side and carefully turn each flower right side out. Place a little stuffing in flowers. Whip stitch edges of slashes together.

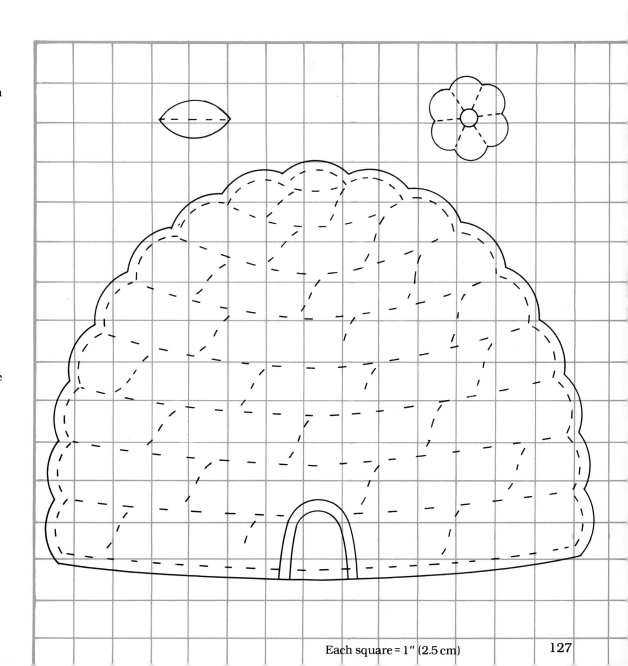

Each square = 1″ (2.5 cm)

The four heirloom bears set out for a **Dejeubears** sur l'Herbe Sunday afternoon picnic. T.R. and Quite A. Small-Bear carried the sandwiches, napkins, plates, and silverware in their new tote-with-pockets-that-unfolds-into-a-picnic-cloth. Bearnice and Buddy are coming with the cooler any minute. (You can see them in applique on the front of the tote.) If you think those cookie-cutter, bear-shaped sandwiches aren't good enough to eat, you should have **been** there.

The pic-pac is all folded up—with the plates, silver, napkins, and wrapped sandwiches and fruit all tucked safely away inside the fitted pockets. It seals itself as a carry-all with Velcro closures in the corners.

128

Pic-Pac

When you unhook the Velcro closures, and open this folding picnic tote on the grass, it measures 58″ (147 cm) square—plenty big enough for a teddy bear's picnic with grown-ups invited. The outside is durable blue canvas with a capacious outer pocket—for a loaf of bread, for example—appliqued with a picture of two bears who love picnics. When opened, the canvas side is down on the grass, and the quilted top reveals all the goodies tucked inside—pockets that double as placemats, and pouches for napkins and silver. As Bearnice would say, "Laziness is the mother of invention."

Materials
2⅝ yards (2.5 m) 60″-wide (152 cm-wide) blue canvas
3½ yards (3.25 m) 45″-wide (115 cm-wide) red-and-white-striped ticking
1⅝ yards (1.5 m) 45″-wide (115 cm-wide) solid white fabric
1¾ yards (1.6 m) 45″-wide (115 cm-wide) blue-and-white print fabric
1 yard (90 cm) 45″-wide (115 cm-wide) red fabric with white pin dots
⅝ yard (60 cm) 45″-wide (115 cm-wide) brown-and-white print fabric
½ yard (45 cm) 45″-wide (115 cm-wide) moss-green-and-white print fabric.
14″x 8″ (35 x 20 cm) emerald-green-and-white print fabric
  Scraps of medium brown, dark brown, yellow, blue, grey, gold, red, yellow and white print, and beige
  Sewing thread to match all fabrics
  Embroidery floss: 1 yard (1 m) each black, red, brown, and green, and 3 yards (3 m) blue
2 yards (2 m) 1″-wide (2.5 cm-wide) Velcro
  Embroidery hoop and needle
90″ x 108″ (2.3 x 1.75 m) quilt batting
½ yard (45 cm) fusible bonding web

Cutting the Pieces
From blue canvas, cut 60″ (152 cm) square for outside of bag, two 5″ x 32″ (13 x 81.3 cm) shoulder straps, and two 15″ x 16″ (38 x 40.5 cm) side flaps. Make patterns for outer border and border pocket following measurements on diagram. Cut 4 outer border pieces and 8 border pockets from ticking. (Make sure to place arrow on grain of fabric, parallel to selvage.) Also from ticking, cut a 15″ x 22″ (38 x 56 cm) rectangle for outer pocket. From blue and white print, cut eight 14½″ x 12″ (37 x 30.5 cm) rectangles for placemat pockets. From brown and white print, for inner borders, cut two 24″ x 5″ (61 x 12.5 cm) strips and two 32″ x 5″ (81.3 x 12.5 cm) strips. From solid white, cut backing pieces as follows: a 24″ (61 cm) square, a 32″ (82 cm) square, and a 15″ x 11″ (38 x 28 cm) rectangle. For napkins, cut four 18″ (45 cm) squares of red with white pin dots. From batting, cut a 32″ (82.1 cm) square, 4 outer borders, 8 border pockets (cut to foldline), four 14½″ x 12″ (37 x 30.5 cm) placemat pockets, and a 15″ x 11″ (38 x 28 cm) outer pocket.

Appliquéing the Center Square and Outer Pocket
Enlarge pattern for center square and the outer pocket following instructions in "Mama Bear's Sewing Basket"; add ½″ seam allowance to edges. Read and follow instructions for making appliqué patterns for Story Quilt on page 112.

Using your patterns, make individual patterns for all appliqued pieces as follows: for center square—sky, ground, picnic cloth, tree trunk, treetop, basket, plates, food, grey pie piece, beige pie piece, underbrim of lady bear's hat, bears (except ears and top arms), lap napkins, bows (including lady bear's hat bow), hats, ears, and top arms; for outer pocket—white basket piece, print basket piece, heart, bear bodies (including arms and legs), bows, underbrim of lady bear's hat, heads, hats, ears.

Pieces should be cut and appliquéd in the above order.

Cut all applique pieces following suggestions in the photograph, or choose your own colors. Look at the photograph and notice which pieces seem to overlap others. Where the shapes come together, extend the part of the one that appears to go under the other by ⅛″ to ¼″ (3 to 6 mm) so that they both can be finished by a single row of zigzag stitching. Note that in the order given above, those pieces listed first go under those pieces listed later.

To applique center square, place sky, then ground on solid white 24″ (61 cm) square. Baste along top edge of ground and around outer edges. Zigzag-stitch along top edge of ground with green. Cut fusible bonding web to go behind appliqué pieces following instructions in "Cutting the Pieces" in the Story Quilt Project. Fuse appliqué pieces in place on square. Using the photograph as your guide, zigzag-stitch around bears with dark brown thread, around sandwiches with beige, and around basket with gold. Zigzag-stitch hatbands to match bows. Zigzag-stitch around other shapes using matching thread. Hand-embroider eyes and nose using 2 strands of floss. Embroider eyes and nose with black in satin stitch, mouth with red in back-stitch, fruit stems with green in straight stitch, pic marks with brown in straight stitch, and leaves with green in lazy daisy stitch.

To appliqué outer pocket, baste solid white 15″ x 11″ (38 x 28 cm) piece to wrong side of half of outer pocket. Cut fusible bonding web to go behind all pieces, and fuse pieces in place on pocket. Using the photograph as your guide, zigzag-stitch around bears using dark brown thread, around basket with beige, and around other shapes using matching thread. Zigzag-stitch hatbands to match bows. Embroider features of bears as for center square. Trace words in place on pocket, and hand-embroider with 2 strands of blue in back-stitch.

Assembling and Quilting the Inside

With right sides together, stitch short inner border pieces to opposite sides of center square. Stitch long inner border pieces to remaining sides and across ends of short inner border pieces.

1. With right sides facing out, place batting between center square and solid white 32" (82 cm) backing square. Pin layers together. Baste ¼" (6 mm) inside inner and outer edges of inner border pieces, above line of horizon, and around outer edge of tree and picnic scene. Using thread to match background fabric, machine-quilt along basting using 8 to 10 stitches per inch.

2. Baste batting to wrong side of outer border pieces; trim batting to stitching. Baste batting to wrong side of lower half of border pocket pieces.

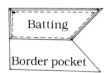

3. Fold border pockets in half with right sides out; pin layers together. Baste along seamlines and topstitch ¼" (6 mm) inside seamlines. Zigzag-stitch along shortest edge.

4. Matching diagonal edges, place a border pocket on each side of each border piece, ½" (1.25 cm) from lower edge of border. Baste pockets in place.

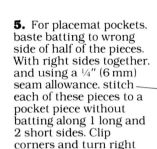

5. For placemat pockets, baste batting to wrong side of half of the pieces. With right sides together, and using a ¼" (6 mm) seam allowance, stitch each of these pieces to a pocket piece without batting along 1 long and 2 short sides. Clip corners and turn right side out.

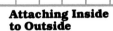

6. Baste together edges of open side. Topstitch ¼" (6 mm) from seamed edges. Draw and machine-quilt a 9" x 6½" (23 x 16.5 cm) rectangle 2" (5 cm) from topstitching.

7. Place a pocket in center of each outer border piece, overlapping border pockets and ½" (1.25 cm) from lower edge. Stitch along side edges of placemat pockets. Stitch the hook half of a 9" (23 cm) length of Velcro to the wrong side of the center top edge of each placemat pocket, and the loop half to the corresponding position on border.

8. With right sides together, stitch borders to center square, starting and stopping stitching ½" (1.25 cm) from edge of center square. Stitch borders together at corners. Press seams open.

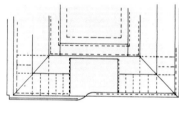

Attaching Inside to Outside

1. Place inside, right side up, in center of wrong side of canvas square. Pin layers together. Turn under ½" (1.25 cm) on edge of canvas, then fold 1" (2.5 cm) over edges onto striped border, trimming and mitering corners.

Baste in place. Hand-baste ¼" (6 mm) from seamlines of outer border, 2" (5 cm) inside center square, along edge of placemat pocket, and on each border pocket where indicated on diagram by dotted lines. With the inside facing up, and using a blue bobbin with white thread on top, machine-quilt along all basting lines.

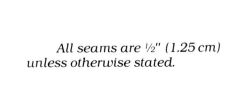

All seams are ½" (1.25 cm) unless otherwise stated.

2. For shoulder straps, press under ¼″ (6 mm) on ends, and 1¼″ (3 cm) on long edges. Fold straps in half lengthwise, and topstitch ¼″ (6 mm) from edges and fold.

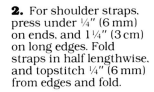

3. For side flaps, press under ¼″ (6 mm) on all edges. Fold in half lengthwise and stitch outer edges together. Sew the hook half of a 15″ (38 cm) length of Velcro to each flap ¼″ (6 mm) from edges.

4. For outer pocket, baste batting to, wrong side of appliqued half of pocket piece. With right sides together, fold pocket in half and stitch, leaving a 4″ (10 cm) opening along lower edge. Clip corners and turn right side out. Slip-stitch opening. Topstitch ¼″ (6 mm) from edges. Baste around bears and basket and machine-quilt along basting.

5. With canvas side out, fold pic-pac in thirds, and then in thirds again in the opposite direction, to make a 19″ (48.5 cm) square. Hold bag with free edge at front top. Place shoulder straps centered on outside top edges 7″ (18 cm) apart, with ends 2″ (5 cm) below top edge. Slip-stitch straps firmly to bag.

6. Position side flaps on back of bag, centered horizontally and vertically; pin in place. Slip-stitch to back. Stitch reserved loop halves of Velcro to front under flaps. When attaching Velcro, don't make side flaps fasten too tightly or your pic-pac won't be able to expand enough to hold all the picnic gear you'll want to pack inside.

CUTTING DIAGRAM

16″ (41 cm)

Place on fold
Border pocket

7½″ (19 cm)

23″ (58.5 cm)

32″ (81.5 cm)

14″ (35.5 cm)

Outer border

58″ (147.5 cm)

Each square = 1″ (2.5 cm)

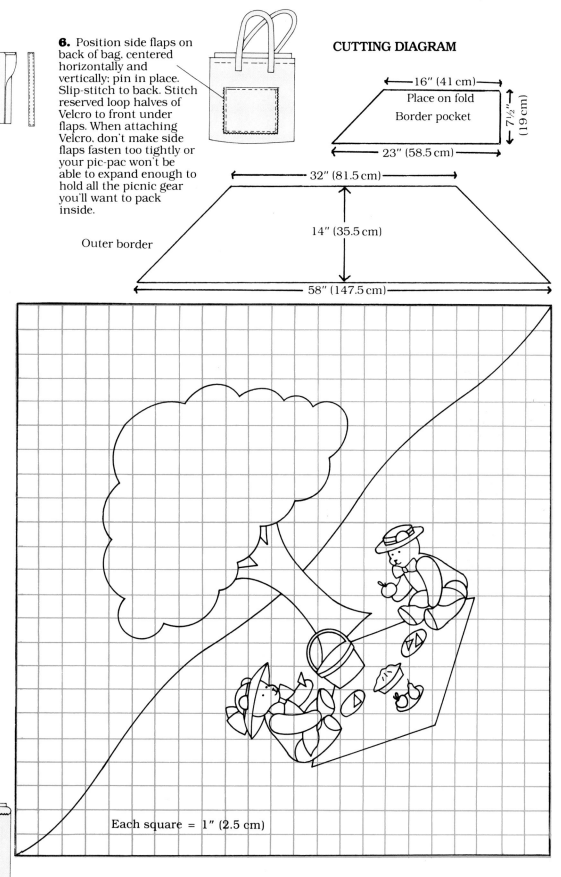

Party Cloth and Napkins

The pattern is stenciled onto the fabric in bright acrylic paints formulated especially for fabric. The cloth measures 56"x 80" (142 x 203 cm)—enough to allow a generous overhang to show the stenciling on a 3'x 6' (1 x 2 m) table. If your table is larger, space out the figures more or repeat them.   Photo on page 135.

Materials and Tools

3¼ yards (286 cm) 56"-wide (142 cm-
   wide) medium-weight, off-white
   fabric (This is enough to make
   1 tablecloth and 6 napkins.)
Off-white sewing thread
20" x 30" (51 x 76 cm) waxed or oiled
   stencil paper
Carbon paper
10" x 14" (25.5 x 35.5 cm) piece glass,
   heavy cardboard, or cutting
   board to cut stencils on
Artist's knife
Paper to protect work table
Masking tape
Pushpins
Acrylic textile paints: brown, red,
   blue, yellow, and black—about
   1 ounce (28.75 grams) each
2 or more stencil brushes: ¼"
   (6 mm) and ½" (1.2 cm) in
   width (It is helpful to have one
   of each size for each color
   of paint.)
Paper towels
Permanent fabric marker: black

Cutting and Hemming Fabric

Wash fabric well to remove sizing. Dry and iron it. For tablecloth, cut an 81" (205.8 cm) length of fabric. Note: if fabric is wider than 56" (142 cm), trim to 57" (144.5 cm) and hem following directions below. For napkins, cut six 18" (45.7 cm) squares. To hem, turn under ¼" (6 mm) twice on all edges of napkins and unfinished ends of tablecloth and stitch hems in place.

Making the Stencils

Enlarge patterns for stencils following instructions in Mama Bear's Sewing Basket. ✂ Transfer patterns to stencil paper. Waxed stencil paper is translucent. Place it on top of pattern and trace design with pencil. Oiled stencil paper is opaque, so you must use carbon paper. Place stencils on cutting surface and carefully cut out shapes using an artist's knife. Cut 2 stencils for each of the 3 bear motifs: one for the bear's body, which will be stenciled in brown; and a second for the inner ears, bow ties, and balloons.

Do not cut out facial features or balloon strings as these will be added after stenciling is complete. Cut separate stencils for lengthwise scallop, crosswise scallop, and corner scallop, leaving ⅜" (9 mm) between side edge of scallop and side of stencil. As scallops are ⅜" (9 mm) apart, this will make it very easy to space them. Mark the center of each stencil at the lower edge to help correctly align it on fabric.

Stenciling

When stencils are complete it is best to test them on scrap fabric first and then make any adjustments necessary. Cover table with paper to protect it from paint that may bleed through the fabric. Tape or tack fabric to work surface. When working on tablecloth, spread out as much of it as possible. Tape the stencil in position. Use paint right out of jar or place a small amount in a bowl. Dip the tip of the stencil brush into the paint. Do not get too much paint on the brush. Hold the brush upright and rub it in a circular motion on a few layers of paper towels to work the paint into the bristles and remove excess paint. Test the brush against a scrap of fabric to determine your results. Place your fingers on the stencil to help hold it against the fabric and to keep the fabric from shifting as you apply the paint. Hold the brush upright with the bristles flat on the fabric's surface. Use a circular motion from the outside edges to the center. Move the brush clockwise and counter clockwise to fill in the entire shape and build up the color intensity that you desire. Apply more paint to the edges than to the center to create a three-dimensional look. (This looks especially good on the balloons.) Acrylic paints dry quickly, so lift the stencil immediately after painting. When the paint is dry to the touch, tape down the next stencil and continue.

Tablecloth

Stencil borders of tablecloth first. There are 13 lengthwise scallops on each long side, and 9 crosswise scallops on each short side. Stencil a corner scallop in each of the 4 corners. Use the ¼" (6 mm) brush for the border scallops, and any small shapes. Use ½" (1.2 cm) brush for larger shapes. For bears, stencil bodies first, and then balloons, ears, and bows. Stencil pattern #1 in all 4 corners, pattern #2 in center of each side, and pattern #3 on long sides between 3rd and 4th scallop from center scallop. Note that all scallops are blue, all bears are brown, and all inner ears are red. Refer to color photo for colors of other pieces. Paint eyes, nose, and mouth using an acrylic brush. Make eyes and nose black, and mouth red. Draw balloon strings and details of paws and footpads with permanent fabric marker.

Napkins

Stencil pattern #4 onto lower right corner of each napkin. Draw balloon strings with marker.

Finishing

Clean brushes with soap and water. Heat-set paint using iron or clothes dryer following manufacturer's directions.

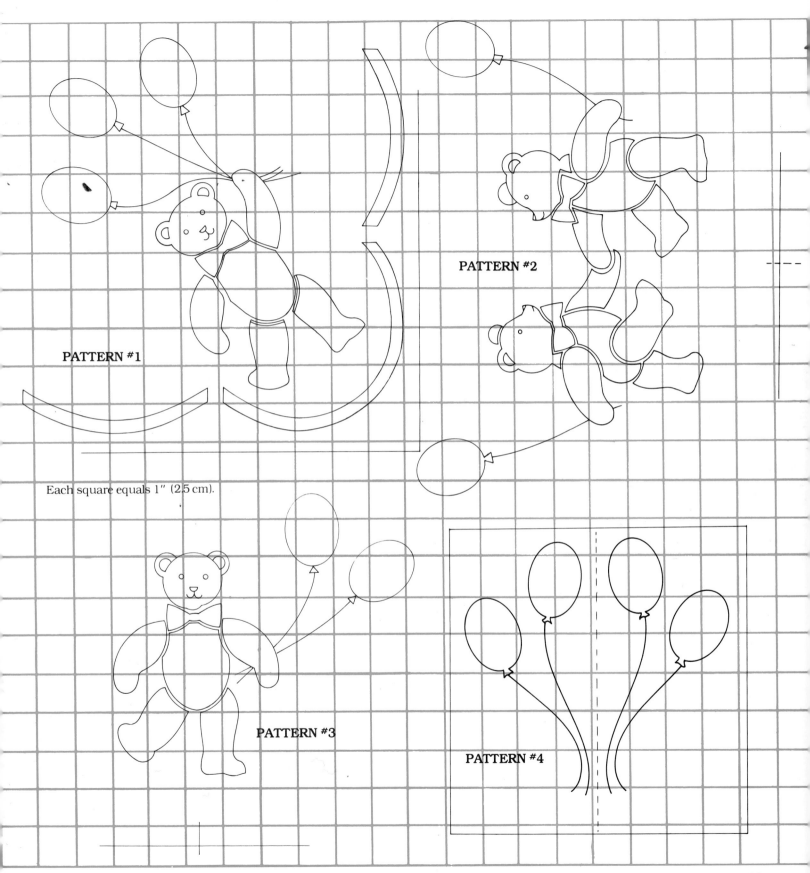

PATTERN #1

PATTERN #2

Each square equals 1″ (2.5 cm).

PATTERN #3

PATTERN #4

133

Hugger-Holders

These 5" (12.7 cm) bears sit up and grip a napkin or placecard at each plate for a party. They will hold bills or letters on your desk, shopping lists or coupons on your kitchen table, or almost anything a spring clothespin will hold. That's their secret; they are made with an ordinary, wooden, spring-loaded clothespin inside. Pinch their shoulder blades and their arms open.

Materials

- ¼ yard (23 cm) 45"-wide (114.3 cm-wide) brown canvas or other sturdy cotton fabric such as denim., twill, poplin, or corduroy (This is enough to make 4 bears.)
- Brown sewing thread
- 6½" (16.5 cm) square of lightweight cardboard for patterns
- 4 wooden, spring-loaded clothespins
- 60" (152 cm) length ⅜"-wide (9 mm-wide) red satin ribbon
- Scrap of brown felt
- ¼ pound (100 grams) of polyester stuffing
- Textile or acrylic paint: black and red
- Small paintbrush.

Cutting the Pieces

Enlarge pattern pieces following instructions in Mama Bear's Sewing Basket. Trace patterns on lightweight cardboard and cut out. Leaving ½" (1.2 cm) or more between pieces, trace 1 side, 2 legs, and 1 inner arm to wrong side of fabric. Reverse patterns and trace pieces again. Transfer markings to right side of all pieces. Cut out pieces, adding a ¼" (6 mm) seam allowance on all sides. Cut 2 ears from brown felt, omitting seam allowance.

Sewing the Pieces Together

1. With right sides together, stitch inner arms to arm areas of side pieces leaving opening between dots. Trim seam allowances to ⅛" (3 mm). Clip side piece seam allowances to dots, and clip both seam allowances along curves. Turn arms right side out.

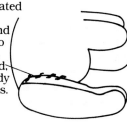

2. With right sides together and arms tucked in, stitch around side pieces stitching together straight edges of inner arms in the process. Be careful not to stitch arm openings closed, and leave opening on back between dots. Trim and clip seam allowances. Turn right side out.

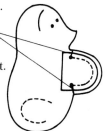

3. Press handle of clothespin to open it and insert one front end in each arm. Push small amount of stuffing in each arm on outside of clothespin. Stuff head and body, keeping clothespin horizontal in body. Turn under seam allowance of opening and slip-stitch edges together.

4. With right sides together, stitch legs together in pairs, leaving openings between dots. Trim and clip seam allowances. Turn right side out. Stuff legs. Turn under edges of openings and slip-stitch together.

5. Place one leg on each side of body as indicated by placement lines. Lower edge of legs and body must be even so bear will sit on table. Using doubled thread, slip-stitch legs to body along placement lines.

6. Make a tuck in center of straight edge of ears as indicated on pattern. Whip-stitch lower edge of ears to head along placement lines. Paint eyes and noses black, and mouth red. Cut ribbon in 4 equal pieces and tie 1 around the neck of each bear.

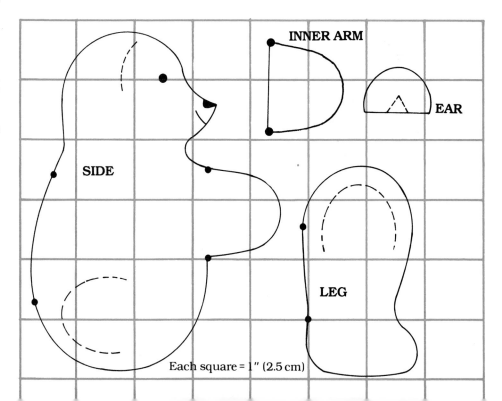

INNER ARM

EAR

SIDE

LEG

Each square = 1" (2.5 cm)

RECIPES

"The recipes I like the best in this chapter are all the cookies (especially the Ginger-Bear Cookies), all the cakes (especially the Chocolate Honey-Bear Birthday Cake with the icing that looks like fur), the Beary Pie, the bread and all the buns (oh! those Strawberry Sticky Buns), almost all the snacks, all the fish and veggies (even), the High Koala Tea (because it's real Australian food, even though the title is corny), all the desserts, of course (the Apple Panda dowdy is a real winner), and all the yogurts, honeys and the Party Bear Punch."

"Why did you say 'almost' all the snacks?" asked Bearnice.

"Because the Forage Porridge tastes like it's supposed to be good for you," replied Quite A. Small-Bear.

Cookies, Cakes, and Pies

Beary Good Honey Nut Cookies

These crisp, honey-flavored cookies are the Bears' favorites. If the Bears have lots of friends in they won't last long. But T.R. and Buddy usually manage to hide a few for later.

½ cup shortening
½ cup firmly packed brown sugar
1 cup honey
2 eggs
2½ cups unbleached all purpose
    flour
1½ teaspoons baking soda
1 teaspoon baking powder
¼ teaspoon salt
½ teaspoon ground ginger
½ cup finely chopped nuts

Combine shortening, sugar, honey, and eggs in bowl and beat with electric mixer until light and fluffy. Mix flour, soda, baking powder, salt, and ginger well. Add with nuts to honey mixture. Stir until well blended. Cover cookie dough and chill several hours in refrigerator.

On floured canvas, using well-floured, covered rolling pin, roll about ¼ of dough at a time to ⅛-inch thickness. Keep remainder refrigerated. Cut with 2-inch round cookie cutter. If you have a scalloped cutter, use it. Transfer to greased baking sheet and bake at 350° F for 8 to 10 minutes. These cookies bake quickly so watch them carefully. Transfer at once to cake rack. If some cookies are difficult to remove, put baking sheet back in oven for a minute or so to warm cookies and then remove. This recipe makes about 6 to 7 dozen cookies. Part of dough may be frozen to bake later, if you wish. Note: This dough can be baked without rolling. Drop a teaspoonful at a time on greased baking sheet. Push batter down with bottom of floured glass. Bake as directed.

Dancing Russian Ginger-Bear Cookies

All the Bears, Bearnice, Buddy, Quite A. Small-Bear, and T.R., are glad they don't have to dance for a living like the Russian bears do. Bearnice says they couldn't because they can't afford to pay the piper. "But by making dancing cookies," she says, "you can be dressing your Russian and eat it too." Quite A. Small-Bear always starts eating his Russian Bear at the feet end so it can get a little rest.

⅓ cup shortening
¾ cup sugar
1 egg
½ cup molasses
2 teaspoons baking soda
2 teaspoons hot water
2¼ cups unbleached all purpose
    flour
1 teaspoon ground cinnamon
½ teaspoon ground ginger
1¾ cups sifted confectioners sugar
1½ tablespoons hot water, about
    Tiny marshmallows
    Raisins
    Red candies
    Colored sprinkles

Put shortening, sugar, egg, and molasses in a bowl. Beat with an electric mixer until light and fluffy. Dissolve soda in 2 teaspoons hot water and stir into molasses mixture. Combine flour with spices and add to molasses mixture, stirring until completely blended. Cover and refrigerate over night.

When ready to bake, cut a paper pattern of a dancing bear about 8 inches tall.

On floured canvas with covered, well-floured rolling pin, roll out about ⅛ of dough in a 9 x 9-inch square ⅛-inch thick. Lay pattern on dough and with sharp paring knife cut around pattern. Remove excess dough. With 2 spatulas, transfer bear to greased baking sheet. (Even if you have non-stick coated sheets, grease them.) Put unused dough

back in bowl and take out enough to make one more bear. Roll and cut as before. Bake the 2 bears at 350° F about 10 minutes. Remove from pan and cool on rack. Continue until all dough is used. You should have 8 or 9 dancing bears. Shape left-over dough into small drop cookies. Bake as directed, checking that cookies do not burn.

To decorate: (frosting)

Mix confectioners sugar with about 1½ tablespoons hot water. Add water slowly so mixture does not get too thin. Frosting should be thin enough to spread, but thick enough so it won't run off.

Starting at the top, put a little dab of frosting at very top of bear's hat. Put ½ a tiny marshmallow in frosting for a pom-pom. Just above where his eyes will be, put a ¼-inch strip of frosting for the fur on his hat. Put a dab of frosting for each eye and stick a raisin on each dab. Put another dab for his nose and on it stick a red candy.

Frost a vest on bear and decorate it to suit yourself. If you like you can give the bear a colored vest by adding some food coloring to the frosting. Cover the vest with sprinkles or add raisin or candy buttons.

Honey Cake

Bearnice would call this a "Jack Sprat" cake since it doesn't have a lot of butter in it. But it does have honey and that should make T.R. and the other Bears happy. Since T.R. was born in the 1800's he'd better put on just a few symbolic candles or he won't be able to find the cake.

Tip from Bearnice: If the layers puff up in the center when baking, cut enough of the top from one layer to make it even. Place that layer, cut side down, on the cake plate first. Add frosting to the layer and put the other layer, bottom side down, on the frosted part; then frost the rest of the cake. Buddy always hopes the cake will rise like that to make a mound in the center because that means the cake will have an extra layer of frosting.

> 1 cup milk
> 1 cup honey
> ½ cup sugar
> 2 eggs
> 2½ cups unbleached all purpose flour
> 1 teaspoon baking soda
> ¼ cup softened butter

Grease and flour two, 8-inch round cake pans.

Combine milk, honey, and sugar in a saucepan; heat and stir until sugar is dissolved. Cool.

Separate yolks of eggs from whites and beat yolks into cooled honey mixture.

In a bowl mix flour with soda. Cut in butter with 2 knives or a pastry blender until a fine mixture is formed. Beat egg whites until stiff. Combine flour mixture with honey mixture, stirring just enough to blend. Fold in beaten egg whites. Spoon batter into the greased and floured 8-inch cake pans and bake at 350° F for 25 minutes or until cake tester or toothpick stuck into center of cake comes out clean. Let stand in pan on rack for 10 minutes. Run tip of a small knife around edge of cake and remove from pan. Let cake cool on rack.

Chocolate Frosting:

Combine ½ cup each bittersweet chocolate chips and butterscotch chips with 6 tablespoons butter in a 6-cup saucepan. Stir over low heat until melted and blended. Gradually stir in 3 cups sifted confectioners sugar, adding milk as needed (about 3 to 4 tablespoons) to make frosting a spreading consistency. Makes enough for top and sides of 2 layers. Keep a sharp eye on the bowl once the frosting is ready to spread if Buddy is anywhere around or you will come up mysteriously short when you frost your cake.

Chocolate Honey-bear Birthday Cake

When a friend of a teddy bear is having a birthday, this is the cake to serve. The cake is chocolate and it melts in your mouth. The frosting is mocha, to match a bear-fur color. It is applied in tiny florettes, made with pastry tube fitted with a #20 or #21, metal, star-tip, applied close together covering the whole cake. The effect is just like fur. A photo of the cake is shown (with pink frosting in the ears) with the Tablecloth and Napkins (stenciled) project in Chapter 4, "Bears in the Kitchen."

> 8 oz. melted semisweet chocolate
> 1⅓ cups honey
> 3½ cups sifted cake flour
> 2 teaspoons baking soda
> 1½ teaspoons salt
> 1 cup room temperature butter
> 1 cup sugar
> 2 teaspoons vanilla extract
> 4 unbeaten eggs
> 1½ cups water

Melt chocolate in a double-boiler; add honey. Sift flour once, measure, add baking soda and salt; sift together 2 times. In a bowl of an electric mixer cream butter and sugar until light and fluffy. Add chocolate-honey mixture and vanilla. Mix well. Add eggs, one at a time, beating thoroughly after each addition; add flour gradually. Grease an 8 x 3-inch cake pan and four cupcake tins. Fill pans half-way. Bake 1½ hours at 325° F. Extra batter can be used for extra cupcakes.

White frosting:

> 2 lbs. 10X sugar
> 2 cups solid shortening
> 2 tablespoons vanilla
> 6 tablespoons water

Combine the above ingredients. Remove ⅛ cup frosting and keep this white. Take ¼ cup of white frosting and add 2 drops of red food coloring for pink. Divide balance into ⅔ and ⅓. To the ⅔ add ¼ cup instant coffee, 2 tablespoons honey, and 2 tablespoons water. To the ⅓ add the same as to the ⅔ plus ¼ cup sifted cocoa powder.

Tips: #20 or 21 for stars
#4 for mouth and eyeballs
#12 for eyes and nose

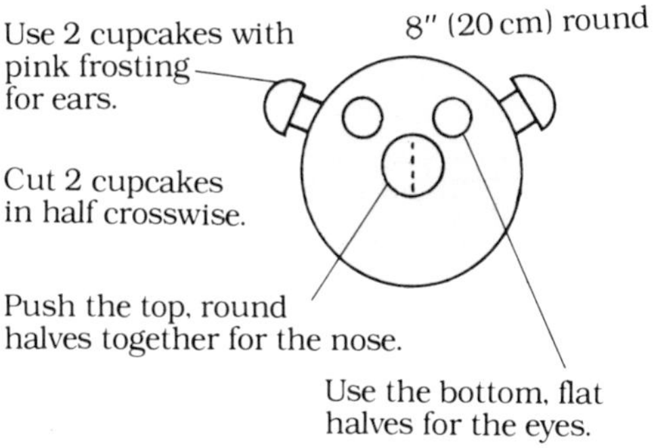

Use 2 cupcakes with pink frosting for ears.

8" (20 cm) round

Cut 2 cupcakes in half crosswise.

Push the top, round halves together for the nose.

Use the bottom, flat halves for the eyes.

Cupcakes

1   2   3   4

Peanut Butter Cub Cakes

These cakes are just the thing for a bear to take along for lunch at school or a bear picnic. They are baked in little paper cups, all ready to be taken out.

> ½ cup shortening
> ½ cup peanut butter
> 1⅓ cups brown sugar
> 2 eggs
> 2 cups unbleached all purpose flour
> 3 teaspoons baking powder
> ½ teaspoon salt
> ½ teaspoon cinnamon
> ½ teaspoon nutmeg
> 1 cup milk
> 12 to 16 2½-inch paper cub cake pan liners
> Orange marmalade or jelly

Combine shortening with peanut butter, sugar, and eggs. Beat with an electric mixer until light and fluffy. Mix flour with baking powder, salt, and spices. Add to creamed mixture, alternately with milk, beginning and ending with flour. Stir only to blend, do not beat.

Place paper liners in 2 ½-inch cub cake pans. Fill ⅔ full of batter. Put a teaspoon of marmalade or your favorite jelly on top of each cub cake. Bake at 375° F for 20 to 25 minutes. Makes about 16 cub cakes.

Beary Pie

Bearnice loves Beary Pie. She has taught Buddy how to make it and now and then he surprises her with half a luscious pie.

 4 cups bluebearies, blackbearies,
    or cut-up strawbearies
 ½ cup sugar
 1 tablespoon lemon juice
 1½ tablespoons cornstarch
 ¼ cup water
    1 9-inch baked pie crust
 ½ cup whipping cream or
 1 cup frozen non-dairy whipped
    topping, defrosted

Clean bearies or wash and cut up strawbearies as needed. Dry well. Combine 3 cups bearies with sugar, lemon juice, and cornstarch dissolved in water. Stir to mix and bring to boil. Cook and stir until thickened and clear. Fold remaining bearies into cooked bearies and pour into baked crust. Chill. Decorate top with whipped cream or non-dairy whipped topping. Makes one 9-inch Beary Pie.

Bread and Rolls

Ginger-bear Bread

Ginger-bear Bread is a favorite of Quite A. Small-Bear. He can eat 2 or 3 pieces at a time, particularly if it has whipped cream sweetened with honey or ice cream on it. Bearnice thinks he's foolish to put honey on it because it ruins the pretty pattern that the sugar makes. "A bear and his honey are soon parted," she says

 ¼ cup softened butter
 ½ cup firmly packed brown sugar
 1 egg
 ½ cup molasses
 1½ cups unbleached all purpose
    flour

 1 teaspoon baking soda
 1 teaspoon ground ginger
 1 teaspoon ground cinnamon
 ½ cup buttermilk
    Lace paper doily
    Confectioners sugar

Combine butter, sugar, egg, and molasses and beat with an electric mixer until light and fluffy.

Mix flour well with soda and spices. Add alternately with buttermilk to molasses mixture, beginning and ending with dry ingredients. Pour into greased 8-inch square pan. Bake at 350° F for 30 minutes. Cool on rack in pan. When cooled, lay a lace paper doily on top of Ginger-bear Bread and, using a fine strainer, sprinkle top with sifted confectioners sugar. To remove doily, lift it straight up so you don't disturb the pattern you made with sugar. To serve, cut into pieces. Makes 6 to 8 servings.

Strawbeary Sticky Buns

Sticky buns are good but they are even better when made with strawbeary preserves. Quite A. Small-Bear can never wait long enough for them to cool before he picks one up. He always drops it because it is so hot, and it always lands on his fur in a place he can't reach with his tongue to lick clean. Bearnice says, "Impatience is its own punishment." It is better to let the buns cool a little before trying to pick them up. That good sticky syrup gets hot while baking and can burn paws and mouth.

 2 cups unbleached all purpose
    flour
 3 teaspoons baking powder
 ½ teaspoon salt
 4 tablespoons shortening
 ¾ cup milk, about
 2 tablespoons melted butter

 ½ cup strawberry preserves
 ¾ cup firmly packed brown sugar
 ½ cup honey
 2 tablespoons butter

Mix flour, baking powder, and salt. Cut shortening in with two knives or pastry blender until texture is fine. Add milk gradually to make a dough that can be rolled. Roll on lightly floured board into a rectangle about 12-inches long ¼-inch thick, and 8-inches wide. Spread with melted butter and strawbeary perserves. Roll, starting with long side, and pinch edges to seal.

Heat together brown sugar, honey, and remaining butter until sugar is dissolved. Pour into a buttered 9-inch round cake pan. Cut rolls into 1-inch slices and place, cut side down, into syrup in cake pan. Bake at 400° F for 18 to 20 minutes. Let cool 5 minutes and turn out on serving plate. Makes 1 dozen.

Bear Claws

These Bear Claw rolls, served with morning tea, last bearly long enough to finish the first cup. T.R. likes to make Sunday breakfast for everyone but he also likes to sleep late. He has learned to use the fast-rise yeast which cuts the time from start to finish in half over regular yeast. It makes it possible to bake up a bear storm more quickly. Bearnice usually helps T.R. to make the Bear Claws. This recipe makes a dozen—3 for each bear—but, somehow, when T.R. makes them by himself the platter never has that many on it when it comes to the table.

Dough:
3¼ cups unbleached all purpose
    flour
 4 tablespoons sugar
 ½ teaspoon salt
 1 package fast-rising yeast
 4 tablespoons butter
 ½ cup water
 ¼ cup milk
 1 egg (at room temperature)

2 tablespoons melted butter

Set aside 1 cup flour. Measure remaining flour into a medium-sized bowl and add 4 tablespoons sugar, salt, and yeast. Mix well.

Heat 4 tablespoons butter with water and milk until hot to the touch (125° to 130° F) or test it on your wrist to be sure it is not too hot. The butter does not have to be melted. Stir liquid into dry ingredients. Mix in egg, beating well. Add enough of the reserved flour to make a soft dough. Knead on a floured board 8 to 10 minutes. Place dough in a greased bowl, turn to grease top, and cover with plastic wrap and a clean towel. Let rise in a warm, draft-free place until doubled in bulk, about 30 to 40 minutes. Press a finger ½-inch into the dough to see if it has risen enough. If the imprint remains, it has. Punch dough down. On a floured board, roll dough into a rectangle about 6 x 16-inches. Spread with 2 tablespoons melted butter and the prune filling. Starting at long side, roll into a long roll, sealing edge to dough by pinching together. Cut crosswise into 3-inch rolls. With back side of knife, press 2 depressions in rolled side of each roll almost to middle of roll, not quite through the dough. Place on greased baking sheet. Cover with towel and let rise in a warm draft-free place until doubled in bulk, about 30 to 40 minutes.

Bake at 375° F for 20 to 25 minutes or until lightly browned. Cool to warm.

To make prune filling:

Cover 1 cup pitted prunes with water and simmer, covered for about 15 minutes or until tender. Drain and add ¼ cup sugar and ¼ teaspoon cinnamon. Chop or whip with spoon until consistency of jam. Cool.

To make frosting:

Mix 1 tablespoon soft butter with 1½ cups sifted confectioners sugar and ½ teaspoon vanilla extract. Add about 2 tablespoons hot water slowly, stirring well. The frosting should be of a spreading consistency. Frost warm baked rolls and sprinkle with chopped nuts (about ½ cup). Makes about 1 dozen.

Breakfast and Snack Ideas

Bluebeary Pancakes

T.R. likes the idea of making pancakes in a bear shape. He has one piece of advice. Be sure the batter for the legs, arms, and head overlaps onto the body when you drop it on the griddle. That way when the bear cake is turned it will not fall apart. If you don't put on the arms and legs, the pancake looks like a snow man...not a bear cake. When T.R. makes them for Quite A. Small-Bear, he leaves off the body, arms, or legs so he can make them fast enough to keep ahead of Quite's appetite. One Sunday morning Buddy ate 120 between ten o'clock and noon. "That's going a smile a minute," said Bearnice.

1½ cups unbleached all purpose flour
3½ teaspoons baking powder
¼ teaspoon salt
3 tablespoons sugar
1 egg
⅞ cup milk (1 cup minus 2 tablespoons)
3 tablespoons vegetable oil
½ cup bluebearies for decoration
Butter
Honey or maple syrup

In bowl, stir together flour, baking powder, salt, and sugar, mixing well. In another bowl, beat egg, milk, and vegetable oil briskly with whisk. Combine dry ingredients with liquids, stirring just to blend. Do not beat.

Heat pancake griddle over moderately low heat. When drops of water bounce off griddle, it is ready to use. Spread lightly with oil.

Form bear cakes as follows: first put a tablespoon of batter in circle in center of griddle. Then put a half tablespoon at top in another circle to make head. Be sure it overlaps body circle a tiny bit. Use 1 teaspoon each for ears, arms, and legs. Cook pancakes about 1 minute, then using wide spatula flop them over and cook about ½ to 1 minute longer. Put two bluebearies on head for eyes.

The pancakes should look like this:

Quite A. Small-Bear makes only the heads with ears, and he adds a berry for the nose. He says that the legs and arms keep breaking when he turns them to cook the other side—even if he tries to be careful. "Besides," he says, "it never looks much like a bear anyway, even if they don't break."

If you have a hungry bunch of bears to feed, put pancakes on cake rack and keep hot in a very low oven (200° F) until you have enough for everyone. This recipe makes 8 bear cakes. Serve with butter and honey or maple syrup.

Blintzes

In Russia they call them *blinyets*; and in New York sometimes they are *blini*, but they are just fancy rolled-up pancakes as far as Buddy bear is concerned. Bearnice has had a lot of experience with making them and offers a few practical hints below.

Blintzes:

2 eggs
¾ cup milk
½ cup unbleached all purpose flour
1 teaspoon sugar
2 tablespoons melted butter

Beat eggs with remaining ingredients to make a thin, smooth batter. Cover and refrigerate for 30 minutes.

Heat an 8 or 9-inch crêpe skillet over moderate heat and grease lightly. Put in 3 tablespoons of batter and tip skillet so batter runs around to fill bottom. Cook about 2 minutes or until lightly browned on one side (you can lift up a corner to peek and see if it is lightly browned) and remove to cake rack. Put a piece of paper towel over blintz and continue frying until all batter is used, stacking blintzes with a piece of paper towel in between each. Cover with a clean towel when finished. Makes 10 to 12.

Filling for Blintzes:

1½ cups (12 ounces) dry curd cottage cheese*
1 egg
1 tablespoon sugar
¼ teaspoon ground nutmeg

If there is any liquid in cottage cheese, drain it off. Then combine with egg, sugar, and nutmeg and beat well.

*If you cannot find dry curd cottage cheese, buy regular small curd cottage cheese and press in a sieve to remove all liquid.

Bluebeary Sauce

2 cups bluebearies
1 teaspoon lemon juice
½ cup honey
2 teaspoons butter
¼ teaspoon cinnamon
1 tablespoon cornstarch
2 tablespoons water

Wash bluebearies and drain well. Combine with lemon juice, honey, butter, and cinnamon. Mix cornstarch with water and add to bluebeary mixture. Let boil stirring until mixture is thickened. Serve warm over Russian-bear Blintzes. Makes 2¼ cups.
P.S. From Bearnice: If you have Bluebeary Sauce left over, serve it to the bears on cake or ice cream.

To put blintzes together:

Lay blintz—browned side up—on clean surface. Put about a tablespoon of filling down center of blintz and fold short sides up over filling. Then fold long sides over to make a little package. Repeat until all blintzes are filled. Brown in small amount of butter, turning to brown both sides. Serve hot with Bluebeary Sauce.

A few hints of wisdom about Russian-bear Blintzes from Bearnice:

Make blintzes as much as a day ahead and store, covered, in refrigerator. Prepare sauce several days in advance. It can be refrigerated and reheated when you are ready to use it.

The filling can be made in advance. But because it is a milk product, it must be refrigerated until ready to use.

Turn all the blintz crepe cakes so browned side is up. Otherwise you'll forget and put the filling on the wrong side!
Tip. If you lightly grease the inside of a cup in which honey or syrup is to be measured, it will pour out more easily.

Forage Porridge

T.R. is always happy when he can cut down on the work load, so when he experimented with this Forage Porridge that needs no cooking he was happy. Quite A. Small-Bear wasn't because T.R. makes a mess getting breakfast and Quite has to clean up when he doesn't cook.

1 cup uncooked quick oatmeal
1 carton (8 ounces) strawbeary yogurt
⅓ cup apple juice
1 tablespoon honey (that's all?)
⅓ cup raisins
2 tablespoons chopped nuts

Combine ingredients and mix well. Cover and refrigerate overnight. Stir and serve with milk. Makes 4 servings.

Grizzly Mix— Dry Trail Foods

Grizzly Mix is for hungry bears to take along when they hit the trail. It is nourishing and tasty. Buddy discovered, though, that it makes a mess in your pocket during a long, sweaty hike unless you put it into plastic or paper bags.

5 cups uncooked oatmeal
1 cup chopped roasted peanuts

1½ cups not-fat dry milk powder
1 cup wheat germ
1 cup raw unprocessed wheat bran or all-bran cereal
1 cup honey
1 cup vegetable oil
2 cups finely cut up mixed dried fruit (prunes, apples, dates, raisins)

Mix oatmeal, peanuts, dry milk powder, wheat germ, and bran in a big bowl. Heat together honey and oil. Pour over mixture in bowl and then spread out in 2 jelly roll pans. Bake at 325° F for 15 minutes, stirring 2 or 3 times. Pour back into bowl and stir in fruit. Cool. Store in tightly covered container. When ready to use, pack into plastic bags, one for each trail-blazer. Grizzly Mix may be stored in freezer if not to be used right away. Makes 14 cups.

Fish and Veggies

Salmon "Gone-Fishing" Steaks

Bearnice taught her bears how to catch salmon at an early age. Since they've grown up, they have learned to eat them cut into steaks and grilled. There are a lot of fancy ways to cook salmon but when you get right down to it T.R. and all the others think grilled over the charcoals is best.

4 salmon steaks (about ½ pound each)
Softened butter
Lemon or lime juice
Salt and freshly ground pepper to taste

Put salmon steaks in an oiled fish grill. (This is a wire, 2-sided grill, with handles and a latch to keep the sides together while cooking.)
Butter salmon and sprinkle liberally with fresh lemon or lime juice. Add salt and pepper to taste.

Close grill and lock handle. Grill 4 inches from hot charcoal 8 to 10 minutes. Turn and spread butter and lemon juice on other side and again lock in grill. Grill 8 to 10 minutes longer or until salmon flakes with fork. Makes 4 servings.

Honeyed Cinnamon Carrots

Buddy Bear took one look at the recipe for Honeyed Cinnamon Carrots and said, "Hmph. You could steam and skin the carrots ahead of time to save two last-minute jobs." Bearnice's reply, "A steam of nine saves time."

9 medium-sized carrots
2 tablespoons butter
4 tablespoons honey
½ teaspoon ground cinnamon

Cut off tops and root tips of carrots and scrub under running water with vegetable brush to clean off any dirt. Rinse well. Place carrots in steamer tray over boiling water. Cover and steam until almost tender, about 20 minutes. Cool cooked carrots enough to handle and brush off skins under running water. Cut carrots in 1-inch chunks.
Heat butter, honey, and cinnamon in 8-inch skillet. Add carrot chunks and cook, stirring, until carrots absorb honey and are glazed. Serve at once. Makes 4 servings.

Vegebearian Casserole

This main dish contains all of the Bear families' favorite vegetables—and then some. It is easy to prepare....and everyone can help.
Be certain to serve it with brown rice, baked at the same time, as that helps make it a complete protein.

1 cup fresh green beans cut in ½-inch pieces
2 carrots peeled and sliced
½ cup coarsley chopped Spanish onion
1 seeded and chopped Italian green pepper
1 cup sliced fresh mushrooms
2 sliced medium summer squash
1 can (10¾ ounces) cream of mushroom soup
½ soup can milk
1 tablespoon chopped fresh basil or 1 teaspoon dried, crushed
1 cup grated American cheese
2 tablespoons butter
½ cup plain or seasoned dry bread crumbs

Butter an 8-cup flat casserole liberally. Layer vegetables in casserole in order in which they are given in recipe. Mix soup, milk, basil, and cheese and pour over vegetables. Use a fork to push vegetables aside to let soup mixture get to bottom of dish.
Cover and bake at 400° F for 45 minutes. Melt butter and mix with bread crumbs; sprinkle mixture over vegetables. Bake uncovered for 10 minutes longer. Makes 4 big Bear-size servings.

Baked Brown Rice:
Put ¾ cup brown rice, 2½ cups water, ½ teaspoon salt, and 1 tablespoon butter in a 4-cup casserole. Cover and bake at 400° F for 50 minutes. Makes 4 servings.

High Koala Tea

The Down Under Koala bear is as cute as a button. If you can get him out of his Eucalyptus tree to come to tea both of you will be very pleased. The menu and recipes are from Australia.

Menu
Iced Tea sweetened
with honey and lemon
Asparagus Sandwich Rolls
Tuna Fisher Fingers
Honey Spice Snaps

Serve the honey and lemon separately so each one can season tea to taste.

Asparagus Sandwich Rolls

Buy thin sliced white bread and trim off the crusts. Butter bread right to the edge. If you like, sprinkle with a little chopped parsley. Put cooked asparagus spears, cut to fit bread, from corner to corner. Bring opposite corners up and roll around asparagus. Secure with a toothpick. Cover sandwich rolls with dampened paper towels and chill until ready to serve. Make as many as you think you will need.

Tuna Fish Fingers

1 can (6½ ounces) drained tuna
  fish
  Mayonnaise
2 teaspoons chopped gherkins
1 tablespoon chopped parsley
1 teaspoon chopped capers
  Whole wheat bread cut into
  finger-length pieces

Toast bread. Blend tuna and enough mayonnaise together to make a smooth paste. (If capers are salted, rinse.) Add gherkins, parsley, and capers. Spread mixture on toasted bread. Makes 16.

Honey Spice Snaps

1 cup firmly packed brown sugar
⅔ cup softened butter
1 egg
¼ cup honey (and hurry!)
2¼ cups unbleached all purpose
  flour
1½ teaspoons baking soda
½ teaspoon salt
1 teaspoon ground ginger
½ teaspoon ground cinnamon
  Granulated sugar

Beat brown sugar, butter, egg, and honey together with electric mixer until light and fluffy. Mix flour, soda, and spices together well and fold into creamed mixture. Chill for several hours.

When ready to bake, shape rounded teaspoons of batter into balls. Dip top of each ball into cold water and then in granulated sugar. Place sugar side up on an ungreased baking sheet. Bake at 325° F for 12 to 15 minutes. Makes 50 to 60

Desserts

Apple Pandadowdy

Apples are one of the Bears favorite foods, which means this Apple Pandadowdy hits the spot more ways than one. Bearnice says "A pandadowdy a day keeps the hunters away."

1½ quarts sliced apples
½ cup firmly packed brown sugar
½ teaspoon ground nutmeg
¾ teaspoon ground cinnamon
6 tablespoons honey (of course)
¼ cup water
3 tablespoons butter
1 cup unbleached all purpose flour
3 teaspoons baking powder
½ teaspoon salt
2 tablespoons granulated sugar
6 tablespoons shortening
⅔ cup milk, about
  Cream

Combine apples with sugar, spices, honey, and water in a well-buttered 1½-quart flat baking dish. Dot with butter.

Mix flour, baking powder, salt, and granulated sugar in a bowl. Cut in shortening with 2 knives or a pastry blender until a fine texture is formed. Stir in milk to make a dough that can be rolled or patted on a floured surface to fit over apples. Transfer with spatulas over apples. Bake at 400° F for 35 to 45 minutes until topping is nicely browned and apples are tender when speared with a knife. Serve warm with cream. Makes 6 servings.

Cinnamon Bear Pears

"Who ever heard of a pink pear?" asked T.R. when he saw Cinnamon Bear Pears come to the table. But then he tasted them. Nobody answered and that ended the conversation because all the Bears were busy eating them.

1 cup water
½ cup red cinnamon candies
⅛ teaspoon ground ginger
4 fresh ripe Bartlett pears

Combine water, cinnamon candies, and ginger in a saucepan just large enough to hold pears. Bring water to a boil, add candies and ginger. Cover and simmer until candies are dissolved. Peel pears, leaving on stem. Remove core from bottom of pear with an apple corer or small paring knife. Add pears to liquid and simmer just until tender, about 10 minutes, turning pears in liquid to color all sides. Cool. Serve with cooking liquid. Makes 4 servings.

Polar B'ars

Polar B'ars combine two favorite bear flavors, banana and peanut butter, with decorations added. Easy to make and easier to eat, these are wonderful winners that T.R. and his friends can make often.

- 6 medium ripe bananas
- 12 wooden sticks
- 1 package (12 ounce) peanut butter chips
- 4 tablespoons vegetable oil
  - Tiny marshmallows
  - Coconut
  - Chopped peanuts
  - Colored sprinkles

Peel bananas and cut in half crosswise. Insert wooden sticks (you can buy some tongue depressors at your drug store) and put into the freezer for about an hour.

In the meantime, melt peanut butter chips and vegetable oil in an 8-inch skillet over very low heat. Blend together. Roll chilled bananas in melted chips, using a spoon to cover bananas completely, if necessary. Immediately roll bananas in tiny marshmallows, coconut, chopped peanuts, and colored or chocolate sprinkles.

Unless Polar B'ars are to be eaten at once, store in freezer until ready to eat. Set them upright in small fruit juice glasses. Do not store for more than 5 or 6 hours.

Polar B'ars can also be decorated with white candied hearts, round candies to make faces, or other edible candies. If the peanut butter coating becomes a little too hard for things to adhere, put a dab of soft coating on and attach the candies. Makes 12 Polar B'ars.

Yogurts, Honeys and Punch

Flavored Honeys

Bears love honey more than almost anything and T.R., Bearnice, and the rest of the family are no exception. But like all of us, they want a change now and then. Here are some flavored honeys they gobble up on cake or ice cream. Sometimes Quite A. Small-Bear uses these to flavor milk.

Chocolate:
- 1 cup honey
- ¼ cup chocolate syrup

Mix honey and chocolate syrup well. If you like, add a dash of cinnamon.

Orange:
- 1 cup honey
- 3 tablespoons defrosted frozen orange juice concentrate.

Mix honey and orange juice concentrate well.

Lemon:
- 1 cup honey
- 3 or 4 tablespoons defrosted lemonade concentrate.

Mix honey and lemonade concentrate well.

Almond:
- 1 cup honey
- 1 teaspoon almond extract

Mix honey and almond extract well.

Pancake Topper:
Try whipping together ½ cup soft butter and ½ cup honey. Use to top hot pancakes. If you wish add some nutmeg or cinnamon.

Yogurts

You can buy plain yogurt or flavored yogurt but the Bears like to mix up their own flavors with plain yogurt. Bearnice says it keeps them out of mischief.

Strawbeary Honey Bear Yogurt:
- 1 cup plain yogurt
- ½ cup sliced strawbearies
- 2 tablespoons honey (and it's about time)

Combine all ingredients in blender and mix for about 45 seconds. Makes 1 serving.

Orange Honey Bear Yogurt:
- 1 cup plain yogurt
- 1 cup orange juice
- 2 tablespoons honey

Combine all ingredients in blender and mix for about 30 seconds. Makes 2, 1-cup servings.

Variation: Add a dash of cinnamon.

Chocolate Honey Bear Yogurt:
- 1 cup plain yogurt
- ¼ cup chocolate syrup
- 2 tablespoons honey

Combine all ingredients in blender and mix for about 45 seconds. Makes 1 serving.

Punch

Party Bear Punch:
Combine 6 cups cranbeary juice, 2 cups orange juice, ½ cup lemon juice, and ½ cup honey. Mix well and chill. Makes 2 quarts.

SCHOOL DAYS

"Shhh," whispered Quite A. Small Bear, "Don't you know you are in the libeary? I'm trying to concentrate."

"But," said Bearnice," I can't find my notebook . . . ."

"And take off your Bearet when you are indoors. That's a dynamite sweater, but I like you better in your pinafore."

"It's *Bearly Passing* and . . ."

"*It's* not bearly passing, *you* aren't."

"I am *too* passing. Those are the words stitched on the cover of my notebook. But let it pass . . . What's that you're sitting on, Quite?"

"That? Oh, just somebody's notebook I guess; someone left it on . . ."

"So!"

"Well you shouldn't leave it lying around. A small bear has to look out for himself."

"And you criticized *me* for my manners. You, you, you *Ursus Naturae!*"*

*Bearnice, who loves her Latin class, meant to pun on the phrase *lusus naturae* which means "freak of nature." But, since "ursus" means "bear" in Latin, and sounds a little like "lusus," she couldn't control herself. What really made her mad was knowing that Quite wouldn't understand the insult, much less the pun.

Twin-bear Sweaters

Child's Sweater Size:
6, adaptable to any chest measurement from 23 to 26" by adjusting length of body, armholes, and sleeves to desired measurement as you work. Garment chest measurement: 27"

Materials:
Knitting worsted yarn: 8 oz. (or three 3½-oz. skeins) main color (MC), 1 oz. white and small amounts brown for bears and red for hearts (we used Brunswick Germantown Christmas Red for MC and hearts, White and Cinnamon). Knitting needles sizes 6 and 8 or ANY SIZE THAT GIVES YOU THE CORRECT GAUGE; 8 yarn bobbins; 2 stitch holders; yarn needle or tapestry needle.

Bearnice is, frankly, in awe of the professional model who is wearing the larger sweater made for a child. In addition to appearing on the cover of Bear's Bazaar regularly, she is a perfect size six. So, naturally, her sweater looks terrific on her—even if the cuffs did have to be rolled up a little bit. Bearnice is thinking seriously about a career in modeling, herself, now. "They say there is quite a demand for 'petite maternals' these days," she claims.

The sweaters are not hard to make at all; they use a simple stockinette stitch throughout, with knitted-in, or duplicate stitch, designs.

Gauge:

5 sts = 1"; 6 rows = 1". To assure correct measurements, check your gauge: On larger needles (size 8) cast on 20 sts and knit 24 rows stockinette stitch (see below). Lay piece flat and measure it; it should be 4" square. If it is too small, try larger needles; if too large, try smaller needles.

STOCKINETTE ST: Row 1 (right side of work): K across. Row 2: P across. Repeat these 2 rows for pattern.

Front:

Wind 3 bobbins with brown yarn, 3 with white, and 2 with red; set aside for working bear panel. Starting at lower edge, with smaller needles and MC, cast on 68 sts.

Ribbing—Row 1 (right side): * K 2, p 2; repeat from * across row. Repeat same row 11 times more—12 rows (2") in all. Change to larger needles. Work in stockinette st until piece measures 8" from beginning, or 2" less than desired length to underarm; end with a purl row. Attach white; carry MC along side edge. Work 2 rows white, 2 rows MC, 2 rows white. Cut MC, leaving a 6" end.

Bear Panel:

Row 1: K 8 white, join first brown bobbin, *k 3 brown; bringing each color across back of work without pulling, k 4 white and 3 brown, drop brown to wrong side, k 11 white; * join 2nd brown bobbin, repeat from * to * once, join 3rd brown bobbin, k 3 brown, 4 white, 3 brown, drop brown to wrong side, k 8 white.

Note:

Bobbins should always hang on purl side of work. When changing colors on row, bring new color under previous color to twist yarns and prevent holes in work. Following chart, work Rows 2 through 6, adding a white bobbin after each bear on Row 4.

Shape Armholes:

Bind off 3 sts at beginning of chart Rows 7 and 8, adding red bobbins

for hearts on Row 7 (carry white yarn across back of heart as you work heart).

Row 9: Slip 1, k 1, pass slipped st over k st (decrease made at beginning of row), continue following chart across to last 2 sts, k 2 together (decrease made at end of row).

Row 10: Purl, following chart.

Row 11: Decrease 1 st each end, as for Row 9, following chart—58 sts. Complete chart, then, cutting off bobbins on first row, leaving 6" ends, work 2 rows white, 2 rows MC, 2 white. Cut white. Continue with MC until armholes measure 3½" above bound-off sts, end with a purl row.

Shape Neck:

Row 1: K 21, join 2nd ball MC, k 16 and slip to a holder, k 21.

Row 2: P across first side; with next ball of yarn, bind off 2 sts at neck edge on second side, p to end.

Row 3: K across first side; with next ball of yarn, bind off 2 sts, complete row. Continuing to work each side separately, decrease 1 st at each neck edge every other row 3 times—16 sts each side. Work until armholes measure 6" straight above bound-off sts, ending with a purl row.

Shape Shoulders:

At each arm edge, bind off 8 sts at beginning of every other row, twice.

Back:

With MC, work as for front, omitting stripes, until same length as front to underarms. Bind off 3 sts at beginning of next 2 rows; decrease 1 st each end of next 2 k rows—58 sts. Work even with MC until same

length as front to shoulders. Bind off 8 sts at beginning of next 4 rows. Slip remaining 26 sts to a holder.

Sleeves:

With smaller needles and MC, starting at cuff, cast on 32 sts. Work 12 rows ribbing as for front. Change to larger needles.

Next Row: Increase 1 in first st, (to increase, k in front and back of st), * k 9, increase 1 in next st; repeat from * ending k 1—36 sts. Purl 1 row, knit 1 row; purl 1 row. Continuing in st st, increase 1 st each end of every 6th row until there are 48 sts across. Work until sleeves measure 11½" from beginning, or desired length to underarm.

Shape Cap: Bind off 3 sts at beginning of next 2 rows. Decrease 1 st each end of every k row 10 times—22 sts. Decrease 1 st each end of every row 3 times—16 sts. Bind off 3 sts at beginning of next 2 rows. Bind off remaining 10 sts.

Finishing:

Sew left shoulder seam. Neckband. With right side of work facing you, with smaller needles and MC, k 26 from back holder, pick up 19 sts along left neck edge, k 16 from front holder, pick up 19 sts on right neck edge—80 sts. Work in k 2, p 2 ribbing until neckband measures 1" Bind off loosely in ribbing. Weave in ends of yarn on bear panel and sew right shoulder and neckband seam. Pin sweater with right sides together on padded board or folded towel; pin sleeves flat in same manner; cover with damp towel and let dry. Sew or weave side and sleeve seams. Sew sleeves in place. Weave in ends.

Abbreviations: k = knit   p = purl   st(s) = stitch(es)

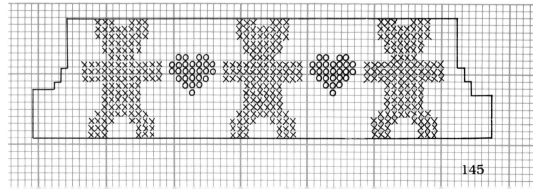

Bearnice's Sweater

This matching sweater was knitted just for Bearnice. See "Heirloom Bears" for instructions on how to make her. Her measurements are:
17" (43 cm) height
8½" (21 cm) length
18" (46 cm) chest girth
17½" (44.5 cm) head girth
So you see that she is a well-proportioned lady bear. Adjust the following instructions if the teddy bear you are going to knit this sweater for has different measurements.

Materials:
Knitting worsted weight yarn: 2¾ oz. main color (MC), 1 oz. white, small amounts brown and red. Knitting needles sizes 6 and 8, or *any sizes that give you the correct gauge.* Crochet hook size F, yarn needle, stitch holder, ¾"-diameter button, 4 bobbins (optional). Note: Bear panel can be knitted in with colors on bobbins or worked in duplicate stitch after the sweater front is completed.

Gauge:
5 sts = 1"; 6 rows = 1".

Back:
With smaller needles and MC, starting at lower edge, cast on 48 sts.

Ribbing:
Row 1: * K 2, p 2; repeat from * across row. Repeat this row 3 times more. Change to larger needles. Work in stockinette stitch (knit 1 row, purl 1 row alternately) for 12 rows, ending with purl row. (Piece should measure about 2¾" from beginning.)

Shape Armholes:
Bind off 4 sts at beginning of next 2 rows.
Next Row (Decrease Row): Slip 1, k 1, pass slipped st over knit st (decrease made), k to last 2 sts, k 2 together (decrease made). Repeat this row every k row 3 times more—32 sts. P 1 row; k 1 row; p 1 row.

Divide for Opening:
Next Row: K 16; slip remaining sts to holder. Work 12 rows, ending at center back.

Shape Neck:
Row 1: Bind off 5 sts as if to p, p to end.
Row 2: K 11.
Row 3: Bind off 4 sts, p across.
Row 4: K 7.
Row 5: Bind off all stitches as to purl. Join yarn at center and work other side to correspond, binding off at neck on k rows.

Front:
Work as for back until first armhole decrease and next p row are completed—38 sts. Join white; cut MC. Continue armhole shaping as for back with white yarn (knitting in bear and hearts with yarn on bobbins, following chart, if desired; when changing colors, twist yarns together once to prevent holes in work). Complete panel of 15 rows white. Join MC, cut white. Work 3 rows MC.

Shape Neck:
Next Row: K 12, slip remaining sts to holder. At neck edge, bind off 2 sts at beginning of every other row, twice, then decrease 1 st once. Work on 7 sts until same length as back to shoulders. Bind off. Leaving center 8 sts on holder, slip last 12 sts to left needle; join red and work to correspond to first side, reversing shaping.

Sleeves:
With smaller needles and MC, starting at lower edge, cast on 36 sts. Work 4 rows k 2, p 2 ribbing as for back. Change to larger needles. Work in stockinette st, increasing 1 st each end of 5th row, then every 6th row twice (to increase, k in front and back of st)—42 sts. P 1 row, k 1 row, p 1 row.
Shape Cap: Bind off 4 sts at beginning of next 2 rows. Decrease 1 st each end of every other row 8 times—18 sts. P 1 row. Bind off 2 sts at beginning of next 2 rows. Bind off remaining 14 sts.

Finishing:
Duplicate Stitch Panel: Each duplicate stitch covers one knit stitch. Following chart, start at lower left of bear's leg. Thread yarn needle; fasten end of yarn on back of work; insert needle from back to front in base of stitch to be covered, then from right to left under 2 threads of stitch above, and to back where thread came out—duplicate stitch made. Work across rows, covering stitches as indicated on chart; do not pull too tightly and guide yarn with fingers as you work to cover stitch completely. Fasten off on wrong side when entire figure is completed. Weave in ends.

Neckband:
Sew shoulder seams. With knit side of work facing you, using smaller needles and MC, starting at left back neck edge, pick up and k 58 sts around neck, including sts on holder, ending at right back neck corner. Work 3 rows k 2, p 2 ribbing. Bind off loosely in ribbing; do not cut yarn. Insert crochet hook in loop and work a single crochet st (sc) at top of back opening, chain 4 for button loop, skip ½" on edge; now sc evenly down one side of back opening and up other side to top of ribbing. Fasten off. Centering top of sleeve at shoulder seam, sew sleeve cap to armhole. Sew side and sleeve seams. Sew button opposite loop. Raise bear's arms up and slip sweater over arms and head.

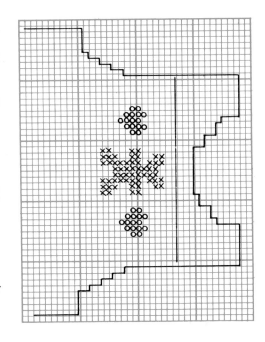

The Dressing Bear (left) is a first grader. Today he dressed himself completely for school. He felt so proud of himself that he went to the blackboard to do the math assignment. Then he turned and said, "How am I doing, fellas and girls?"

It was Bearnice who dreamed up the design for the "Bearly Passing" looseleaf notebook cover (below) as you might already have guessed.

"Bearly Passing" Notebook Cover

Materials

10 ¾″ x 11½″ (27.5 x 29 cm) notebook with a 2¼″-wide (5.5 cm-wide) spine
Cotton fabrics:
⅝ yard (.6 m) blue-and-white print
⅜ yard (.4 m) off-white for backing
Scraps of brown-and-white print, beige with white dots, off-white, yellow, green-and-white print, brown with white dots, beige, and blue
Sewing thread to match all fabrics plus red
Embroidery floss: 2 yards (2 m) each yellow, red, and dark brown, and 1 yard white
Embroidery hoop and needle
25″ x 12½″ (64 x 32 cm) piece quilt batting
Fusible bonding web

Assembling

1. Right sides together, using a ¼″ (6 mm) seam allowance, stitch short blue-and-white strips to top and bottom of appliqué block. In the same manner, stitch longer strip to right-hand side of block, and back piece to left-hand side of block. Press seams away from block. Using red, zigzag around inner edge of blue-and-white pieces.

Right sides out, place batting between cover and backing fabric. Pin layers together. Baste around edges. Machine-quilt outside red zigzag stitching. Trim away excess backing. With blue, zigzag edges for 4″ (10 cm) at center on top and bottom.

Cutting

From blue-and-white print, cut 2 strips 8″ x 2″ (20 x 5 cm) a strip 12½″ x 2″ (32 x 5 cm), back piece 15¼″ x 12½″ (39 x 32 cm), and 2 facings 11½″ x 12½″ (29 x 32 cm) From off-white, cut cover backing 25″ x 12½″ (63.5 x 32 cm) and appliqué backing 8″ x 9″ (20 x 22.5 cm). Enlarge appliqué pattern following instructions in "Mama Bear's Sewing Basket." ✂ Add ¼″ (6 mm) seam allowance all around. Read instructions for cutting the pieces in the Story Quilt Project. Make appliqué patterns and cut pieces from the fabrics given in parentheses. Wall (brown-and-white print), floor (beige dot), chalkboard (green-and-white print, frame (beige dot), bear's body—make patterns following broken lines between paws and legs (brown dot), bow (yellow), bear's head (brown dot), book (blue), pages and balloon (off-white).

2. Turn under ¼″ (6 mm) twice on one 12½″ (32 cm) edge of each facing; stitch hem in place.

3. With right sides together, pin facings to either end of cover. Using a ½″ (1.25 cm) seam allowance, stitch front facing (on end with appliqué) to cover, rounding corners to match notebook. Trim seam allowance. Stitch back facing to cover, leaving inner half of lower edge open. Trim and clip seam allowances along facings. Turn finished center edge of upper and lower seam to wrong side; overcast to backing. Turn cover right side out and place on notebook. Turn under seam allowance on open area of back facing and slip-stitch edges together.

Appliqué

Place wall then floor pieces on smaller off-white backing piece. Baste along top edge of floor and around outer edges. Zigzag along top edge of floor with beige. Cut fusible bonding web to go behind all appliqué pieces following instructions in the Story Quilt project. Fuse appliqué pieces in place on the square. (Note that pieces are put down in same order as given above for cutting them out.) Zigzag around all pieces with matching thread.

Embroider pieces as follows: using 4 strands of floss, back-stitch words on chalkboard with yellow and words in thought balloon in red, and title of book in dark brown. Using 3 strands of floss, embroider ears in back-stitch in dark brown, nose and pupils of eyes in satin stitch with brown, eyes and dots to thought balloon in satin stitch with white, and mouth in back-stitch with red.

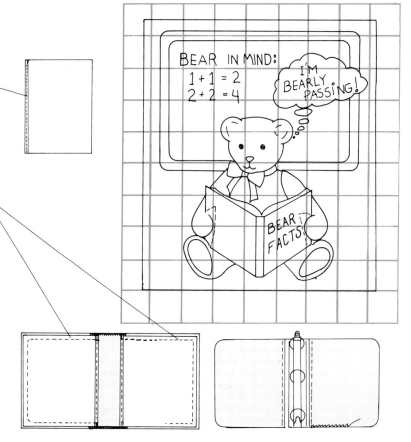

Dressing-Bear

It is a happy day for everyone when a child learns to get dressed for school all alone. These school clothes—a zipper jacket, shorts, and shoes with laces are made to fit Quite A. Small-Bear (see page 48) who learned from them that you don't zip a button or knot a zipper.

Materials

- ⅜ yard (35 cm) 45"-wide (1.2 m-wide) blue canvas for jacket
- ⅜ yard (35 cm) navy pinwale corduroy for pants
- 7" (18 cm) separating zipper (can be cut from longer separating zipper)
- 8" x 18" (20.5 x 4 cm) piece red canvas for shoes
- 1 yard (92 cm) white middy braid
  Blue, red, navy, sewing thread
- 1 large red snap-fastener set
- 14" (36 cm) piece elastic
- 1 red ¾"-diameter (2 cm-diameter) button
- 12" (31 cm) single fold blue bias tape
- 4 red or white eyelets and eyelet tool
  Small pieces of cellophane tape

Cutting

Enlarge patterns for clothes following instructions in "Mama Bear's Sewing Basket." ✄
  From blue canvas, cut jacket back, 2 fronts, 2 sleeves, a 3" x 9" (8 x 25 cm) bias strip for collar, two 3" (8 cm) squares for pockets, and two 3¼" x 4" (8.5 x 10.5 cm) pocket flaps. From blue corduroy, cut 4 pant pieces. From red canvas, cut 4 each of shoe sides, and soles.

Clothes. Use ¼" (6 mm) seam allowance. Zigzag-stitch or overcast-stitch seam allowances of all clothes.

Pants

Lengthen legs of Quite A. Small Bear's shorts, extending side and inner leg seam, see page 56.

Jacket

1. For pocket, press under ¼" (6mm) along one edge of each square; stitch. Press under ¼" (6 mm) along remaining edges.

2. Stitch three pressed sides of each pocket in place on fronts.

3. For pocket flap, press down ¼" (6 mm) on each 3¼" (8.5 cm) edge. With right sides together, fold flap in half so that pressed edges are together. Now stitch across shorter ends.

4. Turn right side out. Top-stitch shorter ends and folded edge. Stitch top edge to jacket front.

5. If you need to shorten zipper, mark a point 7" (18 cm) up from bottom of zipper and hand-sew several times across zipper teeth to make a bar tack.

6. Press under ½" (1.25 cm) on center front edge of jacket. Lap edges over tape of zipper ⅛" (3 mm) from teeth and stitch along edge of fabric. Cut off zipper ½" (1.25 cm) below tack.

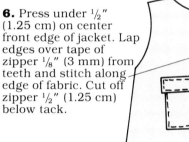

7. With right sides together, stitch fronts to back at shoulders.

8. Fold collar in half lengthwise and stitch seam across shorter ends. Turn right side out. Top-stitch shorter ends and folded edge. Stitch unfinished edge around right side of neck edge.

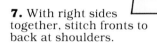

9. Open one fold of bias tape. With tape extended ½" (1.25 cm) at ends, stitch to right side of collar along neckline seam; clip at shoulder seams.

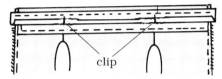

clip

10. Press bias tape toward jacket. Tuck ends of zipper tape under bias; slip-stitch edge of bias tape to jacket.

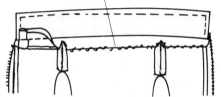

11. Turn under ¼" (6 mm), then ¾" (2 cm) on bottom edge of sleeve; stitch in place to make hem. Make a row of gathering stitches along curved edge. With right sides together, ease top of sleeve to fit arm hole of jacket; stitch seam. With right sides together, stitch underarm seam, starting at sleeve edge; keep going, and stitch front of jacket to back.

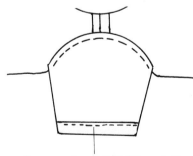

Turn under ½" (1.25 cm), then 1" (2.5 cm) along bottom of jacket and stitch hem in place.
  Following manufacturer's directions, attach large snaps to right hand pocket. Make buttonhole in center of left pocket flap ½" (1.25 cm) from edge. Sew button to pocket under buttonhole.

Shoes

1. Press under ¼″ (6 mm) all around shoe sides. With right sides together, stitch sides in pairs along both long edges. Clip seam allowance; turn right side out.

2. Make sure pressed-under edges are inside and slip-stitch back edges together.

3. Stitch soles together in pairs leaving a 1¼″ (4 cm) opening for turning. Clip seam allowance; turn right side out. Slip-stitch edges of opening together.

4. Whip stitch bottom edge of shoe sides to sole, matching dots and gathering shoe slightly at heels and toes. With right sides together, stitch tongues together in pairs, leaving straight end open. Clip seam allowance and trim to ⅛″ (3 mm). Turn right side out.

5. Sew tongue to placement line on inside of shoe. Following directions with eyelet tool, affix eyelets to circles on shoe. Cut middy braid in half. Thread through eyelets on shoes. Roll a small piece of tape around ends of braid to prevent raveling.

Tic-Tac-Bear Pillow

Materials

Cotton fabrics:
- ⅝ yard (55 cm) red-and-white print
- ⅛ yard (11.5 cm) red-and-white ticking-striped fabric
- ⅛ yard (11.5 cm) blue and white dots
- ¼ yard (22 cm) solid yellow
- 18½″ (47 cm) white square (for back side of patchwork)
- Two 18″ (46 cm) white squares (for inner pillow)
- 18½″ (47 cm) square quilt batting
- 2⅛ yards (2 m) narrow cotton cord
- 1 pound (460 grams) polyester stuffing
- ⅛ yard (11.2 cm) each tan and brown felt
- 1 yard (92 cm) each yellow and blue ⅛″-wide (3 mm-wide) satin ribbon

Embroidery floss:
- 2 yards (1.2 m) dark brown
- 1 yard (92 cm) red
  Red, white, blue, tan, and brown sewing thread
- 18″ (46 cm) red zipper
- ½″-diameter (1.25 cm-diameter) round Velcro fasteners: 5 red and 5 white

Bears

Trace pattern from book and transfer to lightweight cardboard. Cut out template.

1. For bear fronts, trace outlines of 5 bears to each shade of felt, leaving ¼″ (6 mm) for seam allowance around each bear. Draw features on one side. Roughly cut out each shape. Cut 5 pieces the same size from each shade of felt for backs of bears. Pin fronts to back with right sides out and stitch along outline; leave an opening between dots.

2. Trim about 1/16″ (2 mm) from stitching.

3. With a medium width zigzag stitch, sew all around edges—except opening. Stuff bears. Zigzag edges of opening together.

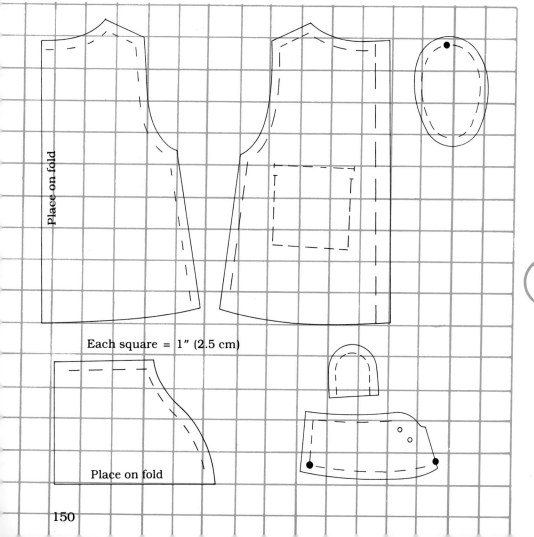

Each square = 1″ (2.5 cm)

Place on fold

Place on fold

With 3 strands of embroidery floss, satin-stitch eyes and nose with brown thread and straight-stitch mouth with red thread. Cut five 6" (15.5 cm) pieces of each color ribbon. Tie yellow bows on brown bears and blue bows on tan bears. Sew loop half of red velcro fasteners to center of red-print squares and loop half of white fasteners to red-and-white striped squares. Sew extra fastener to one corner of blue border. Sew hook halves of Velcro to centers of the bears' backs.

Cutting the Pieces

From red-and-white print cut two 18½" (47 cm) x 9¾" (25 cm) pieces for pillow back, five 4" (10.5 cm) squares for patchwork, and 1½"-wide (4 cm-wide) bias strips to make 75"-long (1.9 m-long) piping case. From red-and-white stripes, cut four 4" (10.5 cm) squares. From blue and white dots, cut two 1½" x 11" (4 x 28 cm) strips and two 1½" x 13" (4 x 33 cm) strips. From yellow, cut two 3¼" x 13" (8.5 x 33 cm) border strips and two 3¼" x 18½" (8.5 x 47 cm) border strips.

Pillow Case Patchwork side.

Sew all seams with right sides together and ¼" (6 mm) seam allowance unless otherwise indicated.

1. Stitch two red-print squares to opposite sides of a striped square; stripes should be horizontal. Stitch two red-print squares to opposite sides of a striped square. Now stitch two striped squares (with stripes horizontal) to opposite sides of the last red-print square. Press seams toward red-print squares.

Matching seam lines, sew strips with striped squares at center to opposite long edges of strip with print square at center. Press seams open.

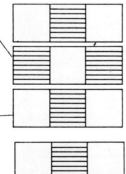

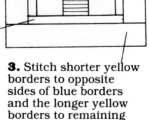

2. Stitch shorter blue borders to opposite sides of patchwork. Stitch longer blue borders to remaining sides of patchwork.

3. Stitch shorter yellow borders to opposite sides of blue borders and the longer yellow borders to remaining sides. Press seams toward borders.

Place batting between patchwork top and backing and pin layers together. Stitch ½" (1.25 cm) from outer edges. With matching thread, machine-quilt along seamlines of squares and borders.

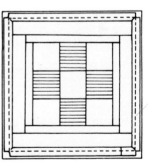

4. Stitch bias strips together on straight grain; press seams open. Press single long strip in half lengthwise and insert cord along fold. Attach piping, make and attach pillow back and inner pillow following instructions for Happy-Stitch Pillow on page 108.

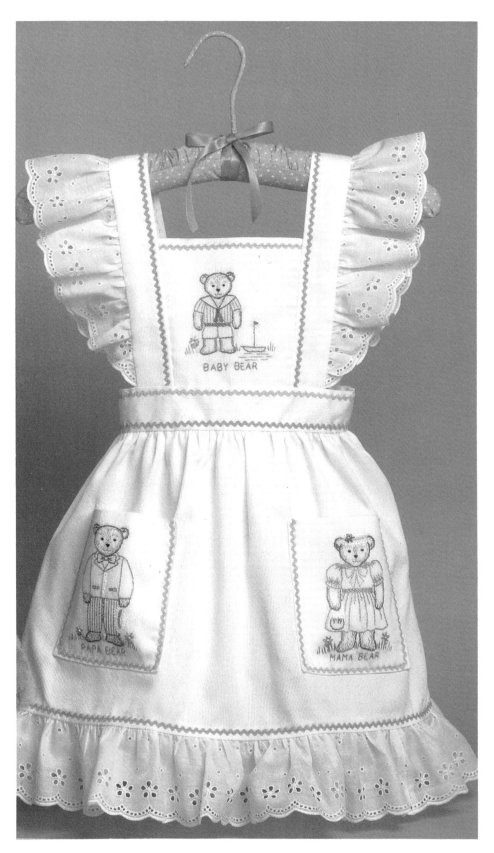

Goldilocks' Pinafore

Decorate a pinafore for your favorite Goldilocks with the three bears embroidered on the bib and pockets. Our pinafore is made from a purchased sewing pattern in white cotton piqué. It is trimmed with ruffled eyelet edging and pink and blue baby rick-rack.

Materials

Embroidery floss
(DMC numbers):
1 skein (8.7 yards or 8 m) each light brown (840), green (3347), blue (809), pink (605), rose (603), yellow (445), light green (996), and gray (414), and 1 yard (92 cm) dark brown (433)
Embroidery hoop and needle

Embroidery

Trace Baby Bear embroidery design to center of bib pattern within seam allowance; omit tiny lines of fur.

Make a pattern for pockets 5″ (12.5 cm) x 5½″ (14 cm) long; add 1½″ (4 cm) to top and ½″ (1.25 cm) seam allowance to sides and lower edges. Trace Mama Bear and Papa Bear to center of pockets about 1″ (2.5 cm) from bottom edge and ½″ (1.25 cm) above seamline; again, omit tiny lines of fur.

Trace pockets and bib, including embroidery outlines, to piqué fabric adding 1″ to 2″ (2 to 5 cm) fabric around edges of pieces. Cut 1 bib piece and two 5½″ x6″ (14 x 15.5 cm) pockets from white cotton fabric for linings.

See "Mama Bear's Sewing Basket" ✂ for embroidery stitches. Insert piece to be embroidered in hoop and stitch the bears in the colors and stitches indicated on pattern. Use 2 strands of floss for stripes of Papa Bear's pants and Baby Bear's shirt, and for flower petals. For waistbands, hatbands, Baby Bear's tie, and Mama Bear's collar, fill in areas with rows of back-stitches made with 3 strands of floss. Use outline stitch for bear's bodies; use 3 strands of light-brown floss. With 1 strand of light-brown floss, stitch tiny lines of fur approximating ones indicated on pattern. Fill in eyes and nose with satin stitches and dark-brown thread. Back-stitch mouths with pink thread. Line the embroidered pockets and bib with lightweight fabric before attaching them to the pinafore.

Key

Stitches

1   backstitch

2   outline

3   straight

4   lazy daisy

5   French knot

Colors

A   light brown

B   green

C   blue

D   pink

E   rose

F   dark brown

G   yellow

H   light green

I   gray

Pattern shown full size

BABY BEAR

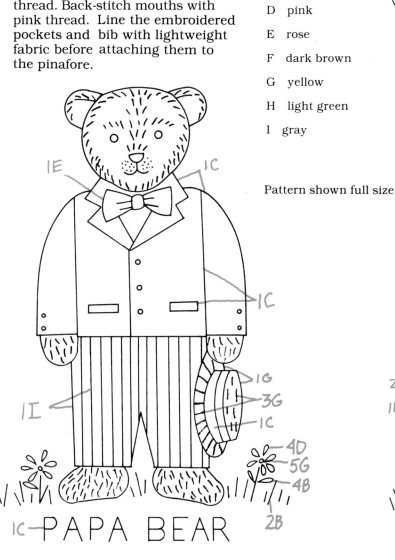

PAPA BEAR

MAMA BEAR

BEARS' BAZAAR

"It's simply making bears in batches," explained Bearnice to the others, "The same way Henry made his Fords. Instead of one person's making one thing all the way through, you, T.R., stack 12 pieces of fabric under the pattern and cut them all out together. Then Buddy will sew them up on the machine, wrong sides together. Quite will turn them right side out and stuff them. Then you all can sit down and decorate them. I'll sell them and collect the money."

"Sounds like a pretty smart way to make a lot of one project quickly," said T.R.

"Sounds smart to me too." said Buddy, "But there is something funny, about it I can't quite put my finger on."

"I know what's funny about it!" shouted Quite. "Bearnice is a *capitalist!* An exploiter of the people! I'm going to *organize* this shop!!"

Quite A. Small-Bear lost his temper when Bearnice asked if he wanted her to teach him how to skip rope.

"I already know how; and, besides, it's 'jump' rope, not 'skip' rope." Whereupon he picked up his old jump rope and whirled it so vigorously that one end of the rope came loose from the handle.

"Well, you needn't fly off the handle," said Bearnice. "Here, I'll make you some new ones shaped like bears." So she did; and there they are.

Jumpin' Rope Handles

Materials

- 7 feet (2.2 m) ¼"-thick (6 mm-thick) rope
- 10" (25.5 cm) square brown-and-orange calico
- Scraps of solid red and beige cotton fabric
- Polyester stuffing
- 5" (13 cm) square woven, non-fusible interfacing
- 2" (5 cm) fusible bonding web
- ½ yard (44 cm) ⅛"-wide (3 mm-wide) turquoise satin ribbon
- Black, red, and brown thread
- White glue

Instructions

You will be making 2 "handle-bears" for each jumprope. Cut calico square in half. Work on a light box or against a lit-up window or lampshade, and trace 2 bear fronts on wrong side of one half. Trace facial features, hearts, and broken lines to right side of fabric. Baste interfacing to wrong side of traced pieces. Cut 2 red hearts, 2 beige muzzles, and fusible bonding web for all 4 shapes. Fuse shapes to front of bears; machine-appliqué along edges. Draw nose and mouth on muzzle. With black thread, machine-embroider eyes, nose, and mouth. Trim interfacing just inside seamline.

With right sides together, place fronts against other half of calico fabric. Stitch along tracing line leaving lower end open between dots. Cut out bears leaving ½" (1.25 cm) seam allowance. Clip curves and turn right side out. Lightly stuff head; with matching thread, machine-quilt ears along broken line on pattern. Stuff upper body; machine-quilt arms along broken line.

Insert rope 1" (2.5 cm) into each bear. Finish stuffing bear, but make sure the rope stays at the center of bear. Pin end in place, and check length of rope; adjust if necessary. Turn under raw edges along opening. Slip-stitch ends together and to rope at center. Machine-quilt legs along broken line, sewing right through the rope. Tie ribbon bow around neck; glue to prevent it from untying.

Teddy Tassels

Materials

- 4" x 8" (10.5 x 20.5 cm) piece lightweight brown leather
- Brown and black sewing thread
- Permanent black fine-line marking pen
- Masking tape

Instructions

For each pair of shoes, trace 4 bear fronts in pencil to half of right side of brown leather; leave at least ¼" (6 mm) seam allowance around edges. Cut out rough rectangles around bears; for the backs, cut corresponding rectangles from remaining leather. Tape edges of each pair together with right sides out; small strips of tape will work best. With about 12 stitches every inch (every 2.5 cm), stitch along outline of bears. Trim leather ¹⁄₁₆" (2 mm) from stitching. Draw face on bear with pen. With black thread, sew ends of shoelace securely to back of bear. Pull tiny stitches through bear's nose.

Cliff-Climber Magnets

Materials

Two 2¾" x 3¼" (7 x 8.5 cm) pieces cotton print fabric
Polyester stuffing
½" -diameter (1.25 cm-diameter) round magnet
7" piece (18 cm) ⅛"-wide (3 mm-wide) ribbon
Sewing thread
2¾" x 3¼" (7 x 8.5 cm) piece lightweight cardboard for pattern

Instructions

Trace pattern from book; transfer to cardboard and cut out to make pattern. Trace bear to wrong side of one piece of fabric. With right sides together, stitch pieces along tracing line. If fabric is tightly woven, cut out bear to ⅛" (3 mm) from stitching (leave twice that if you think your fabric may ravel). Clip seam allowance along curves. On back piece only, cut a small opening as shown on pattern piece; do not cut through front. Turn right side out; stuff and insert magnet. Slip-stitch opening. Tie ribbon in a bow around the neck and glue it in place so it will not untie.

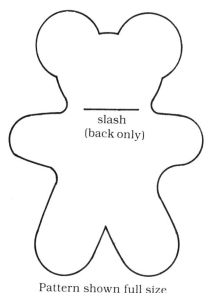

slash
(back only)

Pattern shown full size

Sachet Bear

Materials

10½" x 6½" (27 x 16.5 cm) lace
¾ yard (69 cm) ½"-wide (1.25 cm-wide) lace trim
12" (30.5 cm) ¼"-wide (6 mm-wide) satin ribbon
½ cup (1 dl) potpourri
Three ⅛" -diameter (3 mm-diameter) pearl beads
A few inches of pink embroidery floss
Pink or lavender fine-line marking pen
Lightweight cardboard

Instructions

Trace pattern for bear from book. Transfer outline to cardboard and cut out to make pattern. Trace outline to wrong side of half of lace fabric with pen. Fold lace in half putting right sides together; stitch around outline, leaving space between dots open for turning. Trim seam allowance to ⅛" (3 mm); clip curves and turn right side out. Fill bear with potpourri. Whip stitch edges of opening together.

Beginning and ending where legs meet, overcast lace trim to seam of bear; raw edge of trim should be at back of bear, decorative edge should be at front. Gather lace slightly as you go. Tie ribbon in a bow around bear's neck. Sew on pearl beads for eyes and nose. With 2 strands of pink floss, embroider mouth in straight-stitch.

Place on fold

Beanbag Bear

Materials
1/4 yard (23 cm) blue-and-white ticking-striped cotton fabric
1/4 square of a red bandanna
1 pound lentils
Matching sewing thread

Instructions

Use 1/4" (6 mm) seam allowances. Enlarge pattern pieces following instructions in "Mama Bear's Sewing Basket." ✂ Cut 2 fronts and 1 back and transfer markings to wrong side of pieces. With right sides together, stitch fronts together above dots along center edge. Clip seam allowance along curves; press seam open. Sew darts in back. With right sides together, stitch front to back, matching dot at inner leg. Clip and trim seam allowance. Slash neck along

"One of the things a bean bag is good for," said Buddy, "is to toss it back and forth with a friend who . . .

"Whee!" said the Bean Bag Bear.

". . . is just learning, because it doesn't bounce out of their hands, the way a ball does. Here T.R., catch."

"Wait a minute here!" screamed the bear.

"Or," said T.R., "you can mark a target on the sidewalk, walk off about six strides and draw a shooting line. The person who tosses his Bean Bag Bear closest to the center, without touching someone else's, wins."

"The sidewalk?" moaned the bear in mid-air, "Why wouldn't nice soft grass be just as much fun?"

"Dried beans last forever, too," said Buddy. "First you soak them in water to soften them, then boil them. So if you get really hungry . . ."

"Put me down, you cannibals! Now!! This instant!!!

indicated line at back; do not cut through front. Through neck opening, turn right side out. Fill bear with lentils; turn under edges of slash and slip-stitch edges together. The kerchief is a triangle of bandanna with one end 9½" (24 cm) long and the others each 6½" (16.5 cm) long. Narrow-hem raw edges. Tie kerchief around bear's neck.

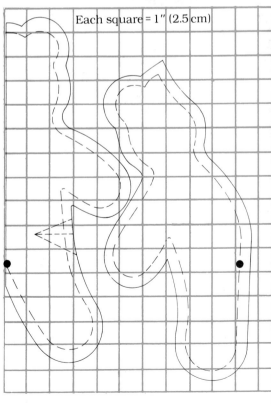

Each square = 1" (2.5 cm)

Angel-Bears Garland

Materials

- ¼ yard (23 cm) fawn-brown velveteen
- 1 yard (92 cm) 4″-wide (10.5 cm-wide) white eyelet edging
- ½ yard (44 cm) 1″-wide (2.5 cm-wide) white eyelet edging
- 1 yard (92 cm) 1½″-wide (4 cm-wide) white eyelet ruffling
- ¼ yard (23 cm) white satin
- ¾ yard (68.5 cm) ⅜″-wide (1 cm-wide) white satin ribbon
- ½ yard (44 cm) ¼″-wide (6 mm-wide) white satin ribbon
- 1 yard (92 cm) ⅜″-wide (1 cm) green-and-white polka dot ribbon
- 2½ yards (2.4 m) ⅝″-wide (1.5 cm) red-and-white polka dot ribbon
- A few handfuls of polyester stuffing
- ⅜ yard (35 cm) ¼-wide (6 mm-wide) metallic trim
- 1 yard (92 cm) each dark-brown, red, and white embroidery floss
- Fawn-brown, red, and white sewing thread.

Bodies

1. Trace patterns from book and transfer outlines to lightweight cardboard. Cut out templates. Trace 3 heads, 3 bodies, and 3 arm pieces to wrong side of velveteen, adding ¼″ (6 mm) seam allowance around each piece. Roughly cut each out. Trace features to right side of head fronts. With right sides together, pin cut-out pieces to uncut velveteen; cut around each outline so you have pairs of matching shapes facing each other. Stitch along traced lines but leave an opening between dots. Trim seam allowance to about ³⁄₁₆″ (5 mm) and clip curves.

Turn pieces right side out. Stuff each piece. Turn under seam allowances of openings and slip-stitch edges together.

2. Use 3 strands of floss to embroider face. Satin stitch eyes and nose with dark-brown thread. Back-stitch mouth with red thread. Outline upper half of eye in white with back-stitch. With brown sewing thread, quilt along lower line of ear with tiny stitches.

Matching centers, stitch inner curve of arms to top of body. Stitch head to upper curve of arms.

Gown

1. For bodice, from 1″ eyelet, cut six 1⅝″ (4 cm) lengths with embroidery details and scalloped edge at the middle of each piece. Pin one piece to center of arms section at front and back of each bear; embroidered edge should go at top.

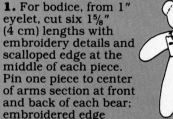

2. For sleeves, cut six 4″ (10.5 cm) pieces of 1½″ (4 cm) eyelet ruffling (measured along binding edge) and six 4½″ (11.5 cm) pieces of ⅜″ (1 cm) ribbon. Center ribbon and sew in over binding edge of eyelet.

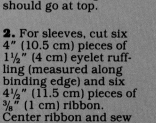

3. With right sides together, stitch ends of eyelet ruffling together from scalloped edge to ⅛" (3 mm) from binding. Do not stitch through ends of ribbon.

4. Slip sleeves over arms and pin ribbon over edges of bodice pieces on front and back. Sew inner edge of ribbon to bear through bodice.

5. For skirt, cut 4" (10.5 cm) eyelet into three 12" (30.5 cm) pieces. Cut three 5" (13 cm) lengths of ¼" (6 mm) white satin ribbon. Make a row of gathering stitches ¼" (6 mm) from raw edge of eyelet. Gather eyelet evenly to 4½" (11.5 cm). Center ribbon lengthwise with inner edge over gathering stitches and stitch along edge. Trim seam allowance to ⅛" (3 mm) from stitching.

6. With right sides together, stitch ends of eyelet together ¼" (6 mm) from edge beginning 1" (2.5 cm) below ribbon. Turn right side out.

7. Place skirt on bear over bottom edges of bodice and sleeve ribbon. Turn under ends of ribbon and eyelet in center back of bear and sew them together. Tack ribbon to bear through bodice.

Wings and Halo

1. Trace 6 wing pieces to wrong side of satin adding ¼" (6 mm) seam allowance around each piece. Roughly cut around each outline. Trace quilting lines faintly to right side of wings. With right sides together, pin cut-out pieces to uncut satin; cut around each outline so you have pairs of matching shapes facing each other. Stitch along traced lines but leave an opening between dots. Trim seam allowance to about ³⁄₁₆" (5 mm) and clip curves. Turn right side out.

2. Stuff wings with a small amount of stuffing. Slip-stitch edges of opening together. Quilt along drawn lines.

3. Place wings on opposite sides at center back; stitch wings securely to bear.

Cut three 3½" (9 cm) pieces of gold trim. Overlap ends to form circle and stitch them together. Place halo atop head and stitch ends to back of head about ¼" (6 mm) below seam.

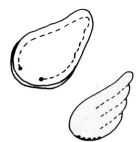

Cut green ribbon in thirds and tie 3 small bows. Sew bows to center front of ¼" (6 mm) white-ribbon waistbands.

4. Cut a 1 yard (92 cm) piece of red ribbon. Sew center of ribbon wrong side up to back of one bear wing. Sew other bears to ribbon with the center of their backs 9" (23 cm) from center. Press ½" (1.25 cm) to wrong side of ribbons; then fold corners of end to center. Sew ends in place. Cut remaining ribbon in half and tie bows. Sew a bow to folded ends of ribbon.

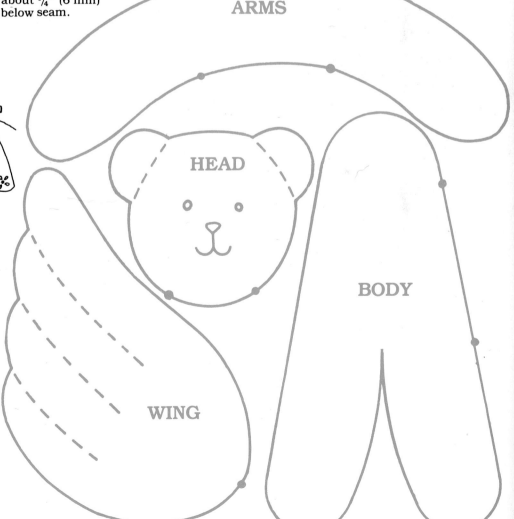

ARMS

HEAD

BODY

WING

Trimming Teddies

Cutting the Pieces

Trace patterns from the book to tracing paper. If you wish to make several teddies, transfer the pattern pieces to lightweight cardboard and cut out templates. Trace pattern pieces and markings to wrong side of velveteen, adding ¼″ (6 mm) seam allowance around each piece. Trace 1 back, 1 side, 1 head center, 2 legs, 2 arms, and 4 ears for each bear. Reverse patterns and cut 1 side, 2 legs, and 2 arms. Add ¼″ (6 mm) seam allowance around each piece and cut out carefully.

Pin outlines together carefully when matching and stitching seams. Sew all seams with right sides together. Clip seam allowances along curves.

Making the Bears

1. Stitch sides together along center front. Trim seam allowance of nose to ⅛″ (3 mm) and press seam allowance open with your fingers.

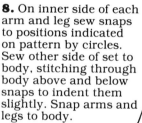

2. Stitch along seam line on top edge of sides; clip to stitching along curves.

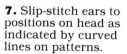

3. Stitch forehead to tops of sides matching center front marking of seams. You may wish to first baste this seam by hand with ⅛″ (3 mm) stitches to help make machine stitches more accurate.

4. Matching centers at top and bottom, stitch forehead and sides to back; leave an opening between dots. Turn body right side out. Stuff firmly. Turn under edges of opening and slip-stitch them together.

5. Stitch arms and legs together in pairs leaving openings between dots. Turn right side out. Stuff firmly. Turn under edges of opening and slip-stitch these together.

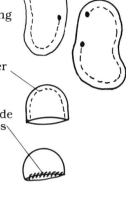

6. Stitch ears together in pairs along curved side. Trim seam allowance to ⅛″ (3 mm). Turn right side out. Turn under edges along seamline; slip-stitch lower edges together.

7. Slip-stitch ears to positions on head as indicated by curved lines on patterns.

8. On inner side of each arm and leg sew snaps to positions indicated on pattern by circles. Sew other side of set to body, stitching through body above and below snaps to indent them slightly. Snap arms and legs to body.

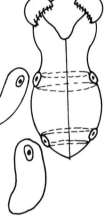

9. With red floss, insert needle at neck where it will be covered by ribbon and pull it out at mouth; embroider mouth as instructed for "Heirloom Bears" in Chapter 1. Knot loose end of floss at neck. Cut eyes from brown felt or leather and nose from black. Draw black pupil in center of eye using a marking pen. Glue eyes and nose to head. Fold ½″-wide (1.25-cm wide) ribbon in half lengthwise; wrap it around neck, unfold the ribbon ends, and tie them in a bow.

To make hanging loop, fold ⅛″-wide (3 mm-wide) ribbon in half and sew ends to back of head.

Materials

9″ x 12″ (23 x 30.5 cm) piece beige or fawn-brown velveteen
Matching sewing thread
Small scraps of brown and black felt or leather
A few inches of red embroidery floss
6″ (15.5 cm) ⅛″-wide (3 mm-wide) green or red satin ribbon
14″ (35.5 cm) ½″-wide (1.25 cm-wide) red-and-green tartan plaid or red-and-white gingham ribbon
4 sets of ¼″-diameter (6 mm-diameter) snaps
White glue
Black marking pen

160

Lapel Pin

Materials

4″ x 8″ (10.5 x 20.5 cm) gold-checked cotton
4″ (10.5 cm) square interfacing
6- strand embroidery floss:
½ yard (44 cm) each brown, black, red, and burgundy
Polyester stuffing
1″ (2.5 cm) long jewelry pin
Sewing thread
Small embroidery hoop

Instructions

Trace bear outline to wrong side of half of gold fabric. Working on a light box or against a lit-up window or lampshade, trace features and bow in position on right side. Baste interfacing to wrong side of front piece. With 3 strands of floss, satin-stitch ears with brown thread and eyes with black thread. Back-stitch eyes and mouth with black thread, nose with burgundy, and bow with red. Trim interfacing close to seam line. With right sides together, sew front and back pieces together along seam line; leave an opening between dots. Cut around bear ¼″ (6 mm) from stitching and clip seam allowance. Turn right side out and stuff bear firmly. Turn under seam allowance of opening and slip-stitch edges together. Sew the pin to the bear's back between his arms.

Pattern shown full size

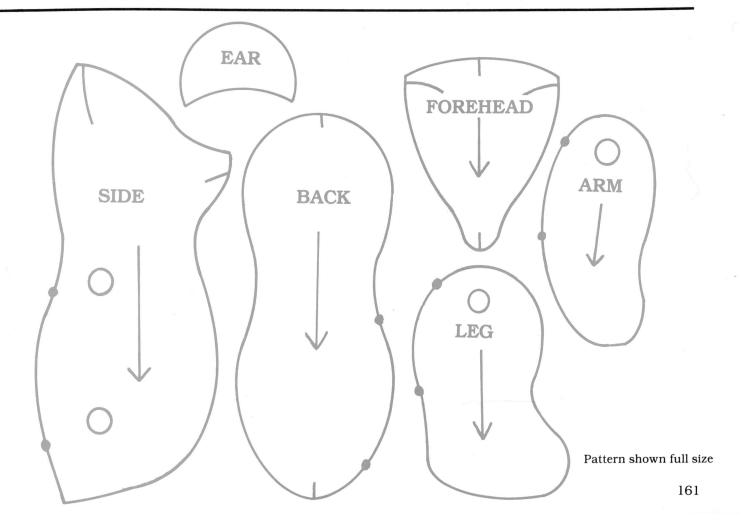

EAR

SIDE

BACK

FOREHEAD

ARM

LEG

Pattern shown full size

Santa Bear Wreath

3. Fold jacket in half to make shoulders; right sides should be together. Stitch side and underarm seams. Clip to inner corners.

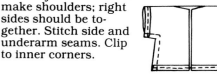

4. Turn right side out. Place jacket on bear and overlap front edges ⅛″ (3 mm). Turn under neckline along broken lines and whip stitch front edges together.

5. Cut ¾″-wide (2 cm-wide) strips of fleece. Fold strips in half lengthwise with right sides out. Zigzag-stitch at a wide setting along edges. Fold strips so zigzag stitches are centered on back.

6. Place a length of fleece around bottom edge of jacket, turn corner at front edge, and continue up to neckline. Make tiny stitches through fleece that both secure fleece on jacket and keep trim flat against velveteen.

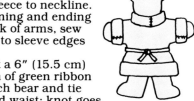

7. Beginning and ending at back of neck, sew fleece to neckline. Beginning and ending at back of arms, sew fleece to sleeve edges also.

Cut a 6″ (15.5 cm) length of green ribbon for each bear and tie around waist; knot goes at center of back.

8. Fold under ⅛″ (3 mm) along long edge of hat and stitch in place. Fold hat in half with right sides together and stitch along raw edges.

9. Turn right side out. Prepare and sew fleece to lower edge of hat the way you did for the jacket.

Materials

- ¾ yard (69 cm) emerald-green velveteen
- ¼ yard (23 cm) beige velveteen
- 5″ x 20″(13 x 51 cm) piece red velveteen
- 4″ x 22″ (10.5 x 56 cm) piece white acrylic fleece
- 1¼ yards (1.2 m) 2″-wide (5 cm-wide) red velvet ribbon
- 1¼ yards (1.2 m) ⅛″-wide (3 mm-wide) green grosgrain ribbon
- 1 pound (460 grams) polyester stuffing
- 1 yard (92 cm) each red and black embroidery floss
  Red, green, beige, and white sewing thread

Enlarge patterns following instructions in "Mama Bear's Sewing Basket." ✂

Making the Bears

1. Make 4 beige bears from the pattern given here, but follow instructions for "Cookie-Cutter Kids." Using 3 strands of embroidery floss, satin-stitch eyes and nose with black thread and back-stitch mouth with red thread.

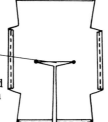

2. Cut 4 jackets and 4 hats from red velveteen. Make T-shaped slashes on jacket. Press under ⅛″ (3 mm) on side, top and bottom edges as shown and stitch in place.

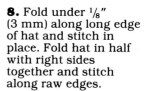

10. Place hat over one ear of bears (put the hat to the left side on two bears, to the right on the others) and bend the corner of each forward. Cut a 3½" (9 cm) piece of green ribbon for each bear. Make tiny bows and sew one to top of each hat, tacking ends of hat to fleece trim. Tack hat to bear's head.

Holly Leaves

1. Trace 10 holly leaves to wrong side of green fabric adding at least ¼" (6 mm) seam allowance around edges. Cut out leaves around outline. With right sides in, pin, then stitch leaves to pieces of remaining green fabric along tracing, but leave an opening between dots.

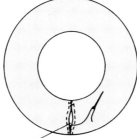

2. Trim seam allowance to ³/₁₆" (5 mm) and clip seam allowance along curves.

3. Turn right side out. Stuff leaves. Turn under seam allowance of opening and slip-stitch edges together. Machine-quilt along center line of leaves.

4. Slip-stitch leaves together in pairs matching ends and first points.

5. For berries, cut five 1¼"-diameter (3.5 cm-diameter) circles of red velveteen. By hand, make a row of gathering stitches.

6. Place a small ball of stuffing on wrong side of circles and gather edges together. Knot thread securely. Sew one berry to the end of each pair of leaves.

Wreaths

1. Cut 2 wreath pieces from green velveteen. With right sides together, stitch wreath pieces together along curved edges. Clip seam allowances along curves.

2. Turn right side out. Turn under ½" (1.25 cm) on both ends and baste hem in place. Stuff wreath firmly. Slip-stitch ends together.

3. To make the big bow, fold ends of a 20" (51 cm) piece of red ribbon forward into a bow shape about 7½" (19 cm) wide. Trim ends diagonally.

4. The center of the bow is a 4" (10.5 cm) length of red ribbon. Fold under ⅜" (1 cm) on both long edges and wrap center around bow. Overlap ends in back and pull tightly around bow so it gathers slightly. Sew ends together in back.

5. Sew bow to wreath over seam. Arrange bears, leaves, and berries around wreath as in photograph and sew them in place with thread doubled in needle.

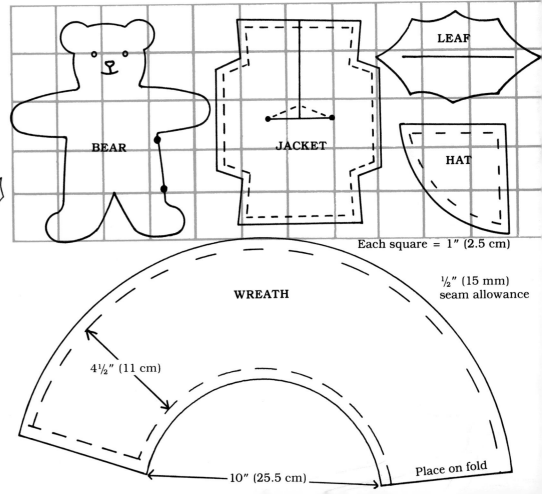

BEAR

JACKET

LEAF

HAT

Each square = 1" (2.5 cm)

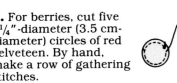

WREATH

½" (15 mm) seam allowance

4½" (11 cm)

10" (25.5 cm)

Place on fold

Trinket Basket

Materials

5" -diameter (13 cm-diameter)
   basket with lid
Cotton fabrics:
8"-diameter (20.5 cm- diameter)
   circle blue-and-white check
Scraps of brown with
   tan dots, tan with white dots,
   yellow, blue, and red
8" -diameter (20.5 cm-diameter)
   circle each interfacing and
   batting
19" (48.5 cm) piece 1¼"-wide
   (3 cm-wide) white ruffle-edged
   eyelet beading
30" (77 cm) ¼"-wide (6 mm-wide)
   yellow satin ribbon (be sure it
   fits through holes in beading)
   Yellow, blue, red, brown, beige,
   and black sewing thread
   White glue
   Fusible bonding web

Instructions

From diagram, make patterns for
balloons, bear, bent arm, belly,
snout, and paw pads. Cut balloons
from red, blue, and yellow; bear
and arm from brown fabric with
tan dots; snout, belly, and paw
pads from beige fabric with white
dots. Cut fusible bonding web to go
behind appliqué pieces.

Baste interfacing to wrong
side of blue-check circle. Center the
design and fuse applique pieces to
position on circle. Using matching
thread, machine-appliqué bear and
balloons to circle using zigzag-
stitch, machine-embroider ear in
beige and face and strings in black.
Baste batting to wrong side of circle
¼" (6 mm) from edge; trim batting
and interfacing close to basting.
Turn under edge along basting and
make a row of gathering stitches
along edge. Center circle over lid
and gather edges to fit; knot thread
securely. Gently remove circle from
lid, keeping gathers intact. Pin
beading around fabric circle so
ruffle extends over edge; start and
stop at bottom of bear. Turn
one end under and stitch it over
other end. Stitch around top
and bottom of beading.

Each square = 1" (2.5 cm)

Weave ribbon through ruffle,
beginning and ending at bottom of
bear. Place fabric cover on lid to
check fit, then remove; spread glue
on sides of lid, and replace cover.
Tie ribbon tightly in a bow and
allow glue to dry.

MAMA BEAR'S SEWING BASKET

. . . is no different from anyone else's. It's a place to put bits and pieces that you hope will turn out to be useful; patterns, stitches, little special folds and tucks to make things neat.

She recommends that you put together her sewer's ribbon which she wears around her neck. Her little snipping scissors are attached to one end, and a pin cushion is attached to the other. She says she can't *bear* to waste time looking for little things that have slid underneath bigger things.

Sewing Ribbon

Materials
5" (13 cm) square and 3½" (9 cm) square off-white aida cloth with 14 threads to the inch (about 28 in 5 cm)

Embroidery floss:
  2 yards (1.84 m) light brown
  1 yard (92 cm) red
  ½ yard (46 cm) dark brown
12" (30.5 cm) ¼"-wide (6 mm-wide) off-white lace edging

Off-white and red sewing thread
32" (81.5 cm) piece 1"-wide (2.5 cm-wide) red grosgrain ribbon with white dots

5" (13 cm) piece ⅛"-wide (3 mm-wide) red satin ribbon
Small embroidery hoop and needle
Polyester stuffing
  1 pair small embroidery scissors

Instructions
Use 3 strands of floss for stitching. Place 5" (13 cm) piece of aida cloth in embroidery hoop and, following photo, work cross-stitch bear in light brown. Eyes are dark brown French knots. Straight-stitch nose and mouth in dark brown too. With red, work one row of running stitches around squares.

Trim front to obtain a 3½" (9 cm) square. With right sides together, stitch squares, leaving a 2" (5 cm) opening on lower edge. Turn right side out and stuff. Slip-stitch edges of opening together. Stitch lace edging around pin cushion by hand or machine.

Turn under ¼" (6 mm) on ends of 1"-wide (2.5 cm-wide) ribbon. Sew one end to center of pin cushion back, ½" (1.25 cm) below top edge. Fold corners of other end to back making a pointed edge, and tack them together. Slip the ⅛"-wide (3 mm-wide) ribbon through one handle of scissors and sew the ribbon ends to wrong side of the pointed ribbon end.

How to Enlarge Patterns and Designs ✂

When the pattern or design for a project is larger than can be accommodated on the book's page, a scaled-down version is printed with a superimposed grid that looks like graph paper.

The instructional text and the legend on the grid will say, for example, "Each square = 1″ (2.5 cm)." This means, simply, that no matter what the size of the grid squares are, each one represents one inch of actual size in the project. If the grid squares are ⅛″ (3 mm) and the legend reads, "Each square = 1″ (2.5 cm)," then the actual parts will be eight times larger than they appear in the patterns. If the legend reads, "Each square = ½″ (1.25 cm)," then the parts will be four times larger than the patterns.

To make an enlargement of a gridded design or pattern with a specified enlargement scale, follow these steps:

1. Lay out your own graph paper or purchase some with the correct size larger grid squares.

2. Count the number of squares the smaller design covers from side to side and top to bottom, and mark off the same number of squares on the larger grid. Put dots at the corners of the rectangular area on the larger grid.

3. To enlarge the design, copy the pattern lines from the smaller grid to the larger grid, one square at a time. Use a ruler to transfer the straight lines and a French curve or a compass to reproduce curved lines. When all the lines are transferred, the enlarged pattern is ready to use.

4. If you are using an unusual grid size and plan to make a number of patterns, you will save time if you draw a master grid on heavy paper or use a single sheet of graph paper. Tape a layer of tracing paper over the grid and draw the pattern on it. When the pattern is complete, remove the tracing paper and save the grid to use again.

5. Pattern on grids can also be photostated to the scale given on the drawing. This process is somewhat expensive. Check your local Yellow Pages for a photostat service in your area.

Transferring Designs and Markings onto Fabric ✂

Trace the design from the book or use the pattern piece you have enlarged. Then use one of the following methods.

1. Insert dressmaker's carbon between the pattern and the fabric and trace over the design with a pencil or tracing wheel.

2. For smooth, light-colored fabrics, turn your traced design over and retrace the lines on the wrong side of the paper with a soft lead pencil. Place the pattern right side up on the fabric and trace over the lines again. The pencil lines on the wrong side will come off on your fabric.

3. Trace the design using a marker or dark lead pencil. Place the fabric over the paper, taping it in place against a window—during daylight hours—or a lightbox and trace the lines on the fabric.

4. To mark dots, darts, and other placement markings on the wrong side of fabric pieces, pin pattern to fabric and insert pin at marking. Lift up edge of pattern and mark fabric with lead or pastel pencil.

5. Use special transfer pens following manufacturer's directions.

Cutting and Pressing ✂

Most fabrics other than fur can be cut with the fabric folded in half with selvage edges together. Pin each piece to the folded fabric one; by cutting two layers of fabric you will get both a right and left side of the body or clothing piece. Be sure to place all edges that say "place on fold" on the fold of the fabric to get one piece that is symmetrical. If you need to cut more than one piece, the number of pieces is indicated on the pattern. Place arrows on the straight grain. Cut out pieces accurately using sharp dressmaker's shears. To cut fur fabric see page 19.

Do not press fur. For other fabrics, press seams, darts, pleats, etc. before joining them into other seams. Press napped fabrics on wrong side or in direction of nap.

Sewing Techniques ✂

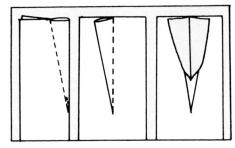

Darts

Fold fabric along center of dart matching stitching (broken lines). Beginning at widest part at edge of fabric, stitch to point. Backstitch to knot thread. For thin fabrics, press dart to one side. For heavy fabrics and fur, slash along center to ½″ – 1″ (1.2-2.5 cm) from the point; press or finger-press open.

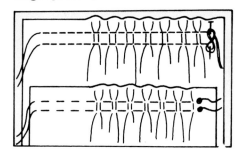

Gathering

By machine: Make 1 or two parallel rows of long straight stitches. Pull ends to gather fabric and secure ends of thread in figure 8 shapes around pins. By hand: Make 1 or 2 rows of small ⅛″-¼″ (3-6 mm) running stitches. Knot 1 end of threads. Pull other end to gather fabric.

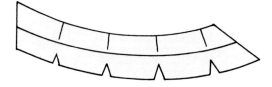

Clipping Seam Allowance

Curved seams must be clipped so that they will lie flat. After sewing, clip to about ⅛″ (3 mm) from the seam in both pieces of fabric every inch or so, depending on the tightness of the curve. Outer curves should be "notched," as in the diagram. The seams may then be pressed open, as shown here, or pressed to one side and the edges overcast.

Mitering

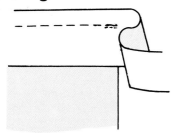

For Binding: 1. On right side, stitch binding to one side of project backstitching at corner.

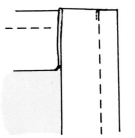

2. Fold binding diagonally to bring it around corner; pin in place. Stitch adjacent edge to next corner. Continue around all edges.

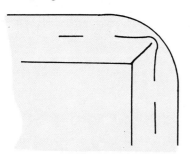

3. Forming a miter on the right side, fold binding over edge to wrong side.

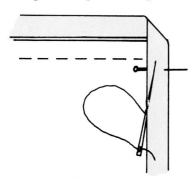

4. Turn under edges of binding along stitching line forming a miter on wrong side of binding with fold in the opposite direction of fold on right side. Slipstitch binding to wrong side and slipstitch edges of miter together.

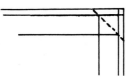

For Hem: 1. Press creases of the desired width along the inside and outside hem lines A and B. Unfold the hem and clip off the corners on the diagonal (dotted line).

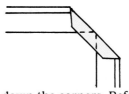

2. Turn down the corners. Refold the hem along lines A and B.

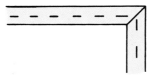

3. Pin, baste and sew the hem, working a slipstitch along each miter at the corner.

Hand Sewing ✂

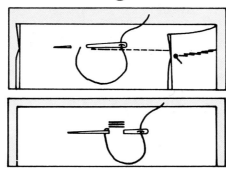

Back-Stitch. Used for sewing strong seams or for attaching trims by hand. Bring needle up from the underside of the fabric and insert it about ⅛″ (3 mm) behind the point where the thread came out. Bring the needle out about ⅛″ (3 mm) in front of starting point. Continue in same manner.

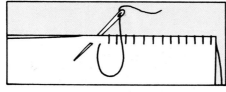

Whip stitch. Used to join 2 edges or to attach a trim or applique. Insert needle close to the edge at diagonal angle from the back to the front; repeat with stitches close together.

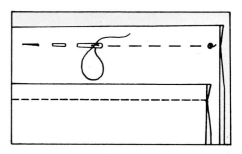

Basting Stitch. By hand, make long running stitches ¼″ (6 mm) or longer. By machine, straight-stitch using longest stitch possible—usually 6 per inch (6 per 2.5 cm).

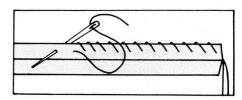

Overcast Stitch. Make diagonal stitches over the edge of fabric to finish edges.

Running Stitch. Weave needle in and out of the fabric 2 or 3 times; pull the thread through keeping stitches small and even. Use for sewing seams by hand, basting, gathering, and quilting.

Tack. Make several small straight stitches in the same spot to hold fabrics, trims, and ribbons in place.

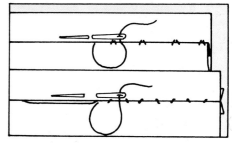

Slip-Stitch. Use even slip-stitches to join two folded edges of fabrics such as openings for turning and stuffing. Make ⅛″ (3 mm) stitches alternating from one side to the other. Use uneven slip-stitches to make a hem. Slip needle through folded edges of top of hem for ¼″-½″ (6 mm-1.2 cm) then take a small stitch under 1 or 2 threads of the fabric beneath the hem. Repeat.

167

Embroidery Stitches ✂

Back-Stitch. Bring needle up from underside of fabric and insert to the right 1 stitch length away. Bring it out at the left 1 stitch ahead. Repeat, keeping stitch length even.

Feather Stitch. Bring thread up through fabric and make a slanted stitch on the right side of line or seam keeping thread in front of needle (similar to blanket stitch). Make next slanted stitch on left side of line or seam in same manner. Repeat stitches alternating sides.

Chain Stitch. Bring thread from underside at one end of line to be embroidered. Inserting needle where thread came out, take a short stitch on the line with thread crossing line in front of needle to form a loop flat against fabric. Repeat keeping stitches the same length.

French Knot. With other hand, wrap thread around needle 2 or more times depending on the size you want the knot to be. Insert needle close to where it came out. Holding knot in place, pull needle to wrong side to secure knot.

Lazy Daisy Stitch. Make stitches the same as a single chain stitch, inserting needle just outside loop to hold it in place. Bring needle up at beginning of next stitch.

Long-and-Short Stitch. Work parallel straight stitches close together to fill in the shape. Vary the length of each stitch so stitches are staggered.

Satin Stitch. Work parallel straight stitches close together across entire area to fill in the shape.

Stem Stitch. Following the line of the design from left to right, insert needle from right to left, bringing it out where last stitch went in; keep thread to same side of needle.

Straight Stitch. This stitch is used as an occasional single stitch scattered in a design, to form letters, or grouped in a ring to form a flower. Each stitch is always separated from the next one.

Chevron Stitch. Work along 2 parallel lines or across a seam in patchwork. Take a stitch on top line and bring needle out in center of stitch. Take a stitch half the length of the stitch taken on the line above. Insert needle to the right and bring it out where last stitch went in. Repeat stitches on bottom and top line.

Cross-Stitch. This stitch is usually worked on crosses drawn on the fabric or on fabric which has threads that can be counted easily. Starting at lower left corner of a stitch and working from left to right, make a diagonal stitch (half cross-stitch) to upper right corner. Continue across, making a row of slanting stitches each going over an equal number of threads or over transferred pattern. Work back over these stitches as shown. You can work each cross-stitch individually and in any direction but they must all cross in the same direction.

✂

Mail-Order Resources

The following categories of materials and utensils referred to in this book may be ordered from the sources listed on this page.

Crown Joints
Fur Fabrics
Glass Eyes
Growlers
Music Boxes

East

The Crafty Teddy, Inc.
168 Seventh Street
Brooklyn, New York 11215

West

Merrily Doll Supply Co.
8542 Ranchito Avenue
Panorama City, California 91402